COMBATTING POVERTY THROUGH
ADULT EDUCATION

CROOM HELM SERIES IN INTERNATIONAL ADULT
EDUCATION

Edited by Peter Jarvis, University of Surrey

ADULT EDUCATION IN CHINA
Edited by Carman St John Hunter and Martha McKee Keehn

COMBATTING POVERTY THROUGH ADULT EDUCATION:
NATIONAL DEVELOPMENT STRATEGIES

Edited by:Chris Duke

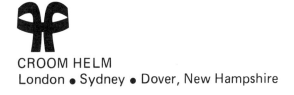

CROOM HELM
London ● Sydney ● Dover, New Hampshire

© 1985 International Council for Adult Education
Croom Helm Ltd, Provident House,
Burrell Row, Beckenham, Kent BR3 1AT

Croom Helm Australia Pty Ltd, First Floor,
139 King Street, Sydney, NSW 2001, Australia

British Library Cataloguing in Publication Data

Combatting poverty through adult education.
   1. Adult education—Economic aspects—
   Developing countries 2. Developing
   countries—Economic conditions
   I. Duke, Chris
   330.9172'4   LC2607

   ISBN 0-7099-0861-X

Croom Helm, 51 Washington Street,
Dover, New Hampshire 03820, USA

Library of Congress Cataloging in Publication Data
Main entry under title:

Combatting poverty through adult education.

   Bibliography: p.
   Includes index.
   1. Adult education – Developing countries – Case
studies. I. Duke, C. (Christopher)
LC2607.C65 1985   374'.9172'4   84-23777
ISBN 0-7099-0861-X

Printed and bound in Great Britain by
Biddles Ltd, Guildford and King's Lynn

CONTENTS

Tables and Figures
Preface

Contents

Contents

Tables and Figures

EDITOR'S NOTE

The Croom Helm Series in International Adult Education brings to an English speaking readership a wide overview of developments in the education of adults worldwide. Books are planned for this series of four different types:

a. about adult education in a single country
b. having a comparative perspective of two or more countries
c. having an international perspective
d. symposia of papers from different countries following a single theme

This book, one of a number to be published in association with the International Council for Adult Education, is a collection of papers examining ways of fighting poverty in the Third World and places adult education in a different context to that in which it is frequently located in the more developed countries. As such, it should prove enlightening reading not only to those concerned with various aspects of adult education but also to those who are more concerned about world poverty and the process of development.

P. Jarvis

PREFACE

In 1980 the International Council for Adult Education (ICAE) convened in Washington a Working Session on Adult Education, International Aid and Poverty, the proceedings of which were published in the Council's journal Convergence (XII, 3, 1980). It was there resolved to prepare and disseminate a series of case studies which would examine the possible role of adult education in reducing or alleviating poverty. The project coordinator entered into correpondence with a widening circle of adult educators - field-workers, scholars, programme evaluators - in many parts of the world. Most worked in the Third World, in Africa, Asia and Latin America, with a scattering from North America, Europe and the Pacific including Australia. Although the intention was to seek case studies on a comparative basis across the great divide between North and South, most energy and interest was naturally generated in the South, where absolute poverty and deprivation remain tragically common. Some 50 relevant programmes were identified for possible study during 1981. A special conference session on the occasion of the ICAE General Assembly in Paris, October 1982, reviewed tentative findings from 15 or 20 studies then at various stages of drafting, and encouraged dissemination of some of these (Convergence, XVI, 1, 1983, pp.76-83). This volume presents one set of such studies, drawn from the three main Third World regions and selected for what they suggest about large-scale, mainly govern-mental, national programmes. The majority have as one major objective reduction of illiteracy in the interests of some kind of development.

The coordinator evolved mainly by correspondence a set of guidelines and a common outline to make com-parison easier. Those working on studies were encour-aged, after an introductory summary sketch, to order their materials and analysis under the following heads:

Preface

the general context of the adult education
  project;
the agency and the project;
aims and objectives;
costs and cost effectiveness;
distinctive features and methods;
issues and analysis (with a number of suggested
  topics);
evaluation and appraisal (as adult education
  and in terms of poverty);
conclusions and implications, including possible
  replicability elsewhere.

Studies took a variety of forms but most of those
included here approximated this framework. Substantial revision generally followed correspondence
between the coordinator and the country authors, all
of whom wrote with authority as participants, in one
role or another, in the project under consideration.
Ultimately, considerations especially of space
obliged the coordinator, as editor, substantially to
reduce the length of most studies. In expressing
appreciation for the willing cooperation and patience
shown by each author, he must also assume responsibility for the final form of these chapters, and for
such ambiguity, through curtailment of evidence or
analysis, as editing may have caused.

Chris Duke

Coordinator, ICAE Adult Education and Poverty Project

Chapter One

ADULT EDUCATION AND POVERTY: POLITICS AND SOCIAL
CHANGE

Chris Duke

What is there to be learned from comparative studies
in adult education? The distinguishing feature of the
studies in this volume is their attempt to address a
common set of questions about the relations between
adult education and poverty, in different countries
and contexts and within programmes having differing
dominant characteristics, philosophies and particular
purposes. Different authors have addressed questions
about the theoretical possibilities of adult education for social change in different practical settings, and attempt to draw conclusions about the
generalisability of findings and the replicability of
experience. The contexts are sufficiently diverse at
least to suggest some powerful common themes and
conclusions. They range from political regimes of the
authoritarian right to the Marxist left, with comparable diversity of economies and culture. Some programmes have literacy as the major practical preoccupation; for others this is a minor element. Most are
governmental, and all are national in scope (although
the particular studies in some instances take a more
local focus of examination). Readers may recognise
one or more of the programmes from accounts elsewhere; where they differ is in addressing specifically the question whether and how in this instance
adult education can be held to have reduced poverty.
    It would be satisfying to be able to demonstrate
conclusively that adult education reduced poverty by
quantities or levels and at cost-efficiencies
superior to reductions in poverty achieved through
other means of spending the same dollars. There was
indeed a hope, maybe a naive expectation, that well
worked case studies would be able to produce such
proof, and some hope at least that sufficient
evidence might be adduced to make a convincing case
with hard-nosed practitioners of the 'dismal science'
of economics, whose influence appears overwhelming

1

among the counsels of those who determine priorities in governmental, intergovernmental and even some non-governmental aid programmes.

The decisive role of education in the adoption of innovation has been well argued and demonstrated before now, albeit at times negatively in terms of non-adoption; one classic positive example is the Tanzanian mass education campaigns such as 'food is life'.[1] It seemed unlikely that further studies would be able to overcome the quite formidable methodological obstacles to proving a direct and measurable effect of adult education upon level of poverty, even with the simplest - and possibly mean-inglessly over-simplified - definitions and measures of poverty. Correlation and interconnection cannot be equated with causation. It is plausibly argued that revolutions tend to follow amelioration of conditions which gives rise to hope, and that mass education, for example, follows rather than causes economic development.[2] Questions were asked of all case study authors about costs and cost effectiveness, though with little expectation that hard proof of relative value per dollar would swing the balance in national resource allocation from agriculture or industry to departments of nonformal education in these or other countries. On the other hand, there was the hope that addressing this question concurrently across different programmes might throw some new light on the dimensions of the problems of evaluation, at least indicating which kinds of investment in adult education by which means in which socio-economic and political circumstances had better prospects of success, and of at the least assisting and accelerating a benevolent cycle of development which might benefit the 'poorest of the poor', as well as the national economy measured for instance by GNP. This set of studies is selected to provide comparison across a number of large-scale national programmes; a second volume will provide comparison across a range of more local, generally non-governmental, programmes. Comparison both within and between sets of studies should prove instructive.

The building blocks for discussion of adult education, development and poverty are not conveniently standardised: one could build different edifices with these elements having no resemblance one with another but shaped more by the ideology, preconceptions and orientations of the builder. The meanings and boundaries of 'education' and 'adult education' have long been fought over. One position is the liberal and individualistic one that education is an end in itself, not for instance a means to

2

development or to the reduction of poverty.[3] This prescriptive position clearly does not describe what is known and funded as adult education in most countries. Especially in the Third World much adult education clearly has other ends. Even accepting that learning occurs in individual persons rather than collectivities, and that it might most desirably take the form of discovery through open exploration and debate, a case may still be made that adult education can confront inequity and thereby contribute to social change. Such would be the social rationale for the tradition of the Workers' Educational Association. Even the human relations experiential learning movement has advanced a similar argument: society is made up of individuals and if they are warm, open and loving, the society too will be a better one and all will benefit.

One difficulty with this liberal and individualistic tradition, whatever form it takes, is its innocence of political and economic realities: it is often levelled at its proponents that there is no such thing as neutrality in education; by accepting the status quo in this liberal-individualistic way one is unavoidably taking sides. There is a growing literature in the western industrialised world which adopts just such a critical perspective upon adult education.[4] In Third World settings power, inequality and absolute deprivation are generally more stark; the individualism of the western tradition appears effete, indulgent and self-seeking. Thus liberal adult education for self-development, leisure and richer personal living, while not necessarily demeaned, is irrelevant for policy purposes. Other elements in the typology of adult education take its place, reversing the priority found for example in Britain. Literacy, usually of a functional kind for 'development', predominates in many countries, as this volume suggests. Practical skills and knowledge for production, whether in a cash economy or for self-reliance of local communities, constitute another important category. To these two may be added various forms of post-literacy and basic (school equivalency) education through to vocationally oriented training at different levels to meet economic development needs; such is the main focus for instance of China's massive system of development-oriented adult education. The third major category comprises adult education for active (and maybe equal, or maybe 'responsible') participation in society. Here the guru remains Paulo Freire, whose 'conscientisation' has been re-interpreted, used or abused, in a hundred different ways.[5] In this category are included adult education for organisation and mobilisation, 'popular education', as well as some of the civic and political education more familiar to industrialised societies.

It will be seen that the studies in this volume span these three major categories, with the weight on literacy, or 'literacy-plus'. The 'plus' may be in the second, 'vocational', category or the third, conscientisation and mobilisation. An important question for the success of Third World adult education concerns the relationship, balance and phasing between these elements; for all are theoretically present in many contemporary large-scale adult education programmes, and most explicitly, among those in this volume, in the case of the Indian.[6] This is not to imply that individual motivation and learning are not also important; most of the studies here pay much attention to these. Only that the purposes are collective: for the development of the group or district, nation or society, through enhanced knowledge and skills, and changed attitudes, of its members. Whether that society, as a political system, is one for which its members can be motivated to learn and work, is another important matter addressed here.

These programmes are mainly governmental, mostly national in scale, relatively massive if not costly for the countries concerned, mostly top-down in their approach. It is therefore important what kind of social change the government wants or will countenance, how far it will confront privilege and inequality in the interests of national (economic) development and the alleviation or abolition of poverty. 'Political will' is a term which has won salience among Third World adult educators in recent years, recognising how crucial is the will and commitment of government if adult education programmes intended to reduce poverty are to be tolerated, supported and successful. The question is also sharply posed whether and for how long the political will and the people's will coincide.[7] 'Participation' is adult education's international password; many see it as a prerequisite for effective learning and effective action. The relationship of participation to political systems and purposes is evident. These studies throw light on the possibilities and limitations of 'participation' for learning in different political contexts. They also illuminate practical and organisational matters about the management of large-scale centre-to-periphery systems relevant to participation, or its absence, including short-course training, teaching methods, curriculum content and local diversity.

4

Adult Education and Poverty

Application of learning to real life is clearly
important if adult education programmes are to affect
the standard of living. This raises questions about
the coordination of strictly educational efforts with
the efforts of other 'development' agencies, both
economic and social-welfare oriented, both national
(including local and regional) and, where this
applies, the efforts of international aid agencies.
Bureaucratic segmentation and resistance to inter-
departmental cooperation appear to be universal
problems of large-scale management. So does the
problem of linking literacy or skill-acquisition to
production possibilities within local cultural,
economic and political realities. If centre-
periphery, planning-diversity and learning-doing
dichotomies cannot be bridged, the prospects for
motivation, effective participation and changed
behaviour of people and systems resulting in
reduction of poverty appear slight.
Another theme implicit in several of the studies
which follow is the relation between international
economic and political forces and poverty at the
village level. Economic development programmes have
had unintended and deleterious economic and social
consequences for those whom they were supposedly most
to benefit; the Green Revolution in India is the
best-known example but by no means the only one: 'it
is difficult to avoid the conclusion that it is not
the lack of growth but its very occurrence that led
to a deterioration in the conditions of the rural
poor'.[8] There are also more sinister, but not
necessarily less accurate, interpretations: that
nonformal education for development is designed and
intended to draw relatively self-reliant peasants
into the international system of exchange and to
pauperise them, economically, socially and culturally, as newly dependent mono-cashcroppers without
the means to feed and maintain themselves other than
at the whim of the world markets for which they
become both producers and consumers.[9] Inevitably,
national conceived and government-led programmes of
the kind featured here tend to lend themselves to
this concern and criticism. Not that there is any
simple answer: not even the smallest Pacific
countries are now successfully islands unto themselves; progress is introducing some to poverty for
the first time. Burma's isolationism has not proved
entirely successful, and China, after extreme isolation and attempted permanent revolution now appears
set for continuous rapid modernisation and an open
door policy. There are however signs of attempted
local self-reliance in both industrialised and Third

5

World societies; some pointers for local-level 'rice-roots' approaches are contained in the second volume of ICAE case studies.

Is there then a place for adult education in reducing poverty? The authors of the following studies all address this question in different ways. None is unduly perturbed by the question 'what is adult education?' or where lie its proper boundaries, questions that have frequently paralysed those in the British liberal tradition. This is just as well: paradoxically, the closer adult education comes to affecting the standard of living and helping reduce poverty, the further it moves from any definition of the purely educational. The Catch 22 is that pure adult education can be accused of being ineffectual, irrelevant to economic and political realities; the nearer it moves, with Freire and others, to having relevance and efficacy, the less acceptable it becomes as strictly individuals' education. Of course the more important contribution might be long-term and indirect, at least in circumstances like the Chilean described in this volume. One reading of the Nicaraguan account is that the indirect long-term effects in the end matter more for the kind of society which will emerge (if international interests so permit) than the immediate skills of literacy gained in those few exciting months. One must also ask the question, unpalatable as it may be in the West, whether the 'target' or 'client' is not the collective, the organisation and the polity, rather than the individual learner. Such appears plausible for the Korean Saemaul Education Movement described below, for the brave strategy intended in the Indian NAEP, and in the religious philosophy of Sarvodaya Shramadana. Readers in the western industrialised world may be tempted to dismiss all this as irrelevant if not unseemly. In fact the issues are universal, and becoming more pressing now in post-industrial societies with their emerging unemployed underclass. Writers like Rubenson in Canada and Sweden, Gaventa in the United States, Gelpi in Europe, Jackson and Lovett in Britain, suggest that the bell tolls no less for the West than for the South.

Two more questions to which this set of studies addresses the reader. The first is the nature of literacy and the effects of preoccupation with it. A decade ago any questioning of the propriety and priority of the massive commitment to massive, yet inadequate, efforts to effect universal literacy would have seemed sacrilegious. Still, today, it appears that Unesco is putting its name to the

concept and target of universal literacy by the year
2000, despite scepticism among its advisers whether
this is a realistic platform from which to launch the
Fourth International Adult Education Conference in
1985.[10] Recently, too, a leading agency dedicated
to assisting adult education for development throughout the Third World has questioned the commitment to
and unintended consequences of mass literacy campaigns: 'let's remove doubtful promises and cope with
the practicable'. This paper asserts that there is no
proof: that literacy was historically a prerequisite
of economic and social development; that literacy
efforts have of themselves diminished exploitation
and poverty; that literacy is a pre-requisite for the
intelligent understanding and handling of life; or
that it necessarily and directly relates to attaining
participative structures, achieving liberation and
abolishing oppression. 'Ever-increasing efforts for
and large expenditure on literacy did not necessarily
lead to a reduction of poverty.'[11]
　　The second question concerns the nature and
meaning of poverty itself. We have moved in these
introductory remarks between abolition, reduction,
alleviation and amelioration: yet poverty itself is
one of those non-standardised building blocks from
which this important but untidy debate is con-
structed. If the debate is unmanageable and inconclusive, little wonder if the actions deriving from it
fail to deliver what is hoped of them. To ask what
poverty means, and thence what causes it, is not to
detract from the fact of absolute poverty or the
likelihood that by the end of the century some 600 to
800 million people will still be trapped in it.[12]
If, as has been suggested above, poverty is actually
at present a product of development and greater
wealth, clearly national development programmes are
not enough. 'Trickle down' appears too slow even in
Third World countries which have enjoyed dramatic
economic growth in recent years, although one might
argue that it is still better than no growth and no
amelioration, even delayed, of the lot of the
poorest. Trends in the affluent West however, give no
ground for hope that some benevolent hidden hand will
eventually do away with absolute or relative poverty.
The question implied here is how to confront the
human causes of poverty. The last two of the studies
which follow clearly suggest that this means making a
new kind of person and citizen, and that the role of
adult education in the abolition of poverty lies in
doing just this.

Adult Education and Poverty

NOTES

1. See for example Hall, Budd L., <u>Mtu Ni Afya.</u>
<u>Tanzania's Health Campaign</u>, Clearinghouse on Develop-
ment Communication, Washington, 1978. <u>Chakula ni</u>
<u>Uhai. An Evaluation Report of the 'Food is Life' Mass</u>
<u>Campaign in Tanzania</u>, Institute of Adult Education,
Dar es Salaam, 1976.
2. See for example Dore, Ronald, <u>The Diploma</u>
<u>Disease. Education, Qualification and Development</u>,
Allen and Unwin, 1976.
3. Paterson, R.W.K., 'Social Change as an Educational Aim', <u>Adult Education</u>, 45, 1973, pp.353-359;
<u>Values, Education and the Adult</u>, R. & K. Paul, 1979.
Lawson, Kenneth H., <u>Philosophical Concepts and Values</u>
<u>in Adult Education</u>, Open University Press, 1979.
4. For example Thompson, Jane L. (ed.) <u>Adult</u>
<u>Education for a Change</u>, Hutchinson, 1980. See also
the Radical Forum on Adult Education, Croom Helm,
series edited by Jo Campling.
5. Kumar, K. and Kidd, R., 'Co-opting the Ideas
of Paulo Freire', <u>Ideas and Action</u>, ffhc/action for
development, 148/5, 1982, pp.4-8.
6. See below, Chapter Four, Ramakrishnan, K.
7. For instance by non-governmental adult educators like S.C. Dutta and Kishore Saint at the international Seminar, 'Campaigning for Literacy', on mass
literacy campaigns, Udaipur, India, January 1982; see
Bhola, H.S. et al, <u>The Promise of Literacy</u>, Nomos,
Baden-Baden, 1983.
8. Ghose, Ajit K., and Griffin, Keith, 'Rural
Poverty and Development Alternatives in South and
Southeast Asia: Some Policy Issues', <u>National Labour</u>
<u>Institute Bulletin</u>, 5-6, 1983, p.183.
9. See for example Mbilinyi, Marjorie, 'Basic
Education: Tool of Liberation or Exploitation?',
<u>Prospects</u>, VII, 4, 1977, pp.489-503; also the
'Political Economy of Adult Education' papers by
Mbilinyi and others available from the International
Council for Adult Education.
10. Apart from this particular question, there
has been tension within Unesco for many years over
the relative standing and significance of literacy
compared with (other) adult education; at times the
former has appeared likely largely to swallow up the
latter.
11. Hinzen, Heribert et al, 'Cooperating or Campaigning for Literacy: Let's Remove Doubtful Promises
and Cope with the Practicable', <u>Adult Education and</u>
<u>Development</u>, 21, Sept. 1983, pp.1-5.
12. The World Bank in 1979 estimated 600 million
trapped in absolute poverty in the year 2000; the
Brandt Commission report estimated the 1980 figure at
800 million.
8

INTRODUCTION

The account of MOBRAL in Brazil, by Lovisolo et al, is the first of several analyses of national literacy in this volume. Second in scale only to the Indian of those described here, it was the most generously financed, and this study by a team of research workers was in turn also the best financed of these studies.[1] Measures of cost, impact and success are thorough and detailed, as regards the literacy objectives of this large-scale national governmental programme spanning a ten year period in a context of national census statistics, economic growth and national development. Altogether this is a methodologically strong, detailed, well documented and thorough account of all aspects of the programme from initial legislation to monitoring and evaluation.

Yet the authors are cautious about the meaning even of the literacy statistics. The period of time, and the resources available for appraisal allow sound judgement, for instance of the lower 'efficiency rate' after the initial euphoria. Basic continuity of purpose and accretion of new programme elements, as needs become apparent, are both explained. The reduction of poverty is only an implicit objective, via the intended 'functionality' of the programme. Literacy teaching and adult education, it is shown, cannot be understood in a vacuum. The economic, political and social context is crucial. Success even in literacy terms requires a coordinated, multi-pronged approach. Note that this was a mass campaign led by a modernising, but right-wing rather than revolutionary or post-liberation, government. The approach was top-down, centre to periphery.

In one of the more critical accounts yet published of the work of MOBRAL this chapter suggests, in muted terms, that community organisation and popular mobilisation are necessary if real, or structural, social change is to occur. By looking at the origins of the programme in times of economic boom it also shows how poverty can actually be caused by and grow out of wealth; hence perhaps the authors' antipathy to human capital theory on which the programme was based. Literacy programmes cannot produce jobs; becoming literate is no guarantee of improved conditions for the individual. The Brazilian economy of the seventies could not absorb the neo-literates. On the other hand one might ask whether, like it or not and in the light of recent liberalisation in Brazil, a trickle-down model of development may not be partly validated by this Brazilian experience.

9

Of particular interest are the differential success rates between women and men, and from region to region, against a backdrop of complex internal migration, rural-rural and urban-rural as well as rural-urban. Brazil is a huge, economically and culturally diverse, country. In the end the authors conclude that only detailed local studies could demonstrate conclusively the connection between poverty and adult education - which would pose in turn the problem of generalising from selected examples. Either way, absolute proof appears impossible. The conclusion is that adult education may be a necessary condition for reducing poverty, but it cannot alone effect that reduction.

There may be an implication that commitment to social transformation on the part of government is essential for a programme like this to bring about the kind of change which will alter the lot of the poor. Methods resembled in some respects those of the then exiled Paulo Freire: to what extent was his pedagogy adopted but, in the words of Kumar and Kidd, coopted?[2] The account shows the tension between intended functionality and centralised national planning: local teachers were meant to make adaptations to suit local needs but, like the learners, reverted to a familiar and traditional scholastic mode of instruction. There was evidently little local variety, little functional adjustment to the needs of different learners and local economic circumstances. Participation thus proved hollow. Another tension was between the individual and the communal: not only does a mass approach contradict individualisation to fit diverse needs; a literacy programme which raises individual aspirations and fosters urban drift in search of non-existent jobs in the urban sector may actually aggravate rather than reduce poverty.

NOTES

1. The full study included a large number of tables omitted from this published version.
2. Kumar, K. and Kidd, R., 'Coopting the Ideas of Paulo Freire', Ideas and Action, 148/5, 1982, pp.4-8. (The original longer version appeared in Political and Economic Weekly, XVI, 1 and 2, January 1981.)

Chapter Two

MOBRAL'S FUNCTIONAL LITERACY PROGRAMME AND THE REDUCTION OF POVERTY

Hugo Rodolfo Lovisolo

Luna Azulay Steinbruch
Terezinho Catarina Pereira Ramos
Isabel de Orleans e Braganca
Anne-Marie Milon Oliveira

SUMMARY

The Functional Literary Programme (PAF) for adults developed by MOBRAL, an Agency of the Ministry of Education and Culture of Brazil, was started in 1970. The law establishing the objectives and operations of MOBRAL dates back to 1967. The main alterations over a ten year period were through programmes set up to complement or support functional literacy activities. Although it gave priority attention to the fifteen to thirty-five year age group, the programme was not devised in terms of ethnic groups, religious faiths, minorities, etc. Aimed at the masses, it was established in favour of lower-income groups (those of slender means, those left 'on the side-lines', the needy, the 'lower classes', etc.) who had not had adequate opportunities of access to the school system or of achieving fairly in that system. In economic and social terms, illiteracy was seen as a barrier to development, its abolition a condition necessary, though not in itself sufficient, to Brazil's economic and social development. For the individual, literacy training and the more general process of continuing education (formal or otherwise) appeared as a key to better income and improved living conditions.

When the PAF programme got under way in 1970 there were 18.1 million adult illiterates in Brazil, 33.6 per cent of the adult population. That was taken as a benchmark for action. The goal was to reduce illiteracy to levels comparable with those of the developed countries, about ten to twelve per cent, within the decade. During the seventies, 14,456,678 persons received diplomas as completing PAF courses out of 33,810,122 enrolled. The percentage of approved to enrolled students was 43 per cent.[1]

The objectives and basic structure of the PAF were not significantly modified, although supporting programmes were generated and modifications introduced to adapt to particular clienteles or groups. These generally related to the modes of action, leaving the main methodological aspects unaltered, for example, utilisation of means of mass communication and greater functionality of content in relation to local characteristics. The mass nature of the programmes and the scale of effort make description, analysis and evaluation of interest but difficult. Insufficiency of data and survey results precludes full answers to some questions about the programme. We therefore give only an approximate reply to the question, what is the impact of the programme on the reduction of poverty; and deal more fully with questions for which we can rely on the experience of MOBRAL, and on available information and survey results, concerning the successes and failures of adult literacy training activities.

THE GENERAL CONTEXT

PAF was formulated and implemented in a context of: high rates of economic growth that prevailed in the years in question; substantial expansion of processing industries; progressive substitution of manufactures; rapid urbanisation; and the continuation through these processes of high levels of illiteracy, although the percentage declined in successive census results. Illiteracy was seen as a barrier to development and a form of social discrimination to be overcome in the interest of equal opportunities for all. The PAF was an initial step of fundamental significance, towards a socially widespread process of continuing education.

Before 1930, Brazil exported minerals, livestock and agricultural products and imported manufactures. Industrial expansion then occurred, with increasing import substitution, gaining headway during the fifties. Early in the sixties there was a setback, but economic growth recovered and gathered particular intensity between 1968 and 1972.[2] Income of the agricultural sector declined, while that of processing industries increased. Agriculture's rate of growth did not, however, lag behind the requirements of domestic consumption and export. Specialists agree about the dynamic role of Brazilian agriculture and its growth, especially in the later seventies.[3]

At the time the PAF was devised and implemented, documents in the planning and education sectors characterised illiteracy as a brake on development and a form of social discrimination to be eliminated by providing equality of educational opportunities. Equalising opportunities may be seen as the preferable way of producing more equitable distribution of income, which is influenced by educational achievement.

The story of illiteracy in Brazil is one of decline in the rate of illiteracy while there has been an increase in absolute numbers.[4] The growth in the number of illiterates between 1960 and 1970 helps to explain the strategy of literacy training and reinforcing elementary education. In 1970 the age bracket relevant in terms of the job market – 15 to 30 years of age – still displayed high rates of illiteracy. For inhabitants in urban areas this was estimated at 9.9 per cent, but for those living in rural areas it was 35 per cent. Brazilian experience indicated that the various programmes aimed at imparting literacy (regional or local, private or public) up to that time had been incomplete for one reason or another. According to appraisals by technical agencies, coordinated efforts were needed to overcome the problem. It was within this context that the Laws and Decrees establishing the function, objectives and structures of MOBRAL and the Functional Literacy Programme were developed.

MOBRAL AND THE PAF

MOBRAL. The institution with responsibility for the PAF was established on 15 November 1967 by Law 5379. Article 1 stipulated that:

> functional literacy training and especially continuing education of adolescents and adults are permanent activities of the Ministry of Education and Culture.

Article 2 regulated the operation of functional literacy programmes by professional and voluntary workers and authorised, under the name of Brazilian Literacy Movement (MOBRAL), a foundation charged with functional literacy training.

According to decree No. 62,455, dated 22 March 1968, the foundation was established to execute the Functional Literacy Training Plan and the task of Continuing Education of Adults and Adolescents. The organisation came into being in 1970. Efforts were made to ensure proper scope of its activities through prior evaluation of educational, social and economic priorities.

PAF was to take priority to the end of the seventies. Concern was felt at all times to afford programme completers possibilities of continuing with the process of life-long education. MOBRAL's programmes were devised and implemented within this concept. This is why, in addition to the Functional Literacy Programme, other programmes came to be implemented in support of the PAF and in response to the needs of the communities themselves: Programmes of Integrated Education, Self-Teaching, Cultural Development, Vocational Training and Community Education for Health.

How the MOBRAL System was Organised.[5] The institution was organised at three different levels; municipal, state and central, with different functions.

The COMUN (Municipal Commission), a juridically autonomous agency viewed as the real executive agent of MOBRAL, was responsible for:

> carrying out the MOBRAL programmes;
> mobilising necessary community resources;
> recruiting illiterates, literacy instructors and promotional agents ('animadores');
> setting up literacy training stations or cultural centres.

The COMUN operates with the participation of the community, and may be assisted by:

> municipal sub-committees/administrative regions;
> supporting groups and community councils.

The State/Territorial Coordination (COEST/COTER) plans, coordinates and controls activities connected with MOBRAL at a state or territorial level, and is connected with the Overall Supervision Sub-System, with Area and State Supervisors.

Central MOBRAL, structurally connected with the Ministry of Education and Culture (MEC):

> operates with the Municipal Commissions through Agreements ('Convenios'), supplying didactic materials and/or hardware for the MOBRAL units, technical orientation and funding to provide stipends for the literacy instructors;
> supervises agreements and evaluates results obtained on a nation-wide scale;

sparks the flow of decisions at a level of nation-wide overview.

At each level an agency was set up, responsible for one or more programmes of the Institution. In the case of the PAF the responsible agency was the Pedagogic Management Department, at central level, the pedagogic agency at the state level and the pedagogic supervisor at municipal level. The system thus developed was responsible for planning, coordination and execution of the programmes. Supervision was assigned to the Overall Supervision Sub-System.

The Functional Literacy Programme (PAF). The Functional Literacy Programme, as its name indicates, had as its central objective, functional literacy training, seen as part and parcel of the process of continuing education. Functional Literacy Training is not necessarily the first stage of this process. It should be built upon the life experience of the population participating in the programme, and its content related to the situations of daily life of those involved.

Functional Literacy Training is understood as that which leads adolescents and adults to make practical, immediate application of the techniques of reading, writing and arithmetic, fostering in them progressive autonomy and the quest for better living conditions. It is aimed at transforming the individual into both agent and beneficiary of the process of development. Functionality is entailed in the response to the basic requirements of the individual.

Alves Ramos e Fonseca, 1979

The objectives of the PAF in relation to Functional Literacy Training are as follows:

to develop in pupils the skills of reading, writing and arithmetic;
to develop a vocabulary permitting mental enrichment of pupils;
to develop the power of reasoning so as to facilitate power to cope with their own problems and those of the community;
to inculcate positive habits and attitudes in relation to work;

to develop creativity, so as to improve living conditions through application of available resources;
to induce pupils to:
get acquainted with their rights and duties and with the best forms of community participation;
engage in preservation of health and improvement of personal, family and community hygienic conditions;
realise the responsibility each one has for maintenance and improvement of public services in the community and for preservation of property and the institutions;
participate in community development, with a view to promoting the welfare of all.

The programmes last five months or 200 hours, usually two hours a day from Mondays to Fridays. The student is not forced to spend five months taking classes. If his rate of learning is faster he will remain only as long as necessary to achieve literacy; if slower, he can enter for the next agreement. (This might lead to dual counting of the same student.) The organisation starts from the principle that the clientele consists of adolescents and adults who, on account of their life experience and the fact that they have already attained a certain stage of maturation and enculturation, as well as motor development and perception, could be successful if encouraged in tasks that call for such skills and take their life experience as a starting point.

From 1976, the duration of the programme was diversified according to the specific characteristics of the population to be served, with special projects drawn up by the State and Territory Coordination offices so as to have the PAF specifically cope with each kind of problem. To establish the programme an agreement is made at the level of each municipality between the COMUN and MOBRAL, setting the goal to be achieved in terms of number of students, literacy instructors and materials needed for development of the programme. To arrive at the agreement, members of the COMUN and other volunteer workers are mobilised to make the course known, and to explain to the communities its advantages and the way it operates.

Mobilisation is by the Municipal Commissions (COMUN) and the communities, with Central MOBRAL and the State/Territory Coordinations also playing a part. The effort is mainly intended to arouse and motivate communities to play a specific and conscious part in the educational activities, joining efforts with MOBRAL to:

   identify those areas where the concentration of illiterates is highest;
   check the number of illiterates;
   develop mechanisms for sustaining the PAF through special strategies;
   foster the organisation of community groups based on the literacy classes, supporting not only the PAF but also the various other programmes of MOBRAL and other entities;
   utilise the resources of the community available locally, to make MOBRAL's mission known in the community.

   The State/Territorial Coordination attends the Municipal Commissions, orienting them towards strategies of mobilisation that involve the community and cooperating substantially towards the better achievement of the State level goals set for PAF. More dynamic participation of the various entities in the task of mobilisation has been a significant factor in the results obtained, embodying, where MOBRAL is concerned, new forms of activity in which the joint action more specifically fits in with the needs and possibilities of the population involved. The support material for mobilisation purposes (posters, information transmitted by mass communications media, etc.), can be generated at any level. The courses are given at points close to the nuclei of the illiterate population. Use is made, for instance, of churches, clubs, schools, even the homes of literacy instructors themselves.
   The selected literacy instructor is a member of the community with a certain amount of schooling to his credit, and in some cases may even be a natural community leader. This is an important factor in mobilisation, thanks to the knowledge he or she may have of the problems and habits of the potential clientele. In an endeavour to encourage instructors to concern themselves with the drop-outs, who are generally numerous in adult literacy classes, MOBRAL introduced a form of payment per student per programme. The literacy instructor received from MOBRAL a stipend proportionate to the number of students attending right to the end of the course. Courses are free of charge, and the distribution of teaching materials to both students and literacy instructors may likewise encourage mobilisation. Literacy instructors receive basic training during

17

which they become familiar with the methodology of the programme and the necessary content in Arithmetic, Communication and Expression, Health, Hygiene, etc. During the course they receive periodical feedback to reinforce the initial contact and basic training, through both supervisors' visits and advice, and the further training of monitors.

Method Adopted for PAF.

The method adopted is based on utilisation of the significant experience of the clientele itself. It uses key words that are derived from the basic requirements of Mankind, which ensures the interest and involvement of the students. The words in question are ones in universal use in the various parts of Brazil.

Koff and Campelo, 1979

For application of the method, a series of steps is recommended: presentation and discussion of the generating poster; study of the key word; study of the syllabic family, based on the key word; formation and study of new words and development and study of phrases and texts. The key words are tied in with basic needs in the fields of education, health, social welfare, clothing, etc. They are presented as significant forms within semantic fields that have to do with fundamental needs. Thus when health is the semantic field, the key words include medicine, vaccine and so on. Ever since it was introduced the method remained unaltered. Such variation as occurred had to do merely with approaches for applying it. Alterations were more marked from 1977 onwards, during the programme diversification phase. The very specific and individual nature of some of these modifications does not lend itself to analysis in greater depth:

greater or lesser emphasis on the use of the generating poster at the time that the key words are being worked on;
use of other materials or resources for decoding the key word;
greater emphasis on the techniques of reading, writing and arithmetic, together with coverage of general subjects connected with the other requirements of the student. This is what ensures overall functionality. It is in this stage, rather than in the previous one, that stress is laid on the performance of out-of-

class activities such as student participation in other MOBRAL programmes. The Coordination offices are at liberty to opt for that form which appears to them most suitable, in developing the process of literacy training.

MOBRAL makes available to students and literacy instructors didactic publications that can be classified into Basic and Complementary. Basic didactic publications are those deemed essential to the objectives and proper development of the programme. They consist of:

the Literacy Instructor's Schedule for Orientation - a didactic instrument that orients the instructor to the proper way of applying the methodology developed by MOBRAL;

the Literacy Instructor's Guide, showing how to use the didactic materials distributed by MOBRAL posters - a didactic instrument that fosters discussion of the theme and meaning of the illustration, so that the key word may be effectively decided;

cards - didactic materials complementing the posters and also presenting the key words;

the student's Reader - intended to give form to the various stages of the method, permitting the acquisition of automaticity and skill in the reading process;

the student's language exercise book - a didactic instrument intended to develop the Functional Literacy Programme in the language field by firmly establishing a grasp of content and encouraging active student participation in the process (reading and writing);

the student's arithmetic exercise book - intended to permit development of the programme in arithmetic, by fostering a grasp of the material and encouraging active participation by the student in the process.

The materials have been produced by a number of different publishing houses, with unity of the various items ensured thanks to the methodology adopted and the quality control techniques applied by MOBRAL. Besides this basic didactic material,

literate students receive complementary materials
consisting of continuing Readers and journals that
help to back up and enrich the process of acquisition
of literacy. In addition, use of radio was introduced
in 1977, followed by PAF by TV in 1979.

Evaluation is conceived as overall, continuous
and all-encompassing. A series of items guides and
assists the literacy instructor in checking whether
or not the student may be deemed to have acquired
literacy. These are direct indicators as to what is
to be expected of the learning process. It has been
stipulated that to be considered literate a student
should be capable of:

identifying the content of the texts and
sentences he reads;
writing texts and sentences that make proper
sense;
solving problems that involve the four operations with one- and two-digit figures, with
and without clustering;
solving problems that involve measures of
length (m, cm, km), calculations of circum-
ference, measures of capacity, measures of
mass (g and kg), measures of value (cruzeiros
and centavos), measures of time (day, month,
hour, etc.), using whole numbers and
fractions.

These are the terminating objectives; participants
should also start by achieving intermediate
objectives. The properly oriented literacy instructor
has complete autonomy as to whether or not he will
consider the student to be literate or otherwise.
This makes it possible, based on recognition of the
rate of learning of each student, to work in terms
of individual differences.[6]

The PAF Clientele. The PAF plan was designed to meet
nationwide requirements and aimed at the adult
illiterate population. It does not specify their
characteristics in economic, social and cultural
terms, but is naturally oriented towards the social
strata of lesser means and income, and those with
the worst living conditions. Even amongst these there
are significant differences of income and of living
experience, mastery of the linguistic code, etc.
Taking into account some of these characteristics
and above all age and degree of urbanisation, MOBRAL
has given priority to a target population:

age from 15 to 35;
located in areas defined as urban, especially
the major cities that have had sharp
population increases in the past three
decades.

The reference frameworks of economics and
education were considered, specifically Human Capital
Theory, to identify the segment of the population
in the best position to take advantage of the
educational process, participate in economic and
social development, and benefit individually in terms
of income and quality of life. Despite the
orientation of PAF facilities towards the segment
to which priority had been assigned, data on
enrolment in agreements and on enrolment in classes,
besides fact-finding survey data, bear out the
predominantly rural participation of students in the
PAF classes; acceptance and participation proved to
be greater in rural areas.[7]
The data on 'agreement coverage' and 'enrolment'
indicate that over 70 per cent of the total students
are from rural areas. In the north-east, the region
of lowest economic and social development, that
percentage exceeds 80 per cent. Data in the fact-
finding survey reveal similar ratios for PAF course-
completers under the 1975/76 agreement.[8] Activities
tend to be concentrated more in the less privileged
areas, as entailed by the double inequality both
between regions and between urban and rural areas.
Hence the north-east region contained 68.5 per cent
of the total number of students, and 73 per cent of
the students from the rural zones. The process may
be characterised as one of specialisation and
'spatialisation' in activity: work with the less-
favoured sectors of the population in social terms,
and work in the less-developed geographical areas.
Obviously there is a close connection between the
two.
A comparison of the distribution of proportions
of illiterate adult population by regions, as
recorded in the 1970 Census, with the data on
distribution of those acquiring literacy, region by
region, through the MOBRAL programme, bears out the
distortion. There is a significant relationship
between the distribution of the students that
completed the course and received passing grades in
the PAF, and the illiterate adults in 1970. The
north-east region, with an illiterate population of
45.9 per cent, was responsible for 57.3 per cent of
the course completion diplomas issued. The PAF
clientele is not a specific social group from an

ethnic, religious or linguistic point of view. There might be a possible correlation between schooling and colour of skin, but elimination of the latter characteristic from the census and from the bulk of fact-finding surveys makes this impossible to determine. Nor do religious differences appear to be significantly correlated with schooling; and linguistic differences, in statistical terms, are practically non-existent. The Portuguese language is practically universal with the exception of the indigenous groups, in very small numbers, amongst which the PAF was not carried out.

In the urban zones, distribution of PAF students is even as between men and women, though there is a slight edge in favour of women in all regions. In the centre-west region, indeed, the predominance of female participation is quite considerable. In rural zones the ratios become inverted. Male participation in the total is 58.2 per cent, while in a number of regions (south-east, 68.8 per cent; south, 67.1 per cent and centre-west up to 62.9 per cent) it significantly exceeds that of women. The most persuasive explanation for this difference is in terms of expectations and practices induced in the respective job markets. In the urban zones, the MOBRAL clientele consists of migrants of both sexes. Migrant women have to take jobs in household employment, which generally means minimum wages and absence of labour guarantees. After incorporation into this first sector of employment, expectations are aroused of getting into the job market with labour guarantees. This generally means tertiary or secondary sector jobs calling for meagre skills, but which require, more for administrative purposes than through any demands of technical procedures, the ability to read and write.

For male migrants, the predominant sector of absorption is the building trade, which usually operates with labour law guarantees. A number of fact-finding surveys confirm that amongst these migrants the idea of building up a small reserve and then returning to the point of origin so as to become a small-holder or to have a small business exercises strong attraction. In the rural areas, factors linked with expulsion tend to affect men more than women. This pressure, allied to the traditional role of women in rural areas, favours as a whole a higher proportion of participation by men.[9]

Distribution of students by age shows that those given priority under the MOBRAL plan really did participate in the PAF courses. In the urban areas, 65 per cent of participants were under 30; in rural areas about 74 per cent. Differences in distribution also show up on an analysis by regions.

Apart from the fact that income levels are low for the sector as a whole, the lower income brackets themselves comprise, in all regions (if those without any income included) a majority of the participants - 87 per cent of the total up to the second category of income levels.[10] It should be stressed that at the time of the fact-finding survey, the current regional minimum wage level was that of May 1975. In monetary terms it was from CR$376.80 to CR$532.80 a month, meaning that the bulk of those surveyed had no income at all, or received less than the minimum wage.[11]

The occupation of PAF course completers mainly involves low wage and low skill activities. In the urban areas, too, groups connected with primary sector activities are significant, such as ordinary farm labourers, 15.0 per cent, and general farm workers, 3.3 per cent. In the rural areas ordinary farm labourers make up 31.7 per cent of the total, 13 per cent being farmers. In both rural and urban areas, though to a lesser extent in the former, the category of those without any occupation (16.4 per cent and 25.1 per cent respectively) is highly significant.

The data presented thus briefly characterise the MOBRAL population. Indirectly, they reflect the economic and social context within which that population exists: rural areas with a predominance of tiny holdings and large estates, and, more recently, capitalistic companies operating in the rural areas; peripheral urban areas whose population tends to be employed in low-wage, low-skill pursuits. All are areas that could be described as poor, with others of relative poverty, within which there are also significant differences in income and occupation. Although the poverty generated by the economic and social mechanisms of production and distribution, and the strata suffering its effects, might appear homogeneous, it is possible to distinguish internal differentiations. These may lead to particular relationships with and applications of educational facilities, to which we refer later.

OBJECTIVES AND GOALS[12]

The predominant objective of MOBRAL activities centred from the start on Functional Literacy Training in the context of a process of continuing education. Reduction in poverty can be considered an explicit objective only if this is included within the concept of 'functionality' of or in the educational process. Functionality of education, especially literacy training, must be understood as the use of literacy training in the life of the individual to improve quality of life. MOBRAL felt that the process of literacy training should be closely connected with the application of its contents, so programme content had to be closely connected with the basic requirements of the individuals and their communities.

In the approach adopted by MOBRAL, poverty features in terms of quality of life; its elimination ought to be a democratic-oriented effect of development. The approach of MOBRAL in the agent-object, subject-object terms of the development process, and in its approach to the autonomy of the individual, etc., emphasised that elimination of poverty implied effort, individual and coordinated, on the part of the agents concerned.

The model of social change devised by MOBRAL went through two stages. In the initial stage, characterised by an excessively individualised view of society, educational action aimed at the individual was viewed as a priority factor for social change and reduction of poverty. In a second stage, education was itself recognised as one of the factors for, social change and reduction of poverty. Seen thus, its success calls for a constellation of other actions, both political and institutional. In fact, the process takes place in the context of a decline in faith in the possibility that economic growth is capable, independently or through the action of the laws of the market, of becoming translated into social benefits, better living conditions, more suitable distribution of income and opportunity. In this respect the second phase points to action by state mechanisms, coordinated and planned activity, and spontaneous or other forms of community organisation in a joint effort to produce social change and vanquish poverty.

The significance of poverty and its reduction seems to run as a thread through the various attitudes of MOBRAL, especially through every programme developed and implemented. There is no way of rendering these meanings explicit. From the purposeful nature of the programme, however, it is possible to deduce the latent and consensual implications. Poverty is tackled within the programmes at both an individual and a community level, even though the generation of poverty is viewed as the result of economic and social factors involved in the production and distribution of social wealth.[13]

This is attempted on two different fronts: first, it is felt that education, by generating greater capability, can lead to better individual placement opportunities in the job market and hence a rise in income levels. In the second place it is postulated that education is capable, also as a result of better preparedness, of improving individual or community application of human and material resources which are being under- or ill-utilised. Hence poverty, at the clientele level, can be at least attenuated by collective and individual action. Poverty, besides being generated by social mechanisms, is to some extent reinforced by social and cultural patterns. Education, in modifying those patterns and expanding the horizon of knowledge, can make possible better individual and collective use of existing resources. In many cases the content of education does not imply new techniques but may comprise technologies of grass-roots origin which had been forgotten but which make it possible to attenuate the effects of poverty.

The relationship between education and poverty, viewed in terms of better placement in the economy, is impaired when the economy cannot provide enough jobs for the capabilities developed. Trained workers go into jobs calling for skills below those they possess. In this context education to reduce poverty concentrates on better application of human and material resources, and especially on organisational forms that make it possible to reduce poverty. This gives rise to community organisation as a form of community action and a way of overcoming, even though only partially, conditions of poverty. (cf. 'Educacao de Massa e Acao Comunitaria', 1979)

The Literacy Training Programme emerged in a context of simultaneous fast economic growth and persisting high rates of illiteracy in the lower income brackets. The struggle against illiteracy came to be thought of, on the one hand as a means of removing an obstacle that prevented the illiterate from enjoying the advantages of economic development, and on the other as a necessity created by that same development and by the community involved. The percentage of illiterates aged 15 or more had been declining but not at the rate hoped for. Institutionalisation of MOBRAL and the Functional Literacy Training Programme reflected the thrust of work done previously: in 1900, 65.3 per cent of the adult population did not know how to read or write; in 1970 that proportion had declined to 33.6 per cent. The Functional Literacy Training Programme needed to be accompanied by renewed effort in the field of regular, especially elementary, education, to put a stop to the process of generating further illiteracy. The PAF acquired the characteristics of a broad literacy training campaign, the underlying idea being that the regular system should acquire the dynamic drive to prevent the generation of further illiteracy.

It was thought of the PAF that education, and particularly literacy training, through its interaction with the job market and the new opportunities of immigration, transportation, mass communication, etc., would be sufficient to produce a significant impact in terms of social change. Such an idea might be thought over-optimistic, but consideration must be given to the feeling of euphoria produced by economic growth and the importance acquired in the fields of education and economic planning by Human Capital Theory. The important role assigned to education as regards both economic growth and its functions in terms of income distribution and remuneration for work, gave rise to a concept of education as a privileged, and often isolated, factor of social transformation in a context of economic growth.

Observation by instructors and participants in the PAF of the effects of literacy led on the one hand to the development of programmes in support of literacy instruction (health, cultural development, vocational training, etc.) and, on the other, to a search, at local and national levels, for agreements for joint action with health agencies, social assistance entities, means of technical diffusion in the rural areas, church activities, etc. The agreements in question were the result of the relatively minor efficiency of literacy training as a factor operating apart from transformation, rather than of an a priori definition of the need for articulation of planning, for coordination and executive action, or for inter-ministerial, inter-managerial and other such efforts for social change. There appears to be more consensus of late in the various government and private agencies. At the same time the need for articulated action by local agencies is generated at local and municipal level. Literacy training groups could thus become a facet of collective action, or of articulation of the joint action of various agencies, with a view to causing significant changes in the economic and social conditions of adults learning how to read and write, and in the lives of their families and the community at large.

COSTS

MOBRAL records costs incurred directly by the organisation. Costs of use of facilities, means and personnel of other institutions and city departments, or communities, have not been calculated. Even to estimate the latter, as to estimate the value of the voluntary work performed, is hard. Such items are, however, highly relevant to the functioning of the programme. We cannot present comparative data on the costs of the regular and nonformal systems to permit a comparative evaluation.

Analysis of expenses over the 1970 to 1980 period, broken down by programmes and including costs of administration and amortisation of loans, shows that most significant, though diminishing with the passing of time, are the direct costs of literacy training (didactic materials, payments to instructors and others), which always add up to over 65 per cent of the total outlay of the institution. The administration item increased with the passing of time, with the development of logistic activities, advisory activities, planned and fact-finding surveys. In 1973 it accounted for 7.2 per cent of total outlays, rising to 18.0 per cent by 1980. Administration may be defined as the group of 'means activities', whereas the programmes comprise the 'end activities'. Average cost per student enrolled through agreement in PAF is calculated at US$12.12 and US$33.83 in the Integrated Education Programme; US$13.18 for the Self-Teaching Programme, US$7.75 for the Formal Training Programme and US$1.08 as the cost of actually placing a candidate in a job through the MOBRAL Job Counter. (Barbosa, 1983)

CHARACTERISTIC DIFFERENCES IN STYLE AND METHOD

The Functional Literacy Training Programme was intended to operate in two apparently contradictory directions. On the one hand it was a mass programme. On the other, it explicitly aimed at relating to different particular needs. These two objectives could be achieved only by active and total participation in the programme of the various parties involved, namely students, literacy instructors, members of the COMUN, the supervisory network and the State Coordination offices.

On the one hand, the participation was supposed to ensure achieving the quantitative goals of the programme, its characteristics of mass impact, by mobilising resources that had not previously been used for the purpose, and creative ability deployed in problem-solving. The scheme operated on the premise that the motivation existed and that participatory action could increase it further, so that it would become possible to achieve the quantitative goals of the programme. At the level of content, on the other hand, participation was intended to permit functional development and adaptation of the programme, to fit in with local requirements and the experience of the participants, the latter acting as a base and multiplier for learning capacity.

In the context of these views operational problems arose. First there was the job of organising the community for participation, hence the establishment of the COMUN, the local agency responsible for the programmes of MOBRAL. In the second place, how were the illiterates to be motivated to participate in the courses? The reply was through various forms of mobilisation, through which the community was supposed to participate. On a more restricted basis there had to be participation by the literacy instructors, the members of the COMUN and the personnel of the Supervisory sector and the State Coordination offices. Third was the problem how to encourage the literacy instructors to view the programme in creative terms, putting functional content into it and meeting the specific requirements of the clientele with which they were working.

MOBRAL reacted to these problems in two complementary ways: by endeavouring to arouse motivation of an ideological type, to be transmitted and developed in training activities, together with the capability to act according to the methodological principles stipulated in the programme; and by paying the instructors on a per student/programme basis for students attending lessons right to the end, independently of approval or otherwise, to induce efforts to keep them in class-rooms through the five month period of the agreement. There was a risk that the instructor, for motives of economic gain, might tend to register 'phantom' students in the control books; the supervisory section was made responsible for detecting such activities. One important source of motivation of instructors lay in the symbolic field. Most are members of the local community, and of the same social standing as their students. To be a literacy instructor, especially in the rural areas, means a form of symbolic differentiation. The fees paid may also – depending on the conditions prevailing in that particular place – generate a form of material differentiation as well.

The process of participation starts with the establishment of the COMUN, therefore, and should extend throughout the five months of lessons, thanks to the provision by the community and MOBRAL itself of the means of sustenance necessary for the educational process and for administrative and material support, such as supervisory activities and feedback, culminating in the celebration of the student passing from a state of illiteracy to one of literacy, in a ceremony generally attended by the municipal authorities (sometimes State dignitaries or representatives of MOBRAL central offices), members of the COMUN, participants in the programme and the community at large.

DISCUSSION AND ANALYSIS

Clarity of Purpose

One frequently criticised aspect of MOBRAL's literacy work is the national use of a single type of didactic material, or of materials with no significant variation from place to place. Does the use of a single type of material run counter to the concept of functionality as the philosophical basis and purpose of the programme?

It is claimed that the application of a common fund of key words does not take into account regional characteristics and local idiosyncrasies, that it tends to cause lack of motivation and to estrange people from the programme. MOBRAL has justified the adoption of a single type of material by two different arguments: a single format was justified through economies of scale reducing unit costs; and the actual 'functionalisation' of content is something to be taken care of by each literacy instructor. The instructor, who usually belongs to the community, especially in the rural zones, would have sufficient knowledge of the culture, problems, basic needs, etc. of the community and of the need to adapt material to local characteristics.

MOBRAL and its critics agree over the principle of functionality as regards adaptation of content to local realities. The need is axiomatic and has become a commonplace in adult education theory: motivation for a literacy training course is the result of proximity between the content of the course and the representations of reality of those involved. Practical outcome of such discussion would depend on the extent to which the specific impact of the active figures, both Directors and students, on their realities was known.[14] It is also difficult to determine to what extent the literacy trainers in fact 'functionalised' the didactic materials.

An endeavour was made to get acquainted with the approaches and motivations of the actors. What were the motives that led to participation in functional literacy courses? What were the motives that led to the voluntary dropping out of students? In the research programme 'Contributions to the Evaluation of the Functional Literacy Training Programme'[15] a question about motives for participating evoked responses such as the following: 'to be able to write letters' 82.9 per cent; 'to make progress', 82.7 per cent; 'to be able to read newspapers and magazines', 81.2 per cent; 'to make more money', 80 per cent; 'to be less dependent on others', 66.1 per cent. The common factor was that they were replies of a general kind, not specific in terms of the lives of those involved. Also they reflected values predominating in society in general about education. In view of the impossibility of penetrating to the specific motives of the clientele, the approach was shifted to research surveys of an anthropological type, intended to uncover motivations.[16] It then became possible to arrive at certain conclusions. This approach brought out a distinction between the symbolic and instrumental value of the literacy instructor and the processes of formal schooling. In rural areas literacy training is not vested with immediate instrumental value. There is considered to be a negative relationship between education and agriculture. Literacy training and schooling are seen as means of getting away from the farm, via migration, and arranging lighter work in the city. The demand of the population in terms of content was for aspects that had to do more with a future prospect of geographical and social change than with present reality.

Surveys based on observation of participants revealed that instructors 'functionalised' programmes only to a very minor extent, also that a concept of schooling had been absorbed and was transmitted by the instructors. This caused rigid adherence to curricula, avoidance of modification, and validation of adult education efforts according to their approximation to formal, regular, school education. Such research is not conclusive. It does however raise questions about the axiom of adaptation and motivation.

Local Power and Leadership
Since MOBRAL reports at the local level to volunteer workers, the opinion of local leaders about the programme, their orientation in relation to it, and their willingness to support or reject it, are

factors of the utmost significance. Local leaders are generally a part of the local power structure of the municipal authorities on whom depend many of the resources needed for performance of the programmes: management, control and material resources. Good relationships with the local authorities are thus a condition for carrying out the programme.

Central Oversight

Because of the scope of the programme, its penetration into rural areas, the distances that have to be covered in order to visit class-rooms, generally by night and over beaten-earth roadways, etc., direct schemes of class-room supervision are hampered (considering supervision not only in terms of control but basically in terms of feedback). Area supervisors generally cover four different municipalities. This means, on average, the need to visit 150 class-rooms a month. In some regions, even at the cost of considerable effort, it is possible to cover only one class-room a day. From the time of the rise in international petroleum prices and domestic prices of fuel, the situation became more and more difficult. Efficient control calls for substantial material and human resources; such resources were too scanty for ideal control and feedback.

Adequacy of Resources

What is optimal in terms of sufficiency of financial resources? Educators tend to consider financial resources insufficient in relation to any ideal system of education. In the case of MOBRAL, the question was never brought up in those terms. Even when endeavours were made to expand the resources available, the approach was always to make best use of existing resources. In terms of material resources, especially physical facilities, needs have always been significantly reduced by the use of existing facilities, schools, churches, literacy teachers' own homes and various others.

It was in terms of teacher training that the major difficulties were encountered. There was a severe deficiency, both quantitatively and qualitatively, in what MOBRAL could provide. In the field of literacy instructor training, comprising the bulk of human resources used, training aimed at overcoming the dearth of trained personnel was combined with the idea that persons in the communities with the illiterates, and also mastering the same codes of activity, could be more efficient

in literacy instruction than workers trained in
normal schools. This may have been both
rationalisation of short supply and an accurate
diagnosis. There is no way of knowing unequivocally
whether this was the right thing to do in pedagogic
terms.

In the survey 'Subsidios para Avaliacao...' (de
Almeida, 1978) levels of schooling of the literacy
instructors were as follows:

Monitors' Level of Schooling	Percentage
First to fourth grades of elementary school (incomplete)	23.4
Fourth grade of elementary school	42.3
Fourth to eighth grade	21.2
Other	13.1

The first three grades of elementary school account
for 91.3 per cent of monitors in rural areas and 71.9
per cent in urban, clearly showing monitors' low
level of formal qualification, and implying the
difficulties involved in literacy training.
Comparison between level of schooling of the
instructors and performance in tests (reading,
writing and arithmetic) by the students, however,
shows no significant and stable relationship, either
negative or positive, between these two variables.
Training of literacy instructors can be analysed at
two levels. To what extent does such training develop
in instructors the values and attitudes of adult
literacy teaching upheld by the agency? In the second
place, to what extent is the training sufficient to
produce a teacher qualified to impart techniques of
reading, writing and arithmetic? With regard to the
latter, no significant relationship was found. As
to the former, it is difficult to check whether or
not the training produced is in relation to the
school-like image of adult education, to effects
arising from traditions and school experience. Adult
education imitates the education of children. The
adult is educated, in many cases, by turning into
reality his or her own image of what studying
implies.

Motivation
Problems of motivation are among the most difficult
in adult education. Motivation to enrol and stay in
literacy courses appears to be present at different
levels. The first comprises motivations developed
within the overall development of society and
stemming from the conditions of economic and social

growth and from ideologies transmitted by mass media about the role and benefits of education in this process. In the economic and social circumstances of its establishment, MOBRAL education was a highly valued channel of social mobility, essentially in terms of a change to jobs in those sectors that operate with advanced technologies and poligopolic markets. Heavy pressure was accordingly developed on the education system. The general context seems to have significantly influenced even those of low income and low educational opportunity. Amongst the illiterate there was a tendency to enter the education system by means of MOBRAL (Functional Literacy Training and Integrated Education) and through the supplementary general education system. In the early 1970s, euphoria about development, added to the large unmet demand for literacy training, probably combined to explain the high number of students under agreement and students made literate early in the programme, with a high productivity rate (defined as the relation between students made literate and those under agreement). This rate fell from 1974 onwards, maybe a result, on the one hand, of a decrease in the level of euphoria and, on the other hand, of partly meeting the demand previously ignored.

At a second level is involved the idea that the various strata comprising the illiterate population have education within their concept of social development. This conditions attitudes towards joining and staying in literacy courses. Those in the urban sectors seek both literacy instruction and continuing education. Preliminary data from the 1980 census placed the proportion of adult illiterates in the urban zones at about 16 to 17 per cent, implying significant progress. However, those answering yes to a census query as to whether they can read · and write are rated as literate, without determining what respondents understand by this. Statements obtained in field work seem to indicate that people understand 'reading and writing' to mean a fluent mastery of these techniques.

Various surveys have indicated that those acquiring literacy through MOBRAL reach a less satisfactory level of writing performance, and that reading performance is characterised by the level of mastery that meets the objectives of the course alone. Rural folk see a negative relationship between agriculture and techniques of writing and reading. These are not necessary or desired for activities in the rural milieu, for either small independent production or for salaried work. Motivation for joining the courses is linked, in these cases, with possibilities of migration. On the other hand those involved define minimum contents to be attained, essentially how to read and how to sign their own names. Learning to sign one's name makes it possible to obtain the required identification papers to exercise the rights of citizenship and to move around and enter the job market. Reading is required for operating in towns and cities, and for relationships with future employers. A minimum mastery of writing, even with bad mistakes, makes it possible to achieve the required written communication, such as writing small notes, writing down addresses, etc. Those who have this level of mastery are inclined to give a negative answer to census queries. It is impossible to establish the offsetting weight of distortion between those who though knowing how to write give a negative answer, and those who do not know how to write, yet give a positive one.

In various parts of Brazil the development in recent years of more intensive agriculture (technified and mechanised) among small producers has been intensifying relationships with the market and commercial circles, financial and technical fields. This increases the demand in rural areas for writing, reading and technical knowledge. It may be that from various points of view the rural areas are becoming belatedly and irregularly urbanised.

Within MOBRAL's framework of objectives, student follow-up activities were carried on in 1975/76.[17] The purpose was to identify changes, based on a group of variables where certain aspects of the objectives and attitudes could be gauged. The variables were migration, income levels, occupation, participation in community activities, participation in associations and continuation of the educational process. The intention was to gauge changes in relation to these variables up to one year after completion of the Functional Literacy Course. The survey suffered serious limitations. On the one hand there was the time-frame limitation: is one year long enough for education to produce its effects? Then there was the limitation stemming from the variables selected themselves. Some of the results are however, worth considering. The survey brought out the fact that shifts from urban to rural areas were as substantial as those in the opposite direction. This to some extent conflicts with patterns observed in economic development, but may be accounted for by the specific migratory features of Brazil. Rural-to-rural migration, or from small localities denoted as urban into the rural milieu, is in line with a historic process of expanding the agricultural frontier, depleting the soil and searching for new places to farm. This process is highly significant in the formation and transformation of the 'peasantry'. And then, according to some, note should be taken of the gradual formation of a rural/urban market in the low labour skills work-force which shifts from one pole to the other in terms of agricultural seasons and the dynamics of investments. At present there is a significant volume of rural labour living in urban areas.

No real increases of income were noted: conversion of nominal into real wages was based on modification in the current legal minimum wage level. However the survey only estimated cash income, and did not allow for in-kind income, which is of great importance in rural areas and especially on small-holdings. Among those that could be classified as wage-earners there were no signs of changes in occupation - from less skilled to more skilled - implying any change in income. Participation in community activities and in associations, though significant, tended to decline with the passing of time after course completion.

The most important factor, change in income and occupation, is conditioned by a number of different factors. As a general rule education, while developing human resources, does not determine the positions to be held. The regular job market lacks the adaptive vigour to incorporate the output of the education system. Though possessing better educational levels, the labour force continues to go into the informal labour market. The job market seems to be somewhat segmented, and each segment has its own particular dynamic of expansion. Secondly, the literacy course does not prepare students for skilled occupations. At most it provides means for joining the regular labour market at the lowest levels of qualification. Penetration into that market can be accounted for less in terms of expected monetary income gains than in terms of possibilities of security and social assistance, through the indirect advantages of association with the labour market. Application of what has been learned within the family unit, as a domestic and production entity, is difficult to gauge. Various survey results seem to suggest that it depends on transformations in the production field, and especially the articulation of loans for agriculture and technical assistance. Application might be assumed in terms of improved living conditions based on reduction in infantile mortality and the birth rate, and on increased life expectancy. It is difficult if not impossible to separate out the effect of education from that of basic sanitation, disease prevention, vaccination and so on.

The third level depends on individual factors, and the form of introduction into the family group. These factors appear to modify general motivations within society, or specific motivations within particular strata and groups, rather than to develop the motivations themselves. In many cases what is found is not so much motivation in favour of education as rationalisations for not moving in this direction. At the level of the family unit in agriculture, moreover, for some members school conjures up an image of division between manual and intellectual work which is negative for the individual member and divisive for the unit.

Indigenous Minorities

Those who are not native Portuguese speakers are members of the indigenous communities. There is no indigenous census, and information on their number varies a great deal. Programmes are only developed with those communities that are in an advanced stage of integration into the national society, or in a process of cultural adaptation to a new one. The Indian National Foundation (FUNAI) has to be consulted in order to carry out any kind of programme with them. Many such programmes have been developed but no evaluation exists of their adequacy or results.

Inter-Agency Cooperation

A number of situations involve relationships with government entities, non-governmental agencies, the communities, and with other programmes. At the central level there are cooperation agreements with various organisations, and directives for their achievement. At the local level there is a great variety of situations, running all the way from those involving close collaboration to those in which there is mutual lack of acquaintance. No clear-cut balance sheet could be drawn up in this respect. The Ministry of Education and Culture has been articulating a closer and more coordinated relationship between its various agencies in terms of a new policy laying greater stress on basic education.

Real-Life Impact?

The difficulties in evaluating the application of what is learned to real life are recognised, as well as those of distinguishing whether application, and especially non-application, depends on problems of inadequacy of content or conditioning factors of other kinds that have not been modified concomitantly. When overall indicators are used for purposes of evaluation, education as a factor in change is not easy to distinguish from other factors. When use is made of case studies, which are highly specific and restricted, selection of the cases raises problems about general applicability.

EVALUATION AND APPRAISAL

Overall Evaluation
The PAF can be evaluated from the point of view of its strictly educational objectives and from that of reduction of poverty. In relation to the former we rely mainly on the survey, 'Review of data from the survey to evaluate the Functional Literacy Program in the North-East and South-East Regions: a comparative study'. To evaluate the effects of the programme on reduction of poverty there is the survey already quoted, 'Education and its effects...'. The survey to evaluate the effects of the programme on poverty contains insufficient information to cover the reduction of poverty in terms other than shifts in income and occupation. There are no surveys directly evaluating the impact of the PAF on the quality of life, conditions in family unit production, and so on. The same can be said of the impact on forms of organisation among the people that lead, via pressure and negotiation, to redistribution of wealth such as may reduce relative levels of poverty.

There are signs that certain practices implied by educational content, health and hygiene, water treatment, disease prevention, nutrition, etc., are being adopted; but such content is also spread through health education programmes and, in the better endowed regions, by means of communication in public and private campaigns. It is difficult if not impossible to distinguish and evaluate the effects of the PAF separately from other programmes and appeals. In the agricultural sector, especially where small-holders are concerned, literacy training starts to produce effects when connected with increase in commercial output, technical and financial assistance, etc. (cf. Lovisolo). This can be seen in rural areas when there is social differentiation between the activities of small farming units and the general process of linking up agrarian activities with agro-industry, industrialisation or relative modernisation of this activity.

MOBRAL's Functional Literacy Programme

Differential Results

In relation to pedagogic objectives and results from the PAF, and the difficulties encountered, there are some analyses available based on samplings of all participants. Performance tests in reading, writing and arithmetic applied in the North-East and South-East regions (the former being the least developed region in Brazil and the latter the most developed) have borne out differences between them. Performance proved to be systematically better for the South-East region. The least difference was observed in relation to reading skills. In both regions reading showed the highest concentration of students with better performance. Reading skills (words, phrases and sentences) may be considered extremely satisfactory. Arithmetical skills rated below those for reading, with better performances in the South-East region. The skills acquired in these two areas were considered satisfactory by the survey workers in terms of day-to-day requirements. Writing results were generally poorer than those obtained for reading and arithmetic, better in the South-East than the North-East. Spelling of words was deemed satisfactory, on the basis of the criteria adopted. Those completing the literacy courses displayed difficulty, however, in writing sentences and texts. The survey report concluded that 'though results were below what had been expected, it may be supposed that those completing the Functional Literacy Program at MOBRAL have at least an initiation into the development of the minimum skills required to acquire the written code of the Portuguese language, thus meeting the requirements of the first two stages of the process of achieving literacy...'.

The same study sought to identify variables accounting for variation in performance. Generally speaking, even if some of the variables are statistically significant, their ability to explain the variance is extremely low, too low to be taken into account. Important variables such as previous schooling, sex, age, schooling of the instructor, prior experience in adult education, etc., were also of low value for purposes of explanation and have low statistical significance.

Reduction of Poverty?

Reduction in poverty, rather than being an explicit objective, is a corollary of the philosophical attitude and theoretical approach adopted in the PAF, which was generated at a moment of educational euphoria, though not educational alone. With the passing of time and the accumulation of experience

38

regarding the attitudes of those involved at various levels of organisation, including the clientele, the view was little by little arrived at that though education may help reduce poverty it is not the main factor. This does not remove the need to make more vigorous efforts in the field of education, since there is a demand for it in the most general of terms. It does, however, mean reconsidering the priorities, the styles involved, and so on; and at the same time, articulating action with activities in the sphere of production, for increase in productivity and more equitable distribution of resources.

Methodological difficulties of isolating the effects of education from other effects are considerable. Orientation towards fact-finding surveys focussing on the performance of those involved in relation to changes produced by education, and follow-up of those changes, appears to be valid; but this has its limitations, including that of subjectivity, such that the changes credited to education, especially in relation to reduction of poverty, are those the various participants believe to have been caused by education. In the end, judgement of success or failure of the programme in terms of reducing poverty stems from social consensus in relation thereto.

An Appraisal

In relation to pedagogic objectives, partial success has evidently been achieved, stemming from the interaction between the programme and the economic, social and cultural characteristics of the clientele in the context of Brazil's development. The clientele takes from the educational content that which in some manner it can convert into instruments for short or medium term use. Its partial appropriation of education perhaps indicates the need to minimise costs. Conditions for appropriation in terms of nutrition, work, jobs, health, age, linguistic habits and so on act as a brake, and increase the costs of the appropriations. Reduction in costs entailed by these conditions is one way of increasing the probability of appropriation. For students to learn better they must be in a better economic and social situation in the first place. Reasoning backs up the circular causation of a number of social processes. Possibly these can be broken down only by acting on a number of different planes at the same time. Since the programme is not directly articulated with the production sector, the effects of such combination have not been felt. Given the characteristics of the programme, undesired effects occur mainly at the individual level (eg, acquire literacy, then migrate, and end up with worse living conditions than before).

Alleviation or Change?

Any educational programme may in principle be merely ameliorative and serve to attenuate social tensions without having direct impact on the political or economic causes producing poverty. Reduction in poverty is above all a political matter. It implies consensus over the allocation of resources, taking into account the limitations that resources impose. Consensus for new forms of generation and orientation of resources can be achieved only through conscious participation by the various parties involved, by negotiation within democratic contexts of operation. Education is a means in this respect, rather than an end in itself. It is only an end to the extent that participation in the educational process by those previously excluded implies better use of resources, generally desired though not attained, that are available to society. It is on the other hand a means to the extent that it increases for these people the possibility of participation and negotiation. In Brazilian life the illiterate is excluded, as though something like a blind person, from public participation, from precisely those sectors in which poverty reduction ought to be a goal, and which are indeed the ones in which reduction of poverty can be achieved. Brazil's illiterates do not have voting rights, though this specific factor may change. Until society 'destigmatises' illiteracy, it will remain a function of the state to develop opportunities for literacy training, even though this implies only the provision of educational opportunities without modification of economic and social conditions. The demand for literacy training is not only economic. It cannot be accounted for solely in terms of the questionable theorems of Human Capital. Basic education and literacy training acquire differing functions, one of which, with all the nuances that ought to be allowed for, will continue to be reduction of poverty.

CONCLUSIONS AND IMPLICATIONS

Evaluation of the Functional Literacy Programme at MOBRAL requires adopting a number of different points of view. By way of conclusion we summarise the more important of these.

MOBRAL's Functional Literacy Programme

(a) Taking into account the task achieved in the past ten years, from the point of view of the overall goal - reduction of illiteracy to a level of about 10 per cent - that goal has been partially achieved. In the areas rated as urban according to census criteria, the percentage of illiterate adults in 1980 exceeds 10 per cent and may be estimated at 17 per cent. In the rural areas, the percentage of illiterate adults is about 47 per cent. Overall the estimated figure is close to 25 per cent.[18] These data should be evaluated in terms of the various interpretations of what literate and illiterate actually mean. When the census question is posed whether the person 'knows how to read and write', a positive answer probably implies a level of schooling covering four to five years of study. Functional Literacy Training, with courses lasting five months, is hardly likely to attain that objective, which is explicitly set in the Integrated Education Programme. Functional Literacy Training calls for mastery of reading, arithmetic in simple terms, and writing of words and short sentences; the second of these objectives is not easily attained. Such considerations bear out the difficulty of evaluating the goals in terms of census data.

(b) In terms of the qualitative aspects of the learning process, the various fact-finding surveys based on performance tests indicate that the objectives have been attained to an extent that can be considered successful.

(c) In terms of reduction of poverty, there is a shortage of information for distinguishing between educational and other factors so as to assign proper weight to the role of education.

(d) Where utilisation of knowledge in the working environment is concerned, literacy training opens up the possibility of penetrating the formal job market, which depends on its growth. As regards the use of learning in urban and rural activities within the formal economy, in family production on the farm, in small businesses, at a level of odd-jobbing work, etc., all this depends on the kind of context within which such activities are carried on, and the specificity of those activities. Only numerous case studies would make it possible to generalise about the effects.

(e) From the point of view of political participation and activities in society, literacy
training makes it possible to commence both
processes: the former in terms of acquisition
of the right to vote; the latter through better
conditions for transitory or definitive
migration. In that respect, its effects are
individual rather than social.

Our opinion is that the process of adult
education cannot sensibly either precede or follow
other economic and social transformations. It is
necessary to act concomitantly on the various levels
or sub-systems of the social structure, and not to
leave coordination of efforts to mere chance, to
maximise the impact of the resources available for
reducing poverty. When literacy training takes place
separately from other transformations at local and
regional levels we run the risk not only of having
what is learned left unused, but also of regression
and resistance to future educational actions. The
only possible benefits are individual ones. These
should not be down-graded or under-valued, but they
are limited in scope, when the basic objective is
improvement of quality of life.
It appears impossible to transfer such
educational programmes to other countries. The only
valid transfers are of philosophic principles and
certain operational characteristics. Perhaps the most
significant principle is not educational per se, but
that a process of adult education can exist only if
it is preceded by the obtaining of a consensus,
especially at the level at which it is to be carried
on. The MOBRAL Functional Literacy Programme has
always operated on the horns of a dilemma. It is
intended to be a mass activity and yet be tailored
to meet individual needs. The proper methodological
mix for this dual objective has been achieved in some
cases but not in others. When it is achieved, this
seems to be thanks to active participants capable of
managing the tension. Thus people with proper ability
and sensitivity to act in adult education are a sine
qua non. The other necessity is to be able to
diagnose precisely how to articulate actions and how
to specify at the local level programmes of nationwide scope. Everything tends to indicate (without
overlooking the factors directly related to the class
room) that it is the mediators (support, motivation,
feedback, etc.), who play the key role in solving the
dilemma.
We need a form of analysis of individual
experience as a basis for suitable comparisons. This

report is in general, overall, terms. Perhaps the greatest value would lie in examining experience in particular contexts. The national picture emerges without our understanding how it is composed. Singular experiences would point to the need, in countries of the economic, social and cultural complexity of Brazil, for proceeding towards decentralisation, for increasing autonomy on the part of the communities in diagnosing and evaluating their education needs, projects or programmes. Effective decentralisation means attending to the economic, social, cultural and personal forces which support centralisation and bureaucratisation, and are opposed to local or regional autonomy. Singular experiences would reinforce efforts to remove such resistance points, alerting change agents to the need for decentralising and debureaucratising our processes of social questioning. Side by side with this, the analysis of singular experiences might provide new criteria in relation to the role of education, to poverty and its reduction, with a determining effect for those who participate in the educational process, and in general for adult education agencies and for the process of reducing poverty. They might determine specifically to what extent the terms used, whether symbolic or material, are connected with the process. This relates to the specific ways in which education can participate in reducing suffering and contribute to improving the pleasure of living.

NOTES

1. A larger number, 33,934,023, of students was covered by operational agreements signed prior to enrolment. 'Students covered by agreements' means the total number supposed to be attending under the agreements, whereas 'enrolled students' means the number actually entering the literacy courses.
2. Gross Internal Product (GIP) doubled from 1968 to 1975.
3. Agriculture represented 24.9 per cent of internal income in 1949, falling to 10.2 per cent by 1970 and rising to 12.2 per cent by 1977.
4. The 13,329,779 illiterates aged 15 or more in 1940 amounted to 56.2 per cent of that population and the 18,146,977 in 1970 to 33.6 per cent.
5. Specific information on the MOBRAL system, its legislation, organisation, functions, resources, other programmes, etc., is to be found in the following documents:
'Ementario da Legislacao Federal referente a Educacao de Adultos no Brasil'

'Educacao de Massa e Acao Comunitaria'
MOBRAL Reports
'Soletre MOBRAL e Leia "Brasil"' - Sete Anos
de Luta pela Alfabetizacao' (Spell out
'MOBRAL', you get Brazil - seven years of
struggle for literacy).
6. See Dauster, T: 'Estudo exploratorio sobre
os criterios de avaliacao do Alfabetizador no Estado
do Maranhao', MOBRAL/SEPES, 1978.
7. See Lovisolo, Hugo: 'Caracterizacao dos
Alunos do PAF', MOBRAL/SEPES, 1978, Rio de Janeiro.
In 1976 28.5 per cent of the 3,386,381 students
enrolled were from urban zones, 71.5 per cent from
rural.
8. Prof. Lovisolo, Hugo, 'Caracterizacao dos
Alunos do PAF' MOBRAL/SEPES, 1978. Rio de Janeiro.
Of a total sample of 9,951, 74.9 per cent were in
rural and 25.1 per cent in urban zones; 6,816, or
68.5 per cent were in the North-East.
9. Based on a group of surveys, many of them
using anthropological methodology. MOBRAL has
developed some activities of this kind as well.
10. In a sample of 9,951, 25.9 per cent received
no income, 41.8 per cent less than 200 cruzeiros a
month and 20 per cent between 201 and 400 cruzeiros a
month. In the North-East these three categories
totalled 94.8 per cent of participants.
11. Showing the value of the minimum wage in
cruzeiros avoids conversion to dollars. International
comparison is irrelevant because of different
purchasing power in different countries. A comparison
between legal or mercantile minimum wages is better
than a comparison through conversion to dollars.
When this survey was carried out, the Government's monetary policy, in order to establish a par
of exchange cruzeiro/dollar, was to determine value
by subtracting the internal inflation from the dollar
inflation. This kind of fixation of the par of
exchange favours the utilisation of current dollars
in any operation. In our calculations we utilise the
rate of exchange in force in each period of the year.
The deflation of values can be obtained by using a
dollar table relative to 1970.
Conversion of cruzeiro to $US measured by sale
of the $US by the Brazilian Central Bank (31 December
each year) moved from 4.95 in 1970 to 9.07 in 1975,
to 65.50 in 1980 and 252.67 in 1982.
12. MOBRAL System Basic Document - Mass
Education and Community Action, MOBRAL Reports,
Legislation.
13. Discussion of education as a variable factor
in wealth and its distribution remains inconclusive.

14. Reality being understood as a social construction, manifested in terms of adequacy and adaptation.
15. Castrol, Monteiro de, et al.
16. Dauster, T. et al, 'O Cavalo dos Outros', SEPES/MOBRAL, Lovisolo, Hugo, 'Unidade de producao familiar na agriculture e educacao: Primeira parte, Da Terra e da Educacao; Segunda Parte, 'Do Trabalho e da Educacao', SEPES/MOBRAL.
17. Lovisolo, Hugo, 'A alfabetizacao e seus Efeitos, O follow-up dos alunos do Programa de Alfabetizacao Funcional', MOBRAL/SEPES.
18. For the period 1970-1980 the 'average productivity' of new literates to those enrolled through agreement was 37 per cent.

SOURCES

1. 'Soletre MOBRAL e Leia Brazil - Sete anos de Luta pela Alfabetizacao'.
2. 'Educacao de Massa e Acao Comunitaria'.
3. Roteiro de Orientacoes do Alfabetizador.
4. MOBRAL Report, 1979.
5. Subsidios para o Desenvolvimento da Metodologia - Programa de Alfabetizacao Functional - Objetivos e Metodologia.
6. GEPED Programs Report, 1979.
7. 'MOBRAL - 7 anos'.
8. Dauster, Tania, et al, 'O Cavalo dos Outros', MOBRAL/SEPES.
9. Lovisolo, Hugo R. 'Caracterizacao dos Alunos do PAF', (Characteristics of the PAF students), Rio de Janiero, April 1978.
10. Lovisolo, Hugo R. 'A Educacao e Seus Efeitos - Follow-up' dos Alunos do PAF.
11. Lovisolo, Hugo R. 'Unidade de Producao Familiar e Educacao'.
    First part: 'Da Terra e da Educacao', MOBRAL/SEPES, mimeographed.
    Second part: 'Do Trabalho e da Educacao', MOBRAL/SEPES, mimeographed.
12. Review of PAF Evaluation data in the North-East and South-East 1, 1980/81 - Terezinho Wiggers de Almeida.
13. 'Subsidios para Estudo da Acao Desencadeado pela MOBRALTECA' (CECUT/SEPES) - 1978-1980 - Hugo Rodolgo Lovisolo.
14. MOBRAL: Teoria e Pesquisa (CETEP - 'Studies and Documents' Series, No.1). Produced by MOBRAL Documentation sector, SEDIN.
15. Sectoral Plan for Education and Culture, 1975-1979.

16. II Sectoral Plan for Education and Culture, 1975-1979, Ministry of Education and Culture, Secretariat General, 1975-1979.
17. Social Indicators - Selected Tables, 1979, Department of Social Studies and Indicators, Superintendency of Geographical and Socio-Economic Studies.
18. Programa de Alfabetizacao Funcional na Regiao Sudest - Subsidios para Avaliacao (Subsidies for the Evaluation of PAF), Terezinho Wiggers de Almeida and others, May 1978.
19. Barbosa, Sergio Marinho 'An introduction to MOBRAL's unitary costs', MOBRAL 1983.
20. Ramos, Odalea Cleide Alves e Fonseca, Maria Stella Vieira da. Por um Sistema de Educacao Permanente, in 'Educacao de Massa e Acao Comunitaria', (Mass Education Community Action), Rio de Janeiro, AGGS Industrias Graficas S/A, 1979.
21. Koff, Adelia Maria Simao Nehme e Campello, Ana Margarida de Mello Barreto. A Alfabetizacao Functional, in 'Educacao de Massa e Acao Comunitaria', Rio de Janeiro, AGGS Industrias Graficas S/A, 1979.

INTRODUCTION

Bekele describes a more recent national literacy programme than the Brazilian, the Kenya National Adult Education Programme (NAEP). The author, whose original draft was linked to an analysis of the literacy campaign in nearby post-revolutionary Ethiopia, draws on field visits and discussions with participants conducted for this study.[1] Her work with the UN Economic Commission for Africa's African Training and Research Centre for Women has been concerned especially with the role and education of women in East Africa; fittingly, one unusual aspect of this Kenyan account concerns the greater take-up by women than men and the ironic worries this raised about 'lopsided development'. Ironic, since it is often said that women - and nowhere more so than in parts of Africa - 'hold up more than half the sky', yet are ignored or disadvantaged in most educational and other development programmes.[2]

Whereas the MOBRAL account relies heavily on official census and programme statistics, Bekele's account is more subjective, her conclusions more impressionistic. In part this is because the Kenya programme, for all its remarkably optimistic aspirations of bringing about complete adult literacy by 1983, is still very new. In co on with the Brazilian study the account, like the programme itself, is anchored in a consideration of national economic, social and educational conditions, and in a government commitment in Kenya from a view that literacy is a prerequisite for economic development.

The account suggests several ironies. The first is the concern arising from its very success in attracting high numbers of women, since the relative disadvantage and pattern of early leaving among girls at school was one source of concern and reason for the programme, and one perceived obstacle to development. A second irony concerns the problems generated by the distinctive strength of Kenya and of this programme: the harambee spirit of self-help and local initiative which ran ahead of the capacities of governmental infrastructures and support systems once the programme was announced. A third, less obvious, irony is that the voluntary teachers on whom the programme relied as a means of holding down costs wanted regular positions and pay, thereby perhaps displaying just that individualistic attitude to advancement which it was hoped the programme might develop in the cause of modernity and development.

As part of Kenya's Third Development Plan, dedicated to the Alleviation of Poverty, this programme had an explicit goal of improving the quality of life, whereas the Brazilian was only implicit. The two economic contexts make an interesting comparison, for instance the significant rural-rural migration in both instances. Both relied heavily on local community effort to achieve an official national programme while containing costs. Community effort is not available, therefore, only to non-governmental programmes. Participation was again highly valued but, despite training efforts through short courses, literacy teachers, like the learners, again gravitated towards formal class-room modes of instruction. By contrast with Brazil, literacy is taught in many of the various languages of Kenya and the traditional local meetings, or barazas, of the chiefs were an important channel for promoting the programme. The NAEP in Kenya placed much emphasis upon functional applications through health, agricultural technology and also promotion of government policy, as well as on literacy and links to certification in the regular school system. Finally one might note the further irony that in a programme clearly meant to serve national economic development there was serious opposition on the part of employers apparently fearful of an educated workforce, and consequently unwilling to free workers to attend classes.

NOTES

1. See 'Reducing Poverty - How Adult Education can Contribute', edited Duke, C., in Adult Education and development (D.V.V.), Bonn, September 1984, which contains edited versions of Bekele's Ethiopian study and of an account by Daniel Wabwire of the Kenyan National Christian Council of Churches' adult education programme in Machakos District.
2. 'Hold up more than half the sky' was adopted by the International Council for Adult Education in the title for the first major publication deriving from the work of its women's network: 'Women Hold Up More Than Half the Sky': a Third World Perspective on Women and Nonformal Education for Development, Gayfer, Margaret and Barnard, Anne, ICAE, 1985. The original expression that 'women hold up half the sky' is credited to Mao Zedong.

Chapter Three

THE KENYA ADULT EDUCATION PROGRAMME

Fetenu Bekele

GENERAL CONTEXT

Despite its natural resources Africa remains the
poorest part of the world. Many of the basic needs,
the satisfaction of which is taken for granted
elsewhere, are yet to be met. Upon independence,
African countries embarked on human resources
development programmes through the introduction of
formal school systems aimed at meeting the needs of
development. Demands by parents for schools as the
principal means of escape from poverty led to further
dramatic increases in provision of educational
opportunities. The beneficiaries in the 1960s and
1970s tended to be urban children; those in the rural
areas were relatively neglected. The advantage
traditionally enjoyed by urban over rural children
in terms of access to schooling was not fully
redressed by the expansion undertaken. Output of
students grew at many times the rate of growth in
wage employment. Although the small modern sectors
of the economies were Africanised much more rapidly
than forecast, the sluggish growth did not help in
absorbing the increasing number of job seekers.

The consequent frustration among youths who had
expected that eight or more years of formal schooling
would provide automatic access to wage employment
led, therefore, to serious doubts among African
leaders about the direction education was taking.
The problem of out-of-school children will be
compounded: at the present rate of increase of school
enrolment, by the year 2000 28 per cent of primary
school age (6-12) and 51 per cent of secondary school
age (12-17 years) youths will be left out of
school.[1] A critical review of the situation in
Africa reveals that 'a large proportion of its
children, for one reason or another, cannot enjoy
the benefit of primary education, that the absolute

number of those who remain illiterate is on the
increase, that large numbers with various levels of
education are idle and the majority of the population
is trapped in a vicious cycle of underdevelopment,
low productivity and low income'.[2]

Realisation of the inherent limitations of
formal schooling and frustration of abortive
development projects lacking the prerequisite
literate and involved population caused some
rethinking of the whole issue of human resource
development in Africa. The neglect of the rural
population has had adverse effects on modernisation
efforts. Economists still debate whether education
is a prerequisite for development or vice versa, but
there is little question that human resource development and improved standards of living are closely
linked. Illiteracy and insufficient education
seriously hamper development in African countries.[3]

African governments, particularly in countries
with agrarian economies and high population
densities, are increasingly aware of the challenge
to unleash people's creative energy, raise their
awareness of the potential of their collective
efforts and help them to organise for self-help and
self-reliance.[4] Providing the entire population
with the necessary skills to meet its basic needs
has become a primary concern: to provide large
numbers of unschooled adults with opportunities to
learn the skills they desperately need to improve the
quality and standard of their own and their families'
lives.

Nonformal education programmes in several
African countries reflect the concern of governments
to find alternative means of education alongside the
formal school system. Nonformal or adult education
is not really new. Different development agencies
and ministries (agriculture, health, etc.) have had
short training programmes for rural people through
their extension workers. Nonformal or out-of-school
adult education is broad and diverse. It includes
all types of training and instruction outside the
formal school system, but which may open the way to
formal schooling, depending on the desire and
opportunities of the learners. It aims to serve
several needs:

  as an alternative for those who lack the oppor-
    tunity to acquire formal schooling;
  as an extension of formal schooling for those
    who need additional training to get them into
    productive employment or to become self-
    employed;

as a means of upgrading the skills of those already employed.[5]

Various short-term work-oriented, technical and vocational training courses, workshops and seminars in skills development, leadership training and cooperatives, etc., fall into the nonformal adult education category. Recognising the potential of even sporadic nonformal education programmes in development, African governments have adopted this method for national programmes which initially take the form of literacy campaigns. Few if any countries do not now have some sort of adult education programme. Literacy campaigns in Tanzania, Kenya, Ethiopia, are well-known. The experiences of countries that have embarked on adult education programmes, and their success in mobilisation and popular participation for development through literacy, appear to be a positive influence on others.

THE CONTEXT OF KENYA

With 57 million hectares of land, of which 6.8 million are of medium and 42 million of low agricultural potential, Kenya is an agricultural nation. Its population of 16 million is 88 per cent rural, with an annual growth rate of 3.9 per cent. There are eight provinces and 41 districts, the largest province being the Rift Valley with 30 per cent of the country's total area and 20 per cent of its population in 1979. As in other African countries, the concentration of social services and employment opportunities in the capital city has given rise to an alarming rate of growth in urban population through migration. From pressure on the land and fragmentation of land holdings came realisation of the need to improve rural farm production and to provide alternative income-generating opportunities in the rural sector. In 1979 almost half the urban population lived in Nairobi. Although rural-urban migration is a continuing phenomenon, the 1979 census shows major rural-rural migration from densely populated parts of the country, especially in the west, to more sparsely populated areas of lower agricultural potential.

Dependent on tea, coffee and tourism, the Kenyan economy has done well of late: GDP at constant prices had increased by an average of 5.1 per cent per annum and 8.8 per cent in 1977. Average earnings have risen steadily in recent years but have been affected by increases in consumer prices, so that real earnings have tended to stagnate.[6] Kenya's 1979-1983 Development Plan, theme 'Alleviation of Poverty', aims at creating income-earning opportunities and providing basic services especially in the rural areas, to improve the lot of the working poor. There have been significant improvements in health and education services in recent years, claiming six and 19 percent of the national budget respectively in 1979 and 1980. Sixty percent of government expenditure on social services goes to education, mainly through the Ministries of Basic and Higher Education.

Primary education claims 65 per cent of educational expenditure and caters for 3,700,000 pupils. Enrolment as a percentage of the estimated 6-12 year population rose from 83 per cent in 1978 to 93 per cent in 1979. In addition, 19 per cent of primary pupils were over 12 years of age. This rapid increase in enrolment has put increasing pressure on school facilities: the average number of pupils per class-room reached 40 in 1979. That year there were 98,000 classes but only 84,000 class-rooms. Despite an additional 4,000 newly-trained teachers every year, the proportion of trained teachers has not risen above 75 per cent of the total. Secondary school enrolment in 1979 was 377,000, up 92 per cent in five years. The proportion of female enrolment declines at secondary level. Forty seven per cent of primary pupils are female but their dropout rate is higher than for boys. While 48 per cent of pupils are girls in standard 7,[7] they constitute only 41 per cent of all secondary enrolments. This is an improvement over former years, when it rarely exceeded 30 per cent, but the increase has taken place largely in unaided community self-help (harambee) schools, of which there are 918 in all. Girls still comprise only 31 per cent of enrolment in government-financed schools, 44 per cent in Form 1 and only 37 per cent in Form IV. The proportion falls further in Forms V and VI, especially in science programmes. Females constitute only 19 per cent of enrolments in science at upper secondary levels, which greatly affects their chances of getting university places. The age range in secondary schools is much wider than in many other educational systems. In 1979, the majority of secondary students were over 16 years, while many more 13 and 14 year olds (710,000) were in primary schools than secondary (45,000). At present less than one in five Kenyans go to secondary school, but this still means that each year 60,000 Form IV graduates and 6,000 Form VI graduates are added to the nation's educated labour force and seek employment in the modern sector,[8] a major problem in terms of employment in either the public or the private sector.

Vocational training institutions and centres include 17 teacher-training colleges, several schools of nursing, two national polytechnics and ten harambee institutes of technology which give training in business, mechanical and electrical engineering, construction, etc. The 250 village polytechnics cater for 17,000 students in carpentry, masonry, motor mechanics and tailoring. The University of Nairobi and Kenyatta University College provide higher level training.

Very few rural people (88 per cent of Kenya's population) receive a full education. Seventy per cent of rural females aged 15 and above are unable to read and write, twice the national male illiteracy rate. Females have formed an increasing proportion of migrants to urban areas in recent years, but constitute only 17 per cent of the labour force; unemployment among females with more than ten years' education is much higher than for males. In view of the limited government resources, the high rate of population growth, the significant contribution of the rural population to development, and their need for an improved quality and standard of living, a President's Directive in 1978 called for a National Adult Education Programme through the establishment of an Adult Education Department in the Ministry of Culture and Social Services. This Programme was envisaged as eliminating illiteracy by 1983. Harambee movements throughout the country and women's organisations (Maendeleo Ya Wanawake) have been positive instruments for the effective implementation of this programme, which is one of the government's basic provisions to alleviate poverty.

PRECURSORS TO THE PROGRAMME

Ever since independence the Government of Kenya has given education high priority. The First National Development Plan of 1964-1969 called for widespread literacy among Kenyans. The Second Plan had similar goals; it stated categorically that literacy for all was a major objective. A Board of Adult Education was established, the main function of which was to coordinate and promote activities in adult education. The following year the late President Jomo Kenyatta launched a national literacy campaign which culminated in the creation of a Division of Adult Education in the Ministry of Education. Its major task was to organise and develop the National

Literacy Campaign as a work-oriented functional literacy and numeracy programme throughout the country, using the development programmes of other institutions as the framework for a literacy element. The programme was geared to improving the general occupational level of the people and was also aimed at making those in the campaign functionally literate at an educational level equivalent to the Certificate of Primary Education (CPE). Based on figures available in 1970, it was projected that illiteracy could be eliminated within a period of 20 years. In the Third Development Plan, 1974-1978, literacy and numeracy were stated as essential for the full enjoyment of life by all the people, to meet national manpower requirements and to prepare citizens for gainful employment. An important long-term objective would be the elimination of illiteracy by promoting all forms of adult education programmes.

The slow progress in the difficult task of eliminating illiteracy remained a concern. In his Jamhuri Day Message (1978), President Moi charged adult education more specifically with eradication of illiteracy and declared the problem as the immediate challenge of the nation. In his Message to the State, the President stated:

> ...we now see that the individual Kenyan cannot become effective enough in promoting development, or participate fully in our social and political system, if he is illiterate. The illiterate Kenyan has difficulty in using our currency, in following instructions for better farming or business practices, in participating fully in discussion about the country, in dealing with ballot papers during elections, and in benefitting generally from the rapid growing means of communication. Inability to read and write must, therefore, be regarded as a serious obstacle to Kenya's development and the attainment of our objective to promote self-reliance and democratic, full and active participation by all Kenyans in all activities of our country. [9]

According to the Second and Third Development Plans, if one were to rely on the eradication of illiteracy along the path set out by the regular formal education together with the literacy campaign, the population of those illiterate would continue to increase instead of decrease in absolute numbers. Because of limited resources, population growth and the slow progress of the process of elimination of

The Kenya Adult Education Programme

illiteracy, even by the year 2000 only 80 per cent
of the people would be literate. The Kenya country
paper to the Eighth Commonwealth Education Conference
in 1980 stated that 'the main target of nonformal
education is the rural masses who constitute well
over 80 per cent of the population. It is in the
rural areas that one finds enormous social, economic
and educational problems - the major ones being
infant mortality, over-population, malnutrition,
constant hunger, poor health services and sanitation,
illiteracy, etc. Rural people, more than anyone else,
need functional education for improvement of their
daily lives. The Government of Kenya, mindful of the
need to solve these has decided that during the
current national development plan (1979 to 1983) it
will expand adult education and its literacy
programmes to alleviate these problems and poverty
through the provision of basic needs. The role of
nonformal education in such an endeavour cannot be
over emphasized.' The President therefore followed
his Message to State with a Presidential Directive
establishing the present Adult Education Department,
the main task of which was to be coordination of all
adult education programmes in Kenya, with the
immediate objective of eliminating illiteracy by
1983. The long-term objective would be to instil in
people a desire for life-long learning to improve
their lot.

    The Directive stimulated a harambee spirit (for
which Kenyans are well known) throughout the country:
both governmental and non-governmental organisations
(church groups, local political leaders and women's
organisations and groups) embarked on a programme
for adults before the newly created government body
responsible for initiating, coordinating and
implementing such programmes could be properly
established. While such motivation and commitment was
lauded it nevertheless caused temporary problems. The
Department needed time to organise itself in terms of
recruitment, development of teaching materials, etc.
It had no control over the haphazard way classes were
started and these later faced set-backs due to
absence of necessary backup services from the
Department.

    In time, the Adult Education Department was able
to recruit its limited staff, develop and disseminate
information and teaching materials and coordinate
adult literacy classes in cooperation with relevant
governmental and non-governmental agencies throughout
the country. Located within the Ministry of Culture
and Social Services and headed by a Director, David
Macharia, the Department directly employs only 8,000

persons. These include (a) professionals and support staff at headquarters, provincial and district levels; (b) full-time; and (c) part-time teachers. The number of staff is small in relation to the number of people to be reached, for effective discharge of its enormous tasks, and especially for the monitoring and evaluation of programmes.

OBJECTIVES AND EMPHASES OF THE PROGRAMME

The Kenya Adult Education Programme is a general adult education programme involving literacy/numeracy and basic compensatory education. It utilises the functional literacy approach, encouraging identification of needs and resources and income-generating activities for community self-help projects. It is intended to provide general adult education for health, agriculture, businesses and citizenship.

Programme content is based on the results of socio-economic surveys in each locality and adjusted to the work and living situations of the learners. It includes the following:

(a) Fundamental or basic education, to enable adults to pursue more detailed adult education programmes, divided into various sectors:

  (i) Adult literacy: teaching adults to read and write for communication and information, and to work with numbers for accounting and record-keeping. This first phase, which lasts for nine months, aims at making adults literate and aware of concepts and ideas taught in relevant subjects based on their needs.

  (ii) Basic health habits: carried out in cooperation with the Ministry of Health, this aims to create awareness of the dangers of poor health and environment, and the causes of certain common diseases. It includes such topics as proper use of latrines, pure water, general personal and environmental hygiene, balanced diet, home and resource management, child development and family planning.

  (iii) Basic agricultural technology: information on and demonstration of the use of improved and appropriate technology for the farm, fertilisers and crop rotation show farmers alternative solutions to their farming problems and enable them to boost production and improve their income.

(iv) Government policy and development pro-grammes: information on national develop-ment policy, the role of the government, the community and the individual and the implications of development plans and strategies are subjects for discussion with adult learners in seminars and barazas (local leaders' meetings). Knowledge about national development plans and projects in their localities as well as existing resources (persons as well as institutions) enables the learners to be informed citizens with rights, obligations and the potential to provide and/or make use of opportunities for development.

(b) Formal adult education for neo-literates or those who dropped out from formal school but wish to continue with their formal education to sit for the Certificate of Primary Education (CPE). An adult-oriented syllabus provided by the Department lasts for about three years after completion of the basic literacy programme.

(c) Higher education. Those who have obtained the CPE are encouraged to read for the Kenya Junior Secondary School Examination (KJSE), which takes about two years after the CPE. Those who wish to continue their education for the East African Certificate of Education (EACE) have to follow the regular syllabus of the Ministry of Educa-tion, as there is no adult-oriented syllabus.

Other nonformal adult vocational education programmes take the form of short seminars and training courses by different organisations and institutions in such subjects as accounting, admini-stration, social welfare and community development, nutrition, clerical and secretarial courses and handicrafts. The University of Nairobi Institute of Adult Education at Kikuyu Campus is one such institution that organises and runs two-week to three-month residential training programmes for organisations and ministries.

The main target of the programme is adult illiterates above the age of 15, with special emphasis on the rural population. This includes rural peasants, nomads, small-scale businessmen and women, fishermen and women, farm labourers, housewives, local leaders, illiterate youth, industrial and plantation workers, with the programme content adjusted for illiterates, neo-literates and school drop-outs or leavers. The National Programme declared in 1978 made use of chiefs' barazas (local meetings), church and cooperative meetings, as well as the mass media (press and radio) for publicity and motivation. The national radio has a three-hours-a-week programme in adult education in four vernaculars and Kiswahili. Mobile film units provided by Unesco and other ministries and agencies, posters and newsletters have been important in reaching people. Special efforts were made to ensure that needy illiterates were well informed of opportunities to become literate at no cost. Free reading and writing materials were made available to all learners. In addition, adult education officers and other government officials, particularly provincial administrators, district commissioners (DC), district officers (DO), chiefs and their assistants have joined with local civic and church leaders in publicising the programme and mobilising adults. Local leaders identify, secure and even build class rooms and teaching facilities. Churches, mosques, community and council halls have been put at the disposal of those who wished to start literacy classes all over the country. Improving the quality of life remains the main goal, with implicit expectations for the reduction of poverty as a result of participation. It is hoped that participants will be exposed to new ideas and opportunities enabling them to look into themselves and their immediate environments for ways and means of improving their lives - better health habits, use of agricultural technologies for better farming and production, better food habits for children and families, venturing into or improving on self-help cooperative projects for income generation, supplementation and preservation, all of which could be built on by follow-up reading.

Kenya's Adult Education Programme is an important part of the government's effort to satisfy the basic needs of the population through the National Development Plan. Needs identified at the initial stage include:

mass adult literacy; free primary education; free milk to school children; increased employment especially for school leavers; massive rural water scheme, etc.[10]

The Kenya Adult Education Programme

An estimated 35 per cent of male and 70 per cent of female Kenyans above the age of 15 were illiterate in 1978. This portion of the population, added to the increasing number of school drop-outs and school leavers, could only be reached through nonformal adult education programmes. The Adult Education Programme addressed itself to all these, especially the rural population.

COSTS

The first phase of the programme, which started in April 1979, had an estimated budget of K.SH.206,945.[11] The yearly budget for the programme was shown as K.SH.1,509,689 in 1979/80 and K.SH.3,546,390 in 1980/81.[12] These figures suggest inadequate provision at the initial stage, somewhat adjusted for the next budget year. Meanwhile literacy classes were started by enthusiastic leaders and groups all over the country before the actual national programme could be made fully operational; ie, before the recruitment of the necessary staff, preparation of teaching and learning materials, etc.

As with most nonformal adult education programmes, there was heavy reliance on existing community physical and human resources. The programme uses existing schools, day-care centres, community halls and churches as training centres and depends on volunteers as teachers. Several self-help schools run by city councils, church groups or women's organisations put pressure on the Department to pay the salaries of the teachers and take over the schools. This of course has budgetary implications.

Adult education teachers recruited and supervised by the Department included full-time teachers (high school graduates who receive about 665 shillings per month), part-time teachers (regular school teachers who receive 150 shillings per month) and volunteers. At the time of writing there were 3,000 full-time, 5,000 part-time and self-help or volunteer teachers. As the initial enthusiasm wore off, fewer and fewer volunteers made themselves available. According to an unofficial report, by March 1981 there were 2,938 full-time, 3,107 part-time and 6,612 self-help[13] (volunteer) teachers.

ISSUES AND PROBLEMS

Preparation and Methods
The Kenya programme uses the participatory discussion method in all its activities: initial planning, curriculum and material development, teaching

methods, monitoring, etc. There are adult education committees at all levels composed of educational and government officers, community and church leaders. Before a programme is launched in a particular locality, a survey is conducted of the socio-economic situation and of the needs and interests of the people, involving the people themselves in the identification of problems, resources and training needs. This forms the basis for preparation of teaching materials for that locality in vernacular languages by headquarters staff, education officers and teachers recruited from the locality. There are primers now in at least 17 vernaculars. Teaching materials thus developed are first tested with selected learners for easy conceptualisation of pictures, figures, etc., then edited by volunteer civil servants before being printed for dissemination.

Teaching in the classrooms also uses the participatory discussion method. Teachers undergo a two week induction course in the psychology of adult learning, the use of participatory teaching method and their role as educators. A set of publications, a foundation course in adult education, is prepared as a follow-up correspondence course to ensure that teachers understand their roles as motivators and facilitators. It has been observed, however, that the adult education teachers, due to their youth, the short duration of the induction course and their long-standing belief in the teacher as all-knowing, revert to the methods of formal education, the way they were themselves taught, and neglect the participatory method. On the other hand, due to the traditional belief that it is only the old who are wise and knowledgeable, the relatively young teachers do not usually command the respect of the adult learners. There are also instances when the publication of well-planned and prepared teaching materials is put aside by printers who give priority to other materials. The consequent delay in securing and disseminating these much-needed materials frustrates teachers and learners.

Conflict of Purpose

The primary objective is to eliminate illiteracy within a limited period of time, and all programme resources are mobilised towards this. For purposes of coordination, several nonformal adult education programmes are in principle under the supervision of the Adult Education Programme. However, the Department had neither the authority, the resources, nor the time to take this on.

Adult learners in literacy classes, particularly in rural areas, are encouraged to form self-help projects in gardening, handicrafts, etc., using land and facilities provided by the city council. While such side-business had positive effects it has also been seen as detracting from realisation of the overly ambitious goal of eliminating illiteracy by 1983, in consideration of the social and economic changes the self-help projects promote in addition to literacy. On the other hand social change is a slow process and literacy by itself may not bring about the lasting change desired.

Management and Resources

There does not now seem to be any problem in relation to local leadership. Early in the programme some political personalities and local leaders started classes by making physical facilities and teachers available at their own cost, with the interest of having as many literates as possible in their constituencies to vote for them. While these people were considered leaders of the programme at the beginning, the classes they started were left in mid-air, hopefully to be slowly absorbed by the Department of Adult Education. Other management matters are resolved through centralisation and cooperation between agencies and ministries.

One problem was the lack of commitment and suspiciousness of industrial employers towards the programme. Not many cooperated in making either time for employees or physical facilities available. It appears that employers are afraid that the result of sending employees to classes may be a demand for higher pay. There is no clear policy of forcing such employers to make the necessary provision and let employees attend classes with pay.

As with all adult education and literacy campaigns, there is heavy reliance on community resources. The yearly operational budget was not adequate. There were too few adult teachers. Teachers were recruited from among job-hunters looking for better jobs, with turnover as these left for other jobs. There may therefore have been lack of commitment on the part of some teachers, aggravated by the insecurity of those who saw their employment terminated by 1983, the target year of the campaign. There was pressure on the Department to take on the self-help classes to which it already provided teaching materials and supervision and the teachers who had initially taken up the task for minimal remuneration. The programme did not have the resources for this added financial burden. A common problem was that of transportation for monitoring, evaluating and even distribution of materials. Motor cycles were obtained as aid for some rural areas, but were quite few in number. There are still places where the villages are totally inaccessible at certain times of the year and this hampers communication.

Traditional Culture and Channels
Traditional culture has had both positive and negative effects on the programme. The existence of barazas (chiefs' meetings), church groups and community leaders helped considerably in the mobilisation of learners. The traditional influence of chiefs and sub-chiefs (the lowest local government authorities, who in some areas are still attending literacy classes) was a motivating factor in rural areas, and there are plans to exploit this better, through special training programmes for these people for outreach and mobilisation work. Church groups and their influence were well utilised. It is considered prestigious to be able to read and write (reading newspapers and family letters) and this has been an incentive for attending classes. Another important traditional-cum-modern organisation which contributed immensely to the success of the campaign is the Maendeleo Ya Wanawake (women in development group). This exists at all levels, with income-generating self-help projects, nutrition education, family planning, literacy and similar programmes. Such women's groups have served as ready-made vehicles for the Adult Education Programme. Most women's groups have built community halls and offices on a self-help basis, and have solved not only the problems of class-rooms but also mobilisation of female learners.

Cultural practices and beliefs having negative effects include the traditional segregation of men and women. This seems to contribute to the low participation of men due to their reluctance to sit in the same classes as their womenfolk. In addition, elders' meetings, drinking habits, social functions and the traditional beliefs that elders (men) are much more knowledgeable than youth and women, are among traditional beliefs and practices limiting the participation of men. The much greater motivation and participation among women than men has been a subject of concern to the government.

What Cooperative Commitment to Development?
The programme had the full support of the government, although the allocated budget was relatively small

The Kenya Adult Education Programme

and relied heavily on the efforts of non-governmental organisations and the community at large. In urban industrial areas, however, there is a need to convince employers to cooperate and release the illiterate labour force to attend classes. Likewise there is need for clear direction in respect of allocation of time for the participation of civil servants who could benefit from the programme. Cooperation of government and non-government agencies occurred over the provision of classrooms, chalk, blackboards (by the Ministry of Basic Education); recruitment of self-help teachers (by church groups, self-help community projects); the services of extension and development workers to teach about agriculture, agricultural technology, animal husbandry, horticulture (by the Ministry of Agriculture); health, nutrition, family planning, sanitation, childcare (by the Ministry of Health); community development, income-generating skills and cooperatives (by the Ministry of Culture and Social Services). Adult Education, like health care, nutrition, water supply and sanitation, is seen as a basic service. Like many adult education programmes, the programme in Kenya encompassed all other basic services in its curriculum; it has thus of necessity had to work hand in hand with other development-oriented programmes.

The local socio-economic and cultural situation was taken into consideration in preparing curriculum content for learners in each particular setting. Since Kenya is an agricultural country, the needs of the agricultural population merit emphasis. Although, according to the Adult Education Department, efforts are made to adjust the curriculum for non-agricultural groups, the content invariably encompasses the following: health, personal and environmental hygiene, family planning, pre- and post-natal care, innoculation, clean water, nutrition, diet for pregnant and lactating women, infant weaning and feeding, identification, production and preparation of local nutritious foodstuff for the family, agriculture, use of improved farming methods, tools, seeds and fertilisers, horticulture and animal husbandry, community development, civic education, mobilisation for self-help projects and income-generating activities. Although learners are encouraged to practise what they are taught in these subjects, it is difficult to assess the extent to which these are internalised and put to practice. However, it was encouraging to see, during field visits and from the observations of teachers, that the learners, especially the women, made extra efforts to look clean and well-groomed when they came to classes. Most of them had uniforms which are used also on public holidays.

APPRAISAL OF THE PROGRAMME

The enthusiasm with which women in particular participated in the self-help projects, which in almost all adult literacy classes run side by side with literacy, can be seen as proof of the relevance of the programme. Full evaluation of the impact of these learning experiences on the lives of the learners needs follow-up and home visits to observe which of the subjects are put to use: how many clean their houses, their compounds, their children; how nutrition has improved as a result of the information and demonstrations by nutritionists, and so on. Such an evaluation needs both time and the cooperation of concerned government agencies. Lack of personnel and transport have so far been hindrances to proper follow-up and supervision. It was only in mid-1981 that the Department started to undertake an evaluation of the AEP.

At the start of the Programme the target adult illiterate population was about 4.5 million; of this 70 per cent were women and 30 per cent men. Table 3.1 shows enrolment of adults in the eight provinces of the country by sex for the period December 1980 to March 1981.

Table 3.1   Enrolment of Adults in Literacy Classes by Sex December 1980 to March 1981

	Province	Men	Women	Total
1.	Nairobi	1,079	2,750	3,829
2.	Central Province	4,675	32,184	36,859
3.	Eastern Province	14,965	64,343	75,308
4.	Nyanza Province	14,094	92,813	106,907
5.	Western Province	11,967	46,462	58,529
6.	Northeastern Province	3,758	2,361[14]	6,119
7.	Coast Province	7,411	17,922	25,333
8.	Rift Valley Province	17,159	34,935	52,094
	Total	74,029	291,120	365,149

Source: Preliminary Report, Adult Education Department, March, 1981.

The Kenya Adult Education Programme

For the period December 1979 to March 1981, preliminary information gave estimated totals for participation as follows:

Year	Total Enrolment
December 1979	412,000
December 1980	399,000
March 1981	365,149
Total:	1,165,149[15]

No official document was available on the number of
people who completed the nine-month literacy
programme. It would also have been useful if data
on the regularity of attendance, age groups of
learners and total population of each province were
available, to show what percentage of which people
have been reached. Discussions with adult education
staff at headquarters, provincial and district levels
and with literacy teachers in the field revealed
problems of irregular attendance mainly due to such
functions as funerals and weddings, or sickness in
the family (eg. eye trouble among elders), or work
on the farms (weeding, harvesting, either working
on their own farms or hunting for seasonal jobs on
coffee and tea plantations).
    As the figures above show, the programme reached
more women than men. Considering that women
represented 70 per cent of the total illiterate
population, the adult education programme has managed
to reach a good proportion of its target group. This
is marred by the low participation of men, a subject
of considerable concern to programme officers.
According to a National Literacy attendance survey
conducted in 1980 by the Adult Education Department
on Why fewer men than women attend literacy classes,
'since the objective of the National Literacy
Campaign is to enhance rapid development, social and
cultural adjustment, understanding and involvement
in socio-political activities by all, the campaign
would be lop-sided if not many men attend the
literacy classes alongside the womenfolk. The success
of the campaign would be further weakened by the fact
that it is the men who have the final say in family
decisions in the society and, however much the
campaign might contribute to the improvement of the
women's lot in the nation, such contributions are
likely to be negated by the men who make the
decisions.'[16] Although it was an explicit objective

to alleviate poverty, in the absence of an overall evaluation of programme impact on the lives of the participants, and in view of the newness of the programme, it is difficult to talk about its success or failure. According to the rate of decrease of illiteracy in figures so far obtained, one can only say that it would take much longer than the deadline of 1983 to eliminate illiteracy as planned.

Considering the high rate of female participation (despite women's heavy burden of work and multiple roles), one tends to assume that the programme content meets women's needs more than it does those of male participants. This indicates one success of the programme. Although not intentional, but only following the stereotyped adult functional literacy programme generally, the mobilisation of women for adult education, more specifically literacy, is definitely a step in the right direction. Considering the crucial role women play in the socialisation of children; in the production, processing and marketing of food (shortage, waste and lack of knowledge in its preparation being among the major causes of poverty in rural Africa); in reaching this segment of the population: the programme has laid the foundation for positive future change. Some local leaders, education officers, extension workers and home economists in the field, as well as learners, were consulted as to the relevance of the programme and its practicality. While the men are preoccupied with the low participation of men in the programme, women participants and women's extension workers and literacy teachers stated that the programme had attracted women who demonstrated their keen interest in knowing and discussing more about nutrition, childcare, backyard gardening, income-generating activities such as poultry, goat and pig-keeping - activities in which, in many cases, they were already involved through their women's groups - and family planning. An agricultural extension worker confirmed findings in Swaziland and other African countries that 'women are more receptive to new farming ideas and methods than men'.

What adult education can contribute to development has been a matter of dispute. Some argue that adult education programmes are merely ameliorative, that they 'take the heat out of the system' by simply alleviating symptoms of poverty without tackling the political and economic causes. Others contend that adult education results in awareness, motivation and acquisition of skills necessary for development. Adult education, even at its first stage of literacy 'by opening the door to the wide world

of printed message, can become an invaluable instrument for consciousness-raising and enhancing popular
participation in the development process, when the
contents and methods are chosen appropriately. If a
large proportion of the adults are illiterate, an
effective and sustained popular participation in
local development is unimaginable without a literacy
component and other adult education activities.'[17]
    Mobilisation and participation of women have
been realised through the programme. Although it is
generally what happens after literacy that determines
the overall success or failure of a programme, it
is my belief that the programme has sown the seeds
for positive change. It has succeeded in reaching
'the unreachables', 'the poorest of the poor', rural
women and men. It appears to have affected the
quality of the lives of its participants through
improvements arising from information and skills
instruction in health, nutrition, agriculture, family
planning and income-generating activities.

NOTES

    1. UNICEF, 1980.
    2. Ibid.
    3. Sheffield, J.R. and Diejomaoh, V.P., 1972.
    4. UNICEF, 1980, p.21.
    5. Sheffield and Diejomaoh, 1972.
    6. UNICEF, 1981.
    7. UNICEF, 1981.
    8. UNICEF, 1981.
    9. President's Message to the State, Jamhuri
Day, 1978.
    10. Paper prepared by David Macharia, Director,
Adult Education Department (1979).
    11. $US1 = K.SH.8, (1980/81). Estimates of
recurrent expenditure of the Government of Kenya for
the year ending 30 June 1980, Government publication,
Nairobi 1979, p.336.
    12. Estimates of recurrent expenditure of the
Government of Kenya for the year ending 30 June 1981,
Government publication, Nairobi, 1980, p.345.
    13. Actually paid by organisations that started
the self-help programme, they saw this as the only
employment they could get. Pressure was put on the
Department to recruit them as full-time workers.
    14. The low female participation here is
attributed to problems such as curfew and nomadic
life.
    15. Not a reliable figure, as some documents
show 1,180,443.

16. Dondo, J.M.C., 1980.
17. UNICEF, 1980, p.27.

SOURCES

1. UNICEF, Assignment Children, 51/52, 1980.
2. Sheffield, J.R. and Diejomaoh, V.P., Nonformal Education in African Development. African American Institute, N.Y., 1972.
3. UNICEF, Kenya, Country Profile, 1981.
4. Kenya country paper to Eighth Commonwealth Education Conference, Sri Lanka, 1980.
5. President of Kenya, Message to the State, Jamburi Day 1978.
6. Macharia, David, Director, Adult Education , Department, Nairobi (personal information).
7. Government of Kenya, statistics for recurrent expenditure for the year ending 30 June 1979 and 30 June 1980, Nairobi.
8. Dondo, J.M.C., Why fewer men than women attend literacy classes, Adult Education Department, Nairobi, November 1980.

INTRODUCTION

The Indian National Adult Education Programme, launched in October 1978 and commenced in the State of Tamil Nadu in mid-1979, has attracted keen interest and generated much discussion in the non-socialist world, partly because of India's huge size and also because of its prominence among those Third World countries reasonably well known in the Anglophone industrialised world. Ramakrishnan's very careful and somewhat depressing study of the Tamil Nadu experience typifies India's scholarship and its community of adult educators: highly professional, deeply committed, often self-critical and critical of failures and disappointments. Given the national and local political and socio-cultural realities of India one cannot but agree with the judgement that the NAEP was naively over-optimistic, echoing Bekele's view of the Kenya programme.

India's NAEP was massive in concept to meet a massive literacy, adult education and social development need. A fine concept fitting the land of Gandhi and of many inspired adult educators and adult education organisations and movements,[1] it was intended not only to provide literacy and functional skills but also to arouse the social awareness of the poor, leading to assertion of their rights and helping to effect social and cultural change. Like other adult education described in this volume it was vulnerable to both national political events and local political interests; for some time after Mrs Gandhi's return to power it was unclear, at least to the non-Indian observer, whether there still existed a national programme, or whether only the name had changed but the commitment been sustained. If the judgement of this Tamil Nadu evaluation is accurately one of substantially frustrated hopes and of failure, a longer time perspective may yet come to suggest that the work of Bordia and his colleagues, carrying the best of the voluntary tradition of adult education into the thinking and decisions of national planning, has not been entirely lost.

The NAEP in the context of the Sixth Five-Year Plan, which called for redistributive justice, was seen as an educational imperative to give 'a fair deal to those in greatest need'. Poverty and inequality were clearly the problem, and adult education including literacy with mobilisation a means to their resolution. One problem according to Ramakrishnan's analysis is that a mass movement - at least in a polity and society like India - cannot be orchestrated and managed from above by the bureaucracy:

perhaps both more and less planning and direction
were needed for success. Ramakrishnan notes for
instance that almost three quarters of the budget,
which he judges inadequate, went on personnel. The
next study, of liberated Nicaragua, may however,
suggest that adequacy of resources is a function of
morale and state of ideology rather than a fixed
measure.

The picture which emerges from Tamil Nadu is of
failure of nerve: mobilisation of the poor seemed too
dangerous; easier, purely literacy, objectives were
adopted instead. Indeed Ramakrishnan found some evidence for regression to greater conservatism among
the literacy workers whom he studies, in the course
of the programme. His close and critical analysis
suggests an almost inevitable failure to motivate and
hold the poor in the programme. What was conceived as
a government-led mass movement, an instrument for
social change, was diluted to the 3Rs with little
application, either, to the functional needs of daily
living - for integration with other development agencies and programmes was also disappointing. There was
rather little diversification to meet different local
needs. Consequently motivation and involvement were
low. Even in terms of pure literacy, success was
limited. Ramakrishnan suggests that the need was
under-estimated. Official figures show high drop-out
and low successful completion, but even these figures
may be unduly favourable to the programme, noting the
methods of data collection and reporting employed. As
to reduction of poverty, the results appear negligible indeed, for reasons which seem inevitable as the
story unfolds.

Of all the studies in this volume, the Indian in
particular must raise sceptical questions about the
comparative international literacy league tables with
which governments and international organisations
frequently make play. The scepticism is at two
levels: about the meaning of literacy statistics when
literacy is surely a moving target,[2] the definition
of which depends on the cultural, economic and technological circumstances of the society; and about the
wisdom of elevating literacy as the only or main
purpose of adult education programmes in contexts of
extreme poverty, deprivation and inequality - if
indeed, as in the Indian case, there is a genuine
commitment to human development. The slippage between
concept and delivery in this case is a powerful
object-lesson.

NOTES

    1. Other Indian studies commissioned as part of this inquiry into the relationships between adult education and the reduction of poverty, to be published in a separate volume, examine two such movements. One by Sugirtharaj is on radical local political action, the other by Dighe is on women's self-reliant local development.

    2. The title of a lead paper on literacy given by Carman Hunter to the International ICAE Adult Education Symposium in Shanghai, May 1984.

Chapter Four

THE INDIAN ADULT EDUCATION PROGRAMME IN TAMIL NADU

K. Ramakrishnan[1]

SUMMARY

In October 1978, for the first time since independence, the Government of India recognised adult
illiteracy as a significant problem worthy of
solution and launched the National Adult Education
Programme (NAEP). The need was obvious: according to
the Directorate of Adult Education, Government of
India, based on the 1971 census data, nearly 66 per
cent of the 460 million persons aged five years or
more were illiterates. The number of adult (age 15
and over) illiterates went up to approximately 210
million in 1971, from the 1961 figure of 190 million
though the literate proportion increased from 24 to
29 per cent. As of 1976, the population of illiterate
adults aged 15 to 35 (considered the most productive
age group) would have been around 100 million. The
Government of India, concerned about such a
situation, prepared an adult education programme to
be implemented by various state governments and
provisionally allocated Rs 2,000 million[2] to be
spent during the sixth plan period (1978 to 1983).

AEP in Tamil Nadu

One of the states of the Indian Union which is among
those states to have implemented the programme more
extensively than the rest of the country is Tamil
Nadu, the coastal state in Southeast India. With a
population of a little over 48 million (1981 census)
and an area of only 130,000 sq km, Tamil Nadu is
nevertheless considered one of the relatively more
developed in the country, with nearly a third of its
state domestic product being accounted for by the
secondary sector and another third coming out of the
tertiary sector. The relatively 'modern' status of
Tamil Nadu is reflected in the fact that the
proportion of urban population is larger, at 33 per

cent, than the country's average of only 24 per cent. In the state's annual budget of approximately Rs10,000 million, nearly 22 per cent is spent on education. Since the launching of the Adult Education Programme in 1978, the Government of Tamil Nadu, through its Directorate of Adult Education, has been implementing the programme through the fully central government funded, Rural Functional Literacy Project (RFLP) as well as through the State Adult Education Programme (SAEP); the funds for the latter come exclusively from the state budget. By December 1982, approximately Rs60 million had been spent at the project level alone, not including the administrative expenses at the district, state and national level. A total of 33,501 Adult Education Centres (AECs) had each completed a ten-month programme with a little more than a million learners reportedly having been enrolled. The share of the voluntary agencies, the universities/colleges and a small number of non-student youth clubs called Nehru Yuvak Kendra, together accounted only for about 4,400 AECs with an enrolment of about 120,000 learners.[3]

The programme in Tamil Nadu had been studied by the Madras Institute of Development Studies (MIDS), an autonomous research institution commissioned by the Indian Ministry of Education to carry out quick appraisals and other in-depth studies as part of a continuing programme of evaluation. The appraisal reports of MIDS and the publications of the Government of India, as well as that of Tamil Nadu, are the basis of this study.

Summary of Assessment

Although the programme was visualised as a means to bring about fundamental change in the process of socio-economic development, 'through literacy, dialogue and action', the appraisal reports of the Tamil Nadu projects suggest that the programme's potential to be an instrument of social change was not realised. The programme had been diluted to the teaching of literacy and arithmetic in a more-or-less formal manner without much attention being paid to heterogeneity among learners; differences in pace of learning; diversity in life styles; or variations with regard to availability of leisure. Consequently motivation among potential beneficiaries was reported to be inadequate. The adult education instructors (also referred to as animators) and other higher level functionaries had not been able to create or sustain enthusiasm among the illiterate adults, since the functionaries themselves were not well equipped either by aptitude or by training to play the role of change agents.

73

The resources provided at the adult education centre level, at Rs1,800 for ten months, to cover about 30 learners, seemed to be too meagre to provide a well developed, needs-based programme of adult education with components to improve functional skills and create social awareness. Even those who were enthusiastic about achieving literacy skills alone seemed to feel that the programme should continue for about two years if effective learning is to take place. The appraisal reports also indicated an absence of integration between the AEP and other development programmes – programmes with specific objectives to ameliorate the adverse effects of poverty and to reduce the number of people below the poverty line. Consequently the programme's potential to serve as a vehicle for development was hampered. Reflecting these weaknesses, the drop-out rate was quite high, and only one in six of the learners who enrolled in the programme seemed to have achieved literacy skills of a level that could be retained and useful. Moreover, nearly 50 per cent of those enrolled were people who had studied anywhere up to fifth standard. Thus achievement, in terms of proportion of people officially counted as 'illiterate' becoming capable of using literacy skills, had been very limited.

The overall assessment of the programme, nation-wide, based on the findings of studies by different research institutions in different states is indicated thus:

> Most of the studies found the achievements of learners in literacy to be very modest; in some projects the achievements appeared extremely low... The situation with regard to achievements in 'functionality' and 'awareness' by and large appeared still more unsatisfactory.[4]

GENERAL CONTEXT

During the three decades since independence, tremendous expansion of facilities for formal education took place in the Indian Union. Many states made school education free of tuition charges, among the first being Tamil Nadu. The budget for higher education increased even more rapidly. But expansion of facilities was least for adult education. Census information indicated that illiteracy for the entire population, including children below five years, which was more than 84 per cent in 1951, came down to 76 per cent in 1961 (69 per cent for Tamil Nadu), to 71 per cent in 1971 (60 per cent for Tamil Nadu), and has been estimated at 64 per cent in the 1981 census (54 per cent for Tamil Nadu). This decrease in the proportion of illiterates in the population over the years, however, seems to be the result of a reported increase in the rate of enrolment of the five-plus age-group in the schools rather than of adult illiterates acquiring literacy skills. In fact the absolute number of illiterates swelled every year as more and more school drop-outs who relapsed into illiteracy joined the ranks of illiterates. According to the estimates of the Directorate of Adult Education of the Government of India, the number of illiterates (excluding the age group nought to four) increased from about 270 million to about 310 million between 1961 and 1971. For the age group 15 and over it went up to 210 million in 1971 from 190 million in 1961. On the basis of these estimates the number of illiterates in the age-group 15 to 35 (the most productive age group according to the planners) was around 100 million in 1976. For Tamil Nadu the corresponding estimate was 6.5 million illiterate adults in the age group 15 to 35.

Past efforts in the area of adult education, dating back to the late 19th century, have been insignificant compared with the massive illiteracy. The five year plans of independent India gave no importance to adult education. Its share in the total plan expenditure on education fell from 4.3 per cent in the first five year plan to 1.5 per cent in the second plan and 0.1 per cent in the fourth plan. The fourth plan expenditure was a meagre Rs45 million. When AEP was launched on a massive scale in October 1978, for the first time the comparatively huge amount of Rs 2,000 million was allocated for adult education.[5]

Efforts to educate illiterate adults in Tamil Nadu prior to the launching of AEP had been episodic. Generally programmes covered only small segments of population. All efforts, excepting 'social education' as part of community development in the fifties and the Farmers Functional Literacy Project financed by the Central Government, had been by private agencies such as the Gandhigram, Ramakrishna Vidyalaya, the Regional Council of Adult Education and the YMCA. Some institutes of higher education had also conducted adult education programmes as part of the social service activities of their students. Most of these programmes had suffered from: (i) lack of motivation; (ii) inadequate resources for production and continuous supply of teaching/learning materials; and (iii) inadequate support by developmental agencies to make the educational programme more integrated. The number covered was unlikely to be very significant in relation to the magnitude of the problem of adult illiteracy and lack of social awareness, though precise estimates of the number of beneficiaries are not available.

Against this back-drop literacy was recognised, in the policy statement, as a prerequisite 'to enable masses to play an active role in social and cultural change'. It was also conceded that problems of poverty and illiteracy were 'two aspects of the same stupendous problem and the struggle to overcome one without at the same time waging a fight against the other was certain to result in aberrations and disappointments'.[6] However, an examination of the policy statement reveals that the concurrent attack on poverty through AEP has not been articulated in any concrete and specific manner. The statement also indicates that the target group of beneficiaries was illiterates, 'belonging to the economically and socially deprived sections of the society'. The higher illiteracy rates among women and still higher rates among the groups referred to as Scheduled Caste and Tribes were recognised and it was emphasised that special attention must be paid to these groups.

Of the Tamil Nadu population of a little more than 48 million, 40 per cent were in the work force. Only 22 per cent of the female population were classified full-time 'workers'. Cultivators and agricultural labourers together accounted for 60 per cent of the workers. The bulk of the population (67 per cent) lived in the rural areas where illiteracy rates were higher. The per capita income at 1970/71 prices was about Rs 700. The economy was marked by fairly high income as well as asset inequalities. In 1970/71 the top 10 per cent owned nearly 80 per cent of the total movable and immovable assets held by rural households. The top 1 per cent held 39 per cent of the total assets.[7] Of various estimates of people below the 'poverty line', some indicate the proportion to be at times as high as 68 per cent.[8] An unacceptably large proportion of the population is eking out an income which does not even provide for the daily minimum calorie requirements for themselves and their dependants. Politically, Tamil Nadu stands out from the rest of the country with regional parties being in power since 1967. In every village, and even in hamlets, one cannot fail to notice the flag posts with the flags of the two major parties, and probably those of a few other national parties too. Tamil Nadu may be politically 'more aware' than some other states. However none of the political parties seemed to have an adult education programme. Note also that in Tamil Nadu politics the influence of the medium of film, a major entertainment and a significant industry, is important. Many adult illiterates expressed as one of the motivations for their enrolment in the programme the desire to be able to read the books of movie lyrics.

This in brief constitutes the national and state level context for the AEP. In Tamil Nadu the programme got off to a start in the middle of 1979. The major burden of implementation was assumed by the State Department of Education, through its Directorate of Nonformal and Adult Education, and some part was played by 30 voluntary agencies funded to run about 2,300 centres. Political parties, trade unions and religious organisations were excluded from the scheme of assistance for adult education, as a matter of policy. By December 1982, the Tamil Nadu Directorate programme resulted in 29,100 centres completing ten months of activities. The universities and Nehru Yuvak Kendra accounted for 2,161 centres, and voluntary agencies for 2,230. During this first four years of implementation of NAEP, a little more than a million adults were reportedly enrolled in these 33,501 centres. The original plan for Tamil Nadu indicated that of the 6.5 million illiterate adults in the age group 15-35, about three-fourths or 5.1 million adults would be reached by the programmes of the various agencies during the period 1978/82.

AEP AIMS AND OBJECTIVES

The Programme was launched in October 1978 by the Government of India. This government had come to power under circumstances unprecedented in Indian politics. It was the first time that the party which had ruled the nation since independence found itself rejected by the electorate. This was probably considered as the harbinger of major social transformation; the new government apparently saw adult education as crucial in accelerating social transformation, as some pronouncements in the policy document seem to suggest.

The policy statement seems to suggest that the major objectives of the AEP were to

1. impart literacy skills to the illiterates in the age groups of 15 to 35;
2. facilitate upgrading of their functional skills; and

77

3. create social awareness among the poor and illiterate citizens for the purpose of enabling them to ascertain their rights and help bring about social and cultural change.

While the policy statement does not explicitly articulate any expectation of the AEP as an instrument for the reduction of poverty, it can be seen that the role of literacy and education has been considered crucial for socio-economic development, as can be inferred from the specific pronouncement in the policy document that the'government have resolved to wage a clearly conceived, well planned and relentless struggle against illiteracy to enable the masses to play an active role in social and cultural change':

NAEP is visualised as a means to bring about a fundamental change in the process of socio-economic development; from a situation in which the poor remain passive spectators at the fringe of the development activity to being enabled to be at its centre, and as active participants. The learning process involves emphasis on literacy, but not that only; it also stresses the importance of functional upgradation and of raising the level of awareness regarding their predicament among the poor and the illiterate.[9]

Similarly the strategies formulated for implementation also reveal expectations of the AEP as something much more than a programme meeting a basic educational need. They visualised AEP as a time-bound mass movement, which on its completion would have created conditions for a different process of socio-economic development. Accordingly they argued that the AEP could not be organised by the education ministry alone: 'every effort must be made to involve other ministries and departments with a view to sharing the responsibility for organisation of adult education programmes'. The NAEP was expected to establish mutually supportive linkage with the other developmental activity. On this point:

it is important that the adult education move-should be closely linked with the planning strategy, ...For this purpose a close cooperation should be created with the dominant development activity of the area, whether it

goes under the rubric of Integrated Rural Development or Integrated Tribal Development or
Employment Oriented Area Planning or DPAP, or
whatever.

The policy planners talked of the necessity to
provide special programmes for special groups based
on special needs. Programmes to train rural youth
in scientific methods suited for small-scale production and to prepare urban workers for securing
their rightful claims and for participation in management were examples in the policy document. Thus we
can justifiably suggest that the programme formulation at least strongly implied objectives such as a
change in the standard of living and the quality of
life, albeit in the long run, as well as reducing
illiteracy. We now defer analysis of planners'
orientations and their implicit assumptions regarding
adult education, and turn to how the programme was
organised.

PROGRAMME ORGANISATION

The objectives of AEP were expected to be achieved
through educational activities in a number of adult
education centres, the basic administrative unit for
the programme. Each adult education centre (AEC) was
to be organised by an animator or instructor who
would run it for about ten hours a week for a
period of ten months. It was expected that each
adult learner would spend at the centre between
300 and 350 hours over this period. The animator was
to be a part-time worker receiving an honorarium of
Rs 50 per month for his or her services. A number of
AECS together constituted a 'project'. 'As far as the
responsibility for working the projects is concerned', the 'most appropriate body would be the
various voluntary organisations engaged in programme
of education or social development'. In addition it
was expected that education institutions (particularly universities and colleges), local bodies,
(panchayats and municipalities) and employers could
be made responsible for the organisation of adult
education activities and follow-up programmes. In
areas where none of these agencies was able to assume
the responsibility it was suggested that the responsibility would have to be shouldered by the State
Government.
However, in Tamil Nadu the State Government and
voluntary agencies agreed that the major burden
should be carried by the State Government. The voluntary agencies sector which was expected to educate

nearly 300,000 adults during the first two years of the programme, had only about 2,400 centres sanctioned for that period. Although it received applications from more than 800 agencies for financial assistance,the state government did not recommend and forward to the central government most of the applications. By October 1980 only 33 agencies were given approval, and only 30 agencies finally availed themselves of the assistance and implemented the programme.[10] The smallest adult education project consisted of 30 centres. Full-time supervisors were appointed for every group of 30 centres. Full-time project officers were also appointed to administer projects comprising 100 AECs or more. The animators were trained for periods ranging from one to three weeks, while supervisors and project officers were exposed to orientation programmes of a few days.

The AEP directly within the government sector was through different projects – the Rural Functional Literacy Project (RFLP), which was centrally funded, and the State Adult Education Programme (SAEP).[11] The programmes at field level were identical except that for the RFLP, each district constituted a project with the project officer being in charge of 300 AECs spread over three to four development blocks whereas the project officer in SAEP was responsible for only 100 AECs confined to one development block. The RFLP project officers were provided with a jeep and a driver to facilitate their functioning. Some of the voluntary agencies provided their project officers with two-wheelers. The SAEP project officers were not provided with any vehicle.

All the projects in a district were formally under the coordination of the District Adult Education Officer (DAEO). According to the AEP policy guidelines and the report of a working group on adult education, the role of the District Adult Education Officer was to <u>assist</u> the District Collector (the head of the government administration at the district level, with whom the primary responsibility for the programme formally rested), to coordinate and monitor the programme implementation. However in practice the administration of the government programme was entirely by the Directorate of Nonformal and Adult Education, the state level body under the Department of Education which central and state funds were routed to the programme.

The RFLP was launched in Tamil Nadu in April 1979. The AECs began to operate by June/July 1979 and the first ten-month phase ended in March/April 1980. Subsequent phases of RFLP were held in development blocks other than those in which the programme had taken place in the previous phase, thus denying continuity of the programme in the same community. By December 1982 the ten-month programme under the RFLP had been completed in 10,800 centres and was in operation in another 5,600 centres in twelve districts, accounting for more than 90 per cent of the rural population of the state. The SAEP was implemented in 61 development blocks at the rate of 100 centres in each block. All the districts, except Madras which does not have any rural population, had been reached by SAEP. The first phase of the SAEP began in January/February 1980. By December 1982 SAEP had accounted for 18,300 centres where the programme had been completed. SAEP was operational in the same development blocks in the subsequent phases too, and consequently a fraction of the centres were repeated in the same locations where the programme had gone through one phase.

COST AND COST EFFECTIVENESS

The financial pattern for the programme was evolved by a group of experts from the central planning commission who estimated that the per-learner cost for the ten-month period would be Rs 60, excluding expenditure for evaluation, monitoring and research. The planners had calculated this cost with reference to the number of persons enrolled, not those who would successfully complete the programme. On account of inevitable wastage through drop-outs, it would be safe to assume that the per-learner cost would not be less than Rs 80. The expenditure on central and state administration, evaluation, research, etc., was estimated to be around ten per cent of the total arrived at on the basis of the aggregate of per-learner costs. The policy document even mentioned the need to provide for expenditure on follow-up programmes for continued education of neo-literates, estimated at around 20 per cent of the total expenditure.[12]

According to the guidelines of the Scheme of Assistance, expenses at the field level worked out to about Rs 1,800 per centre with 30 learners. The scheme provided for expenses of lamps, blackboards, and such teaching/learning materials as charts, primers and slates. The total was shared between various components in the following proportion:

Physical facilities such as blackboard, lanterns and fuel for lighting or electricity charges	16%	
Teaching/learning materials	16%	32%

Honorarium for animators	29%	]
Supervision	11%	] 65%
Project administration	14%	]
Training of functionaries	11%	]
Miscellaneous	3%	3%

The honorarium for the part-time animators, the intended key to the programme, was fixed at Rs 50 per month for the ten months. Since so far the programme has not continued after one phase of ten months in more than 90 per cent of the locations, the animators have not been able to be employed beyond the ten months. However, the supervisors who were paid Rs 500 per month for twelve months had their tenure continued, especially in the case of the programme by the Directorate, when the subsequent phases were conducted. The number of supervisors for a project of 100 centres could be increased to four provided the total payment on salaries and travelling allowances was within the overall limit prescribed. Similarly some flexibility was provided by letting the project administrators use any savings generated for other purposes such as additional training or ad hoc payments to subject-specialists in agriculture, animal husbandry and village industries. No specific provisions were made for activities designed to enhance income-generation by the learners.

Rs 60 per learner for a period of ten months is very little compared with the allocation for formal education. For instance the cost per pupil (based on expenditure and enrolment in 1975/76) in the case of school eduation is worked out at Rs 150 per year, and in the case of college education Rs 698 per year. In a state where the government has made schooling up to twelfth standard free, an individual who did not make use of this schooling opportunity had saved the state approximately Rs 1,800; but when such an individual would like a second chance the state is willing to spend less than five per cent of the saving that resulted on account of his or her staying away from school, even though by staying away from school the individual not only saved the state the expenditure on education but, in many cases, also contributed to the state domestic product by being productively employed. In terms of aggregate expenditures in the year 1979/80, out of a budgeted expenditure of Rs 2,050 million for education in Tamil Nadu the expenditure (excluding the fund provided by the central government) on adult education was an insignificant Rs 15 million.

In spite of the plan to make NAEP a programme 'relevant to the environment and learners' needs' and 'flexible... and diversified in regard to curriculum, teaching and learning materials and methods', the scheme appears too frugal and too rigid to achieve the desired objectives. Evaluation studies also reveal that both the inadequacy of the resources and the rigidity (in terms of specific number of learners, number of centres, etc.) with which resource utilisation patterns were prescribed, adversely affected the programme.

Did the decisions of the policy-makers with regard to resource allocation for the programme and its various components reflect the intentions of the planners to make the programme a potential facilitator for bringing about changes in the process of socio-economic development? Some early critics of the AEP policy pointed out the shortcomings with respect to resource allocation. These criticisms may be summarised:

1. The measure of cost-per-learner (estimated at about Rs 60 per learner considering only field costs and at about Rs 80 per learner including all the overheads of administration above the level of field functionaries) has been grossly under-estimated.

2. Even if the under-estimated cost-per-learner were the basis, the resource allocation for the programme to cover all the target population of estimated 100 million illiterates would have to be much more than the Rs 2,000 million for the sixth plan period.

3. The allocation of resources within the project indicated that an overwhelming portion of the committed resources will not be spent on the poor and the deprived, but on administrative structures, salaries, vehicles, allowances and the (secretariat expenses) of the top-heavy bureaucratic set-up proposed for the National Adult Education Programme.

4. The break-up (of the project expenses) implies that contrary to the assertions made, the chief component of the adult education programme will probably be pure literacy.[13]

Looking at the proportion of field expenses allocated to the various components we see that as much as 65 per cent is earmarked for items related to functionaries' salaries and training. Taking into account the costs of administration at levels above that of the project, almost three-fourths of the cost per learner is spent on personnel.

The experience of Tamil Nadu gives substance to apprehensions expressed above: only one in six of the learners who had completed the programme was able to read and write at a level capable of retention, boosting the effective cost per learner close to Rs 500. In the case of the government programme the allocation intended for teaching materials and equipment was not entirely utilised for that purpose, whether on account of procedural delays or for other reasons. On the other hand, allocation for salaries to project officers and administrative staff exceeded estimates because in-service people with long service and consequently higher salaries than envisaged were in position as project officers. Even when savings were generated in costs for lighting fuel by resorting to electrification, these savings had not been utilised for expenditure in connection with activities such as craft training or organising cooperatives, because no provision had been made for such expenditure. Thus the programme had largely been reduced to just literacy with all the problems, such as lack of interest on the part of learners, which had contributed to the early demise of literacy programmes in the past. In such circumstances the concept of 'cost-effectiveness' has very little relevance.

DISTINCTIVE FEATURES AND METHODS

The Adult Education Programme in Tamil Nadu, India, has been the victim of a unique, albeit mistaken, notion of the policy planners that mass movements can be planned and orchestrated in the minutest detail. Though the planners seem to have been aware of the differences between mass and selective programmes, they nevertheless wished that AEP should be a 'mass programme with the quality of planning and implementation of a selective programme'. Further, they become quite euphoric, wishing that AEP should become a mass movement through the involvement of youth and student population. However, the field experiences suggest that such ambitions were hard to realise, partly on account of the fact that the programme, with a rigid scheme of assistance (worked out to the last detail of expenditure to be incurred on an individual learner's requirement of learning materials) had been launched across the

country without adequate attention paid to the pre-
paratory planning; and partly because the very
economic conditions of the poor which were to be
ameliorated through the AEP proved to be the major
cause for their non-participation in the programme.

A related feature was the standardisation of
methodology for the 'education' in the Tamil Nadu
Programme. The curriculum for the ten-month programme, the primers and the teaching methods, were
all centrally designed at state level rather than
being evolved at village, block or at least the
district level. The standardisation was stretched
to the limit when even learner evaluations were
through question papers, designed again at the state
level, with numerical scores assigned to each
question and cut-off scores adopted to report
learners' achievements. Thus the objectives of a
need-based education obtainable at a pace appropriate
to one's own learning abilities remained unachieved.
Consequently an innovative programme which raised
expectations of all concerned was reduced to a narrow
literacy programme. Not only was the programme thus
reduced but it was also characterised by some attri-
butes which are by now considered undesirable even in
the context of formal education for the young:

1. the fixed entry point (in terms of the
    time of launching the AEC);

2. the fixed duration of the programme,
    ignoring individual differences (eg. in
    terms of pace of learning, or variation
    with regard to availability of leisure)
    among learners;

3. the lack of flexibility and spontaneity
    in the curriculum to suit the needs and
    moods of a variety of learner groups
    (noting that 'curriculum' is used in the
    very broad sense of a set of related
    activities that the learners and the
    animator do together, rather than in any
    narrow sense such as 'topics for
    discussion' or 'literacy instruction').

As a result, the programme failed to attract the
intended beneficiaries in large numbers. Even among
the few who participated only a very small proportion
could be said to have gained literacy skills. The
small gain will be of permanent value only if the
efforts with respect to post-literacy are also
increased much more than has occurred so far.

Another distinctive feature of the programme was the planners' recognition of the need for evaluation and applied research concurrent with programme implementation:

> the importance of systematic monitoring and evaluation cannot be exaggerated. It must permeate the entire programme and should provide feedback for introducing necessary correctives from time to time. It is also important to have inbuilt arrangements for applied and coordinated research so that the experience of NAEP is systematically analysed and provides guidelines for future action... Universities and institutions of higher education as well as SRCs will have an important role to play in evaluation and applied research. Monitoring and evaluation mechanisms should get built at the district and project levels also, for it is mainly there that the feedback has to be used for introduction of correctives.[14]

Even this study based on evaluation reports would not have been possible but for the recognition of the need for concurrent research. However, research and feedback at the field level were not well built into the system, resulting in mere filing of statistical reports to superior officers.

EVALUATION AND APPRAISAL

The adult education programme in Tamil Nadu was studied by the Madras Institute of Development Studies with the object of providing feedback on such aspects as:

1. the profile of the participants in the programme;
2. the expectations of the target groups, the extent of fulfilment of such expectations and reasons for non-fulfilment;
3. the reasons for non-participation and drop-out;
4. the perceptions of functionaries regarding the strengths and weaknesses of the programme and suggestions for strengthening the programme;
5. the effectiveness of the programme in terms of the level of achievement of literacy skills and the degree of awareness of issues relevant to the adult learners; and

6. the effectiveness of processes such as the training of functionaries and internal evaluation practices.

The studies, called quick appraisals, were confined to (i) gathering information through questionnaires about each project; (ii) personal interviews with functionaries at different levels; (iii) visits to adult education centres in operation; and (iv) interactions with learners, drop-outs and non-participants.

Extent of Achievement

Recall that by December 1982, four years after the official launching of the programme, those reached by the programme amounted to about one million, or about a sixth of the estimated target population of 6.5 million. The sample studies indicate that 50 per cent of those enrolled were school drop-outs, and less than one in six of the sample learners had reached a level of literacy skills which can be considered useful and retainable. The limited nature of the quantitative achievement is evident. Under the circumstances, it does not seem very meaningful further to consider issues such as the drop-out rates and actual attendance. Turning to qualitative aspects of the programme, it is again evident that the impact of the programme was marginal: only a third of learners claimed that their expectations were fulfilled and even among these the more easily measurable literacy performance was unsatisfactory. Both learners and functionaries complained that facilities such as space and lighting were unsatisfactory. Although the programme was intended to benefit mature adults whose education was expected to lead to increased productivity, the majority of learners were found to be adolescents under twenty years of age. The pattern of responses of people who did not join the programme and of those who dropped out revealed that preoccupations with work, either for income or for housekeeping, prevented many from participating on a regular basis at fixed times.

Problems of Initiating the Programme

The responses of animators and supervisors during the appraisal studies indicated that persuading adult illiterates to join was very difficult. Typically only five to 15 per cent of the eligible population could be persuaded even to enrol themselves. In a significant proportion of the locations where adult education centres were needed they could not be run on account of the unavailability of suitable persons to perform the function of animator. This problem was more acute in the case of scheduled caste and tribes and females, among whom illiteracy rates were the highest. Thus the impact of the programme even in conventional adult education terms was very marginal. Only about one per cent of the real target group could be equipped with minimum literacy skills, and even these might be lost on account of inadequate follow-up programmes.

Impact on Reduction of Poverty

In the area of reduction of poverty, the impact must be considered negligible. While a few instances had been reported where the animators or supervisors had taken some personal interest to help participants receive benefits such as loans for buying cattle through the ongoing development schemes, and a few instances whereby some voluntary agencies gave priority to participants of adult education for a very limited number of work opportunities in some cottage industries, such instances were few in number compared with the enormity of the problem of poverty. Neither has there been enough evidence to say that the programme provided the stimulus or initiative to create new income-generating opportunities, or create conditions likely to lead to redistribution of assets of incomes. Thus the AEP in Tamil Nadu cannot be called a success or said to have successful tendencies, either in conventional adult literacy terms or in terms of its potential for bringing about fundamental socio-economic change as envisaged by the planners. Possible reasons for this outcome are discussed below.

ISSUES AND ANALYSIS

Programme Objectives

The AEP in Tamil Nadu was implemented according to the formulation of the programme by the policy planners in central government. Accordingly it is appropriate to analyse the objectives as articulated by the policy planners and comment on their relevance, flexibility, etc., in the light of the experience of Tamil Nadu. The policy document emphasised the need to recognise the quality of the problem of illiteracy and poverty, each causing and reinforcing the other. It also held that fundamental socio-economic changes in favour of the deprived could not be effected by eradicating illiteracy alone; in fact it was recognised that motivation for getting out of the status of an 'illiterate' cannot be created by conventional literacy programmes. Nevertheless the planners, while identifying the target group and assessing its size for purpose of implementation, confined themselves to those deemed 'illiterates' according to the census definition of literates: 'one who can both read and write with understanding any language is a literate'. An enumeration process in which individuals are merely questioned on their literacy status rather than being tested may significantly underestimate illiteracy, given that 50 per cent of those who joined the adult education programme had a few years of schooling. Thus there was lack of clarity with regard to programme objectives: adult literacy vs adult education.

Other policy statements and the pattern of resource allocation indicate that the programme, while being called an adult education programme, was designed to be a literacy programme. The types of programmes suggested do not reveal whole-hearted commitment to the social transformation premise:

- Literacy with assured follow-up.
- Conventional functional literacy.
- Functional literacy supportive of a dominant development programme.
- Literacy with learning-cum-action groups.
- Literacy for conscientisation and formation of organisations of the poor.[15]

All except the last item are meant to 'educate' adults to 'perform better' within the existing framework. The last item, which seems like an afterthought, does not seem to make sense anyway; one can understand the idea of programmes for conscientisation and formation of organisations of the poor, but not the primacy of literacy for this process.

The resource allocation pattern also clearly reveals that the planners, in spite of their avowed commitment to something much broader than a conventional 'literacy programme', had not operationalised their intentions by providing for expenditure to be incurred in creating new skills and income-generating opportunities. They seem, mistakenly, to have entertained a notion that fundamental socio-economic changes can be set in motion by a massive bureaucratic programme to impart literacy skills to millions of poor illiterate adults. The ambition to reach 100 million illiterate adults within five years, at the end of which period they expected to have an infrastructure capable of educating 35 million adults in a wide variety of areas, as part of life-long education, can at best be characterised as naive, to go by the experience of Tamil Nadu. By

the end of 1982, only about a sixth of the 1976
estimate of 6.5 million illiterates in the 15 to 35
age group had been exposed to the programme.
Moreover:

1.   The illiterates in the 15 to 35 age group
       represent only about 60 per cent of the
       illiterates in the group '15 and above'.
2.   About 50 per cent of those who were
       enrolled in the programme happen to be
       school drop-outs, who probably are not
       identified as illiterates in the census.
3.   Only less than a fourth of those who were
       enrolled seems to have achieved meaningful
       levels of literacy skills, as the assess-
       ment of a sample of learners reveals.
4.   Even those who may not be considered
       'illiterates' may have to be educated in
       order that they become functionally
       competent and socially aware.

     In other words, the target population itself
had to be considered much larger than the estimated
6.5 million, if the spirit of the adult education
programme were to be truly followed. While the
numerator for the ratio of real beneficiaries to
potential beneficiaries seems to be over-estimated,
when we merely take enrolment figures, the denomin-
ator is under-estimated. Even with such incorrect
estimation, which leads towards a favourable image of
the achievements, only a sixth of the 'target' (that
too the 'quantitative target' alone) was reached
during the first four years of the programme. The
evolution of such a target-based policy led to strategies wherein number of learners, number of centres,
number of blocks, number of districts, etc. became
important, not the qualitative achievements. The
purposes of the programme got confused: inflated
statistics of literacy status or genuine improvement
in people's competencies and consciousness of their
status and role?

Nature of Leadership Provided
While the policy planners at least paid lip service
to the need for creating awareness among poor
illiterate adults so that they could participate in
the process of bringing about desirable socio-
economic change, the leadership down the line was
more wary and was even in favour of the status quo,
as indicated by several pointers. Many top level
functionaries responsible for implementation felt
that creating awareness should not lead to conflicts;

should not disturb social stability; and should be done slowly and delicately if there were problems. Such attitudes were revealed during personal inter- actions and discussions during seminars and work- shops, rather than in what finally appeared in the form of minutes and proceedings. Thus, during the programme 'awareness creation' was confined to dis- semination of information on family planning, savings habit, cooperation, nutrition, infectious diseases, personal hygiene and so on. The relevance of these topics in an adult education programme cannot be questioned, but discussion only of such topics would not suffice to achieve the expectation that 'the illiterate and the poor can rise to their own liber- ation through literacy, dialogue and action'.[16]

The diffidence of the leadership at state level to extend beyond literacy and some non-controversial dissemination of information naturally permeates downwards. The evaluation study shows that district level officers, project officers, supervisors and even the animators (who were economically at a level considerably above that of the adult illiterates in most cases), considered 'awareness creation' as too sensitive an area to be handled through the pro- gramme. It seemed all these functionaries were apprehensive that such creation of 'awareness' would lead to conflicts resulting in the programme being terminated by elites in the locality. Many function- aries' attitudes towards the poor also appeared not conducive to their playing the role of change agent and facilitator. Responses from a sample of animator/trainees revealed that more than 80 per cent entertained opinions and attitudes such as the following:

1. lack of effort on the part of the poor and their way of life are the causes for their poverty;
2. most of the rural population is illiterate because the rural folk do not realise the worth of education;
3. illiteracy is the major factor which prevents the poor from getting the benefits of the development efforts of the government.

Unfortunately the training programmes for animators, conducted by the supervisors and the project officers, had not changed such attitudes of those who were expected to provide leadership for the liberation of the masses. On the contrary the train- ing programmes might even have strengthened some 'oppressor attitudes' as Freire would characterise them. Thus, 63 per cent of a sample of animators thought before the training programme that education to develop an awareness of justice, and an attitude to fight for it through collective action, was more important than literacy training; only 57 per cent thought so after the training.[17]

In brief, the leadership provided for the formulation and implementation of the programme did not reflect a commitment to or even a genuine understanding of the fact that the reason for the 'exclusion of a vast majority of the people from the process of education' is the concentration of power, financial, political and social, among a few; and that fundamental change is not feasible without a change in the power structure. Indeed the decision to exclude political parties and trade unions from participating in the programme rather clearly reveals the biases of the leadership.

Resource Allocation for AEP

Resource allocation can be discussed by looking at three dimensions of the issue:

1. adequacy of total resources made available in a given time span (eg, the annual outlay) in relation to desired objectives;
2. adequacy of resources allocated to an individual project (or adult education centre) in order that the outcome of the project be significant and long-lasting; and
3. flexibility of utilisation of the allocated resources in a manner most appropriate to local needs.

In all three respects, the strategies adopted were far from satisfactory. Only a very small percentage of the target population (size probably underestimated) was covered by the programme. Unless resources several times the amount allocated were committed to adult education, significant results were not likely to be obtained in the relevant future. In the same vein, the resource allocation per project or per adult education centre was not adequate. More resources were needed to sustain the programme and to cover all of the 'target' population; and resources would need to be increased to improve the effectiveness of the programme through better facilities, larger size of better paid and better trained cadres, etc.

The Indian Adult Education Programme in Tamil Nadu

Coordination with Other Relevant Agencies

The adult education centres were expected to disseminate information and to channel the development
programmes of the various departments of the government. Such expectations were not realised to any
significant degree. A development block had the
benefit of the services of extension officers and
other village level workers of as many as ten to
twelve departments, such as agriculture, health,
cooperation, animal husbandry, poultry development
and village industries; but visits by development
officials were infrequent. Based on the information
provided by the Directorate, a performance index,
in terms of the number of visits by all development
officials taken together during the ten-month
programme, expressed as number of visits per 100
centres, works out to only 108. Assuming that each
development official (about eight of them on an
average) visited each AEC at least twice in the ten-
month period, the total number of visits should have
been 1,600 for every 100 centres (8 x 2 x 100). The
actual level of activity was not even one-twelfth
of this, which could hardly be called adequate. The
inadequate integration of AEP with other agencies
thus also prevented the AEP from performing as an
instrument for reduction of poverty.[18]

Motivation of the Potential Beneficiaries

As a consequence of such weaknesses it was revealed
in the evaluation research that the interest evinced
in the potential beneficiaries was very low:

1. Almost all animators and supervisors
    conceded that they found it difficult to
    enrol the minimum number of 30 adults to
    start the centres. Most of the animators
    complained that learners were extremely
    irregular in attending the centre.
2. Almost 50 per cent of those enrolled seemed
    to be school drop-outs rather than those
    who had never been exposed to any school-
    ing.
3. A significant proportion of the enrolled
    were teenagers rather than mature adults.
4. Many learners, animators, supervisors and
    even project officers perceived the need
    for providing incentives such as refresh-
    ments or certificates of merit (which
    according to the learners must be instru-
    mental in getting a job!) to the learners
    in order to ensure participation in the
    programme.

More important still is the fact that the functionaries most often chose not to continue the programme
in a given village for a second phase, on account of
insufficient response.[19] Considering that in the
first phase the average attendance was generally not
more than 20 individuals, and that of them only 15 to
20 per cent achieved a level of literacy skills which
could be useful and retained, it is clear that even
in the locations where centres had been run once,
more than 90 per cent of the target population (which
easily numbered 100 or more individuals in each
habitat) were yet to benefit from the programme. In
spite of this, if the programme had to be discon-
tinued for lack of enrolments, its potential to
facilitate radical social transformation cannot but
be questioned.

ADULT EDUCATION AND REDUCTION OF POVERTY: SOME CONCLUSIONS

The case of the Adult Education Programme in Tamil
Nadu shows that, for a variety of reasons traceable
largely to the formulation and partly to the manner
of implementation, the programme became just a ritual
incapable of achieving even conventional literacy
objectives. Possibly some marginal improvements could
be effected through larger allocation of resources,
increased flexibility and innovative programme strategies. However, the major question as to its potential for reduction of poverty will have to be faced
squarely: 'in developing countries where incomes are
low, absolute poverty is generally reflected mainly
in inadequacy of food intake and the consequent
under-nourishment on a mass scale'.[20] Is the
existence of such 'absolute poverty' a direct consequence of factors such as illiteracy, lack of
productive skills and lack of education? Or a consequence of lack of opportunities, perpetuated by an
inequitable distribution of productive resources
which seems to be getting more and more inequitable
at the expense of the poor, as a result of the
'development' strategies followed by the respective
governments? This is the important question to be
answered.
    The unrealistic expectation that adult education
programmes can be a significant instrument for reducing poverty within the existing structure of the
society arises from a misguided notion. Proponents of
development through education do not seem to recognise that most of those in the developing countries
either do not own any productive resources or own too
little to make a living. Consequently they are forced

to sell their labour, the remunerative use of which can be feasible only if the small section which owns the non-labour productive resources finds this attractive enough. Under such circumstances labour power gets rewarded by the resource-owning affluent minority just enough to make mere sustenance and continued availability of such cheap labour assured. All the measures designed to create more opportunities for the absorption of the abundant labour force (concessions to industries, liberalisation of imports, subsidised inputs such as fertiliser, power and transport) which can be utilised only by those who own resources, lead to increasing concentration of resources within a smaller and smaller section of society. The natural growth rate of the labour force aggravates the problem further. Under these circumstances, while collective efforts such as those of the trade unions or agricultural labourers can wrest some concessions from the owners of non-labour resources, even such efforts may not be effective beyond a certain point, on account of the ability of the resource-owning section to curtail such efforts either through the state machinery or by measures like the denial of access to the productive resources. This will lead to deprivation of earnings of the labour force and force capitulation. Hence reduction of absolute poverty will have to be the result of fundamental changes in the structure of the society which redistribute non-labour productive resources in such a way that the control and use of those resources and the consequent generation of income and wealth gets distributed widely for the benefit of the entire society. Can adult education programmes by the government or by those who depend on government funds help to create an awareness of these issues among the learners? Can they pave the way for collective action to bring about the necessary structural changes? Can adult education thus indirectly contribute to the reduction of poverty? It seems unlikely. A government which has not implemented to any significant extent already legislated reforms such as the redistribution of surplus land, is not likely to encourage mobilisation for structural change. The Tamil Nadu experience seems to confirm this.

The AEP in Tamil Nadu has not been extended significantly beyond literacy and dissemination of information on matters such as personal hygiene and nutrition. The primers used for literacy instruction and the topics for discussions emphasise only changes to be brought about in the individual's behaviour and attitudes, completely ignoring the ways in which the individual is inexorably linked to the society, and how these links are barring the poor from progress. While the usefulness of changes in individuals cannot be denied, these cannot be ends in themselves:

> Many programmes of non-dialogical education can achieve their limited objectives without affecting the underlying social structure, not making any impact on the problem that spawned the programme in the first place. It is possible to increase knowledge of nutrition or change attitudes towards fertilizers without increasing health or food production.[21]

For an adult education which affects the underlying social structure, it is necessary to emphasise educational processes such as mobilising, organising and struggling for individual and collective liberation. Such a process of education and awareness creation may not be possible through programmes run by government, which has a vested interest in the status quo. One cannot help concluding that for a vast majority of the population, which is in the grips of absolute poverty, the amelioration of that poverty, by direct relief and development of opportunities for income augmentation, is a pre-requisite for adult education to be relevant. In the context of such absolute poverty, the idea of reduction of poverty through adult education can be as incongruent as the apocryphal folklore of Tamil Nadu which is alluded to as 'Kokku Thalaiyil Vennai Vaithu Pidippathu'.[22]

This may seem too pessimistic a note on which to end. This conclusion is only with respect to the rather mechanistic role of adult education as an instrument for reduction of poverty. On the other hand if we were to look upon a desired educational status of a society as an end in itself rather than a means to economic objectives, then we can easily see that adult education must be visualised as a continuous activity, and not as a time-bound project, on a par with such welfare measures as health care and formal education. In the early phase of such adult education activity measures to reduce absolute poverty may justifiably be considered an integral component of plans to spread education, since reduction of poverty seems to be a pre-requisite to educational activities becoming relevant. As the grip of absolute poverty over large sections of society eases, the focus should change too, and in the mature, continuing stage, adult education will serve to:

1. enable individuals to acquire new skills when they find their old skills have become obsolete on account of rapid technological change; and/or
2. facilitate individuals to cultivate an interest and involvement in spheres other than that related to their work.

The recognition of such a perspective will hopefully pave the way for a more realistic set of expectations of adult education, and consequently a more realistic formulation of programmes.

NOTES

1. The opinions expressed in this chapter are the author's personal opinion and in no way reflect the views of the Madras Institute of Development Studies or of any other individual connected with it. The author is grateful for the very valuable suggestions by some colleagues on earlier drafts. It has not been possible to do full justice to all the comments, and the author is solely responsible for the weaknesses remaining. The analysis in this document is based on the situation, in 1982. Subsequently some quantitative expansion of the programme, both nationally and in Tamil Nadu, has taken place. Some revisions of a marginal nature have been introduced at the beginning of 1984 but the major thrust of the analysis is not likely to be altered. Hence no updating has been attempted.

2. For the purpose of convenient understanding of the order of magnitudes, one Rupee may be considered equivalent to $US0.1, though the official exchange rate is slightly different.

3. Adult Education in Action, DNAE, Madras, 1982, p.2.

4. Mathur and Premchand, 1981, p.35.

5. Bordia, 1980, pp.4-6.

6. National Adult Education Programme, An Outline, MESC, New Delhi, p.9.

7. Kurien, 1982, pp.23-24.

8. Ahluwalia, p.17.

9. National Adult Education Programme: An Outline, p.9.

10. Madras Institute of Development Studies, 1980, p.39.

11. The Self-Sufficiency Scheme of the Tamil Nadu Government was designed to create basic infrastructure and meet other basic needs such as drinking water, roads and school buildings, on a project basis in each of the 376 'development blocks' into which

The Indian Adult Education Programme in Tamil Nadu

the state had been divided for the purpose of
development administration. Several of these blocks
constituted an administrative 'District'. The state
of Tamil Nadu is divided into 16 'Districts' with
populations ranging from 0.6 million to 4.5 million.
12. N.A.E.P.: An Outline, pp.23-24.
13. Bahn, 1980, pp.123-125.
14. N.A.E.P.: An Outline, p.16.
15. N.A.E.P.: An Outline, p.12.
16. N.A.E.P.: An Outline, p.1.
17. Madras Institute of Development Studies,
1982(2), p.34.
18. Madras Institute of Development Studies,
1982(1), p.34.
19. Madras Institute of Development Studies,
1982(1), pp.89-90.
20. United Nations, 1975.
21. Etherington, 1979.
22. This adage which is in Tamil language
alludes to the foolishness embedded in a suggestion
to catch a stork: place a lump of butter on the head
of the stork; the butter will melt, even while the
stork is patiently waiting for its catch of fish,
and run down into the eyes of the bird which thus
blinded can be caught easily!

REFERENCES

Ahluwalia, Montek S., Rural Poverty in India: 1956/57
to 1973/74, World Bank Staff Working Paper No.
279.
Bahn, Susheela, 'The National Adult Education Pro-
gramme: A Critique' in A.B. Shah and Susheela
Bahn (eds.) Nonformal Education and the NAEP,
Oxford University Press, New Delhi, 1980.
Bordia, Anil, 'The National Adult Education Pro-
gramme: Background and Prospects', in A.B. Shah
and Susheela Bahn (eds.), Nonformal Education
and the NAEP, Oxford University Press, New
Delhi, 1980.
Bordia, Anil, 'Planning and Administration óf
National Literacy Programmes', The Indian
Experience, International Institute for
Educational Planning, Paris, 1982.
Census of India, 1971.
Census of India, 1981. Series-20, Tamil Nadu, Provis-
ional Population Totals.
Director, Evaluation and Applied Research, Government
of Tamil Nadu, Tamil Nadu: An Economic Apprais-
al, 1979, Madras, 1980.
Directorate of Adult Education, Literacy Statistics
at a Glance, New Delhi, 1978.

Directorate of Nonformal and Adult Education, Adult
    Education in Action, Report prepared for the
    UNESCO/IIEP Workshop at Madras, 1982.
Etherington, Alan, 'Conscientizing the Evaluator'
    Commonwealth Conference, New Delhi, 1979.
Kurien, C.T., Dynamics of Rural Transformation: A
    Study of Tamil Nadu 1950-1975, Orient Longman,
    1982.
Madras Institute of Development Studies, National
    Adult Education Programme: An Appraisal of the
    Role of Voluntary Agencies in Tamil Nadu, 1980,
    (mimeographed).
Madras Institute of Development Studies, Adult
    Education Programme in Tamil Nadu: An Appraisal
    of the State Government, 1982 (mimeographed).
Madras Institute of Development Studies, Adult
    Education Programme in Tamil Nadu: An Appraisal
    of the Programme for Training the Functionaries,
    1982 (1) (mimeographed).
Madras Institute of Development Studies, Adult
    Education Programme in Tamil Nadu: An Assessment
    of the Internal Evaluation Practices, 1982 (2)
    (mimeographed).
Mathur, R.S.,and Premchand, Adult Education Pro-
    gramme: Analysis of Strengths and Deficiencies,
    Directorate of Adult Education, New Delhi, 1981
    (mimeographed).
Ministry of Education and Social Welfare, Government
    of India, National Adult Education Programme:
    An Outline, New Delhi, 1978.
Ministry of Education and Social Welfare, Government
    of India, Education in India 1975/76, New Delhi,
    1978 (pp.45 and 162).
Ministry of Education and Social Welfare, Government
    of India, Scheme of Assistance for Voluntary
    Agencies in Adult Education, New Delhi, 1978.
State Resource Centre for Nonformal Education, Adult
    Education in Tamil Nadu in the Sixth Five-year
    Plan: An Outline, Madras, 1981.
United Nations, Poverty, Unemployment and Development
    Policy: A Case Study of Selected Issues with
    Reference to Kerala, 1975.

Appendix

Table 4.1

Illiterates in the Indian Population*

Year		Illiterates in the Population Aged 5 and Above			Illiterates in the Population Aged 15 and Above		
		Persons	Males	Females	Persons	Males	Females
1961	Total	267 (71.7)	115 (59.6)	152 (84.7)	187 (72.2)	78 (58.6)	109 (86.9)
	Rural	236 (77.5)	102 (65.7)	134 (89.9)	165 (77.4)	70 (65.4)	95 (91.8)
	Urban	31 (45.6)	13 (34.0)	18 (59.5)	22 (45.3)	8 (31.5)	14 (62.8)
1971	Total	307 (65.6)	132 (54.0)	175 (78.0)	209 (65.9)	86 (52.3)	123 (80.6)
	Rural	269 (72.1)	116 (60.5)	153 (84.5)	183 (72.9)	76 (59.4)	107 (87.0)
	Urban	38 (39.8)	16 (30.2)	22 (51.2)	26 (39.6)	10 (27.6)	16 (54.5)

* Population figures in millions; figures in parentheses indicate percentage to the corresponding population.

Source: Literacy Statistics at a Glance, Directorate of Adult Education,
Government of India, New Delhi, 1978, pp.7-8.

INTRODUCTION

Valerie Miller's passionate account of the Nicaraguan
literacy crusade makes exhilarating reading.[1] She
was one of the overseas volunteer-expert-sympathiser-
co-celebrators to join the leaders of the successful
liberation movement which had toppled Somoza in 1979.
The contrast with the Kenyan and Indian - also
national, centrally planned, governmental - campaigns
is dramatic. The Nicaraguan crusade was announced
fifteen days after liberation and ran, after seven
and a half months of planning, from late March to
mid-August 1980. By then, it is claimed, illiteracy
had fallen from 50 to 13 per cent.
     Again the political context of adult education
is obviously crucial. Whereas leading adult educators
in India were unable to carry through the full
commitment to adult education for redistributive
justice, despite a formal Plan commitment to it, and
suffered further set-backs with changing party fortunes at the national polls, in Nicaragua we see one
of those rare historic moments when there is a close
approximation, perhaps almost complete if temporary
coincidence, between the political will and the will
of the people (though even here not of all the
people, as Miller's references to resistance and
attempted subversion show). Nicaragua's story thus
resembles other classic literacy-out-of-liberation
experiences of newly liberated societies - the Soviet
Union and China, Tanzania, Cuba and Vietnam. The
approach is still centrally planned, moving out to
the periphery, nationally coordinated and directed.
Resources were very limited, since the civil war had
left the country virtually bankrupt, and almost
isolated in an economically, ideologically and
militarily hostile region - a predicament which
continues to threaten the existence of revolutionary
Nicaragua. The obvious success in mobilising and
motivating, in the process incidentally channelling
the possibly destructive exuberance of victorious
young freedom fighters, demonstrates that lack of
resources, and a centrally planned, possibly very
directive, approach are no bar to success if the time
and the will are right. Sadly perhaps, the previous
Indian account is perhaps more pertinent, with more
object-lessons, for most countries facing extremes of
poverty and educational disadvantage, than is the
Nicaraguan.
     As to the key question whether this adult
education - essentially literacy - programme successfully addressed and reduced poverty, again the story
is unique to this place and time. It is presented in

the terms professed but not carried through of the Indian AEP - structural transformation of the society and of the attitudes and values in which it is anchored. Miller's account is redolent with expressions about the making of a new society, the restructuring of attitudes and values especially of the young, urban, middle class literacy workers who went to live and teach in the country and to learn traditional values and ways from rural folk, meanwhile, it was hoped, gaining a political education and a new respect and socialist consciousness for the people and their ways.[2] Though she does not use these words, there is evident a hope that the dichotomy of (urban) middle class - (rural) working class would be broken down, and a common citizenry forged, committed to justice and participative development. It remains to be seen what will be Nicaragua's fate as an element, and largely a pawn, in the regional realpolitik of its most powerful neighbour, although the threat to survival might unwittingly provide the conditions to sustain revolutionary fervour, keeping the political will and the predominant popular will as one, and so continuing the process of building a new society which reduces differences and abolishes poverty, as the Crusade and its architects intended.

NOTES

1. The original draft had to be reduced in length. In the process some of the indignity addressed at the conduct of the Somoza regime and enthusiasm for the crusade has also been lost.
2. Curiously echoed below in the Saemaul study from the anti-socialist Republic of Korea. Sending or persuading young educated city people to work in and learn from the country in an effort to remake their attitudes and values is a common theme in Asia, from the retrospectively defined disaster of China's Cultural Revolution to the various student rural service schemes of many non-socialist Asian countries.

Chapter Five

THE NICARAGUAN LITERACY CRUSADE: EDUCATION FOR TRANS-
FORMATION

Valerie Miller

SUMMARY

The Nicaraguan Literacy Crusade was part of a
national programme of social transformation intended,
to benefit and empower the poor and disenfranchised.
For nearly a year it galvanised the nation's attention and energies, reaching deep into Nicaraguan
society and laying the foundations for a new, equitable form of development. Approximately a quarter of
the population were immersed in the intense learning
experience; directly or indirectly, through family
and friends, the campaign touched almost the entire
nation. Some 400,000 Nicaraguans mastered elementary
reading and writing skills, studying their history
and revolution in the process. By 1981 the number was
expected to reach 500,000. Official statistics
indicated that illiteracy fell from 50 per cent to 13
per cent. The skills and experiences acquired were
intended to serve as a force for national
development. Through the Crusade over 50,000 urban
young people and their families learned about rural
poverty and peasant culture. Close to 20,000 teachers
and members of the National Literacy Crusade and
participating organisations learned similar lessons
and confronted their assumptions about education.
More than 25,000 urban dwellers, who served as
literacy teachers in the cities, acquired a new
understanding of their community and workplace.
        On one level the campaign was a social and
cultural exchange programme which brought citizens
together to learn about one another and develop a
new understanding of themselves, their relationship
to the world and their culture, sharing songs, poems
and history, learning about health care, malaria
control and basic sanitation. On another level, it
was a programme of economic education and job
training, teaching about underdevelopment and the

challenge of reconstruction, and providing skills necessary for more effective participation in the workplace. Thirdly, it was a political project to forge national unity and demonstrate the commitment and ability of the new government to respond to the needs of the poor and disenfranchised, thereby earning legitimacy and credibility nationally and internationally. The greatest political significance was as a development project aimed at reducing poverty and disparity. The Crusade helped lay the basis for redistributing the nation's power and wealth. By attacking illiteracy and inequity, it directly confronted major obstacles to the effective participation of large sectors of the population in national development, preparing them for social transformation and the new political and economic structures which this would bring.

The Crusade provoked a strong reaction from members of the ousted regime. The massive nature of the Crusade affected the quality of volunteers' teaching skills. A gradual regional model of implementation zone by zone would have made possible a better training programme. Implementing the campaign so soon after victory meant relying heavily on organisations and institutions with almost no experience in administration or management. As a result however, regular teachers received training in new educational approaches, with the opportunity to put them into practice, while institutions and organisations were able to develop managerial capacities and improve their operations.

CONTEXT

Historical Foundation

Nicaragua is a small Central American nation of considerable economic potential. Some 57,000 square miles in area, it is an agricultural country of great diversity. Unusually high quality soils produce coffee, cotton, lumber, cattle and basic grains such as corn, rice and beans. The Nicaraguan people are relatively homogeneous racially and culturally, sharing a mestizo Caucasian and Indian heritage and a common hispanic culture.

The Nicaraguan Literacy Crusade emerged from a liberation struggle begun in the early twentieth century by General Augusto C. Sandino against foreign intervention in the nation's economy and the military occupation of the country by foreign troops. His struggle and that of his peasant army provided the inspiration and established the initial commitment to universal literacy which was later taken up by the Frente and the government of National Reconstruction.

The Nicaraguan Literacy Crusade

The conflict originated over the proposed US construction of an interoceanic canal through Nicaraguan territory. After Liberal President Zelaya refused construction rights in 1909, the US provided support to the Conservative opposition who seized power in 1912, agreeing to a permanent US military presence and US domination of the economic system through control over the national banking, railway and customs operations. Following increasing tension, general elections were agreed to in 1927 and a National Guard established to maintain the peace. US Marine Commandants took charge and Anastasio Somoza Garcia was appointed as one of the Guard's first officials. The Liberal General Augusto C. Sandino refused to accept the settlement. He and his peasant army fought and the Marines withdrew in 1933. Sandino signed a peace treaty and retired to organise peasant cooperatives in the North. The United States then installed Somoza as head of the National Guard. A year later Somoza had Sandino assassinated, his cooperatives destroyed and their members and families exterminated, leading to the longest dynastic dictatorship in Latin American history.

Sandino had continually sought people's social and economic development: he set up cooperatives for agricultural production and created a special department in his army for adult education, encouraging his troops to learn to read and write:

I can assure you that the number of our illiterate officers can now be counted on fewer than the fingers of one hand. Unfortunately due to a shortage of people who can teach, progress among the soldiers has been almost negligible.

During the early 1960s the Frente Sandinista de Liberacion Nacional (Sandinista National Liberation Federation) took up Sandino's military and educational challenge. The organisational efforts of the Frente Sandinista coupled with decades of military repression, inequity and foreign domination, finally led to a massive civilian rebellion in 1978. Under the direction of the Frente, Somoza fell and liberation was declared in July 1979.

The National Planning Context: Society in Transformation

The Frente leadership had always been committed to a programme of profound structural transformation and human development, believing that the institutions and structures of the old order had not met basic human needs or served the interests of the majority of Nicaraguans. They pointed to the dependency of the Somoza system vis-a-vis the international economic structure as a major cause of the nation's poverty and inequality. The new government proposed a development strategy of rapid social change directed at improving the living conditions of the poor, together with expanding trade and diplomatic relations, increasing production and redistributing power and wealth. Government programmes were designed to benefit the majority preferentially, and means for their participation encouraged. Expropriation of Somoza's properties, agrarian reform, improved social services, national planning, new international markets, progressive taxation, nationalisation of banks, universal literacy, public and private economic enterprises and austerity were among the elements involved in the strategy.

Popular participation through a network of citizens' and labour associations was considered fundamental, with economic enterprises and political structures managed and directed by workers and community members. This evolving network would work closely with government to set priorities, plan and coordinate national development. Participation was to be further encouraged through a representative legislative body, the Council of State, and a variety of public forums which would promote open debate and dialogue between government and citizens. Such a programme implied recasting the inherited systems and structures and also meant transforming the cultural traditions and human values which the dictatorship had legitimised. The passivity and sense of inferiority of the poor, and of superiority in the upper classes, were to give way to values and attitudes of initiative, creativity, community service, sacrifice, austerity, dignity, self-worth and humility.

The young government faced a decades-old legacy of debt and destruction and a deeply engrained system of inequity and corruption. In the struggle against Somoza 40,000 to 50,000 people had been killed and 40,000 children orphaned. The dictator escaped with all the reserves in the Central Bank except $3.5 million, and left an international debt of $1.6 billion. The roots of poverty were deep in the society's structure of power and wealth. Under Somoza Nicaragua was run as a family plantation; development focused narrowly on agro-exports. Under this economic system national projects, often financed by international agencies such as USAID or the World Bank, were essentially used to enrich Somoza's personal fortunes. Despite the rhetoric of benefiting the poorest of the poor, they served primarily to buttress the regime, enlarging the bureaucracy and providing Somoza's partners with business opportunities. Isolated sectors of the population benefited from the programmes, but the root causes of economic disparity and political injustice were never addressed. Ultimately development projects expanded the patronage system and further impoverished and repressed the majority.

The wealth of the nation was very unequally distributed. The majority of Nicaraguans lived in grim poverty and misery. About half had an income between $US200 and $US300 per person per year, in a land where prices for food and clothing resembled those of the United States. The average annual income for the rural population was less than $US120 in 1975 and in 1978 USAID estimated that over half the rural dwellers lived on less than $39 a year. Access to education, health care and public service was poor. Most people lived in inadequate housing and survived on a meagre diet. Life expectancy was low even for this region: it was some ten years shorter than for the area as a whole in 1979, and 18 years shorter than for the regional leader, Cuba.

This poverty and disparity was reflected in the educational system, in which learning opportunities for the poor had been very restricted, and which had served to enforce inequitable economic and political power relationships while depending upon a system of incentives which promoted graft and incompetence. Educational disparities were stark. Of the 70 per cent approximately of elementary school-age children who entered primary grades in 1976, over half dropped out within a year. Half the population lived in rural areas, but two thirds of enrolled students were from urban centres. During the 1970s only five per cent of those who entered primary school in the countryside completed their studies compared with 44 per cent in cities. During 1977, 17 per cent of the secondary school age population (13-18) was enrolled in high school; 8.4 per cent of the 19-24 age group attended institutions of higher learning. The curriculum in these programmes, whether for city or village, had an urban focus and a heavy US influence. Rural studies and traditional peasant culture were largely ignored. Teaching standards were low and opportunities for staff development restricted. Some officials had phantom teaching appointments which allowed them to collect double salaries. In rural areas political favourites were assigned to village schools and allowed to absent themselves for most of the year. For the majority of students and teachers alike, the social order and its corresponding educational system affirmed values of passivity and competitive individualism: for the poor, feelings of inferiority; for the wealthy and middle class, attitudes of superiority.

Illiteracy was both a condition and product of this situation. In 1979 a special census revealed over 50 per cent national illiteracy, rising above 85 per cent in some rural areas. Under the dictatorship the promotion of universal literacy was neither politically advisable nor economically necessary. Export agriculture depended upon a large pool of unskilled workers and neither required nor encouraged an educated labour force. Politically speaking basic education would have provided the poor and disenfranchised with the tools to analyse and question the unequal power relationships and economic conditions under which they lived. Under Somoza church-sponsored groups organised small community literacy programmes, the leaders of which were often harassed. The Frente also held literacy classes, while training in the mountains. The government conducted a literacy programme as well, used as a cover for counter-insurgency operations in the North. The 'Plan Waslala', according to the Ministry of Education's own report in 1978, appointed over 100 literacy teachers to act as spies and identify peasants sympathetic to the Frente. Many singled out by this operation later disappeared. Waslala itself was the site of an infamous concentration camp where hundreds of peasants died.

Organisational Setting

The Literacy Crusade was designed and implemented amidst the creative chaos of a society in revolutionary transformation. Institutions were new and the leadership, while committed and dedicated to social change benefiting the poor, inexperienced in public administration. Organisations and their management were constantly being reviewed for their effectiveness and restructured or relocated. As further needs were identified, new institutions and programmes were created. Because of the scarcity of trained personnel, many of the bureaucrats from the old system were kept, and committed professionals placed in key positions of authority. This particularly affected the Literacy Crusade. The majority of teachers were considered conservative politically and pedagogically, and a significant number actually reactionary. Some of the country's most experienced practitioners and theoreticians of adult education were chosen for other responsibilities: one, for

example, to be Vice-Minister of Labour and another
for agricultural training. Despite these problems,
national enthusiasm for the campaign and government
commitment to the programme made it possible to use
the necessary professional personnel although many
were inexperienced, and also made possible cooperation between institutions and organisations.

THE AGENCY AND THE ADULT EDUCATION PROGRAMME

The National Literacy Crusade formed part of the
Ministry of Education but functioned as an autonomous
agency managed by a single executive body, the
National Coordinating Office, under the direction
of Father Fernando Cardenal, S.J., the national
Crusade coordinator. The office was responsible for
planning and implementing the campaign and coordinating the efforts of the participating citizens' and
labour organisations. There were six divisions: (1)
Pedagogy; (2) Production and Design; (3) Organisation; (4) Publicity and Public Relations; (5) Financial Promotion and (6) Administration. The Pedagogy
Division, with four sections - Curriculum, Research,
Training and Library/Museum - was designed to provide
educational expertise. The Organisation Division
served as a support and control structure for the
literacy volunteers, and provided liaison with the
different sponsoring organisations. It had five
sections: Statistics and Census; the Popular Literacy
Army (EPA), the Urban Literacy Guerillas (GUAS); the
citizens' and labour organisations; and the Internal
Technical Secretariat. The Administration Division
was separated into two departments: Logistical
Support (Supplies, Health, Food Distribution, Transportation, Communication and Maintenance and Plant
Maintenance) and Administration which contained
Control, Accounting, Personnel and Budget. A special
sub-division was also established to design and
implement the bilingual Crusade programme in three
languages. The state and county offices were each
structured along lines similar to the national -
Pedagogy, Statistics and Census, Logistical Support
and Publicity.
     The Crusade Office operated in consultation with
a National Literacy Commission, presided over by the
Minister of Education with delegates from 25 public
and private institutions, workers' associations and
citizens' groups, for mobilisation and coordination
of resources. Parallel commissions were formed at
state and county levels with representatives from the
same institutions and organisations as nationally.
Sub-commissions were established at village and

neighbourhood levels. The overall national administration and organisational network was complemented
by the operational structure in the field. The field
network was managed by a variety of organisations and
coordinated by the Crusade through the Literacy
Commissions. For the rural work, the Sandinista Young
People's Association was responsible for the organisation, enthusiasm and discipline of the education
brigades. These high school and college students,
known as the Popular Literacy Army (EPA), formed the
bulk of the rural teaching corps. Where possible the
Farmworkers' Association (ATC) organised a small
teaching unit called the Peasants' Literacy Militia
(MAC) that worked alongside the EPA.

ANDEN, the Nicaraguan Educators' Association,
was responsible for the professional support staff
of teachers for the Brigades and Militia. Each Squad-
ron of about 30 volunteers was assisted by from one
to three supervising teachers. ANDEN was also in
charge of the Quincho Barrilete project, a literacy
and basic education programme for child street
vendors, and the Retaguardia, a summer day-care programme for primary school children. Cultural Brigades
of some 450 students directed by the University and
the Ministry of Culture were organised to collect
oral histories, promote local culture and conduct
research studies. Locally the citizens' associations
and workers' groups coordinated accommodation, mobilisation, distribution of supply and security for the
Brigadistas. In urban areas the teaching corps was
organised into two main forces: the Urban Literacy
Guerillas, housewives, working students, professionals and private citizens coordinated directly by the
Crusade; and the Workers' Literacy Militia (MOA) of
factory workers, office personnel, market vendors and
government employees directed by the Sandinista
Worker Federation.

Emerging from Sandino's historical commitment to
literacy and adult education, the actual Literacy
Crusade was first proposed by the Frente Sandinista
during the liberation struggle. One priority programme once victory was won would be to teach
literacy. In the month prior to victory the Frente
asked two highly respected educators, Carlos Tunner-
man and Miguel de Castilla, to develop a project
proposal for a nationwide campaign. Fifteen days
after the triumph of 3 August 1979, the new government announced the Crusade. After a planning period
of seven and a half months the official campaign was
launched on 23 March and ended on 15 August 1980. A
community programme, managed locally, carried on the
efforts afterwards, providing continued learning

opportunities for those who had not finished their studies and consolidation for those who had. Bilingual campaigns in English, Miskito and Sumo were conducted in late 1980, and a supplementary literacy programme planned for 1981 to incorporate people who did not participate originally.

The programme concentrated on literacy, mathematics and the study of the nation's past and present reality. Specific learning materials consisted of the elementary literacy primer, Dawn of the People; a teacher's manual, The Teacher's Guide for Literacy Volunteers and an arithmetic workbook, Arithmetic and Economic Reconstruction: One Single Operation. Teaching games emphasising learner creativity, such as a type of syllable scrabble, were developed and distributed, and during 1980 the national match factory produced all matches in special boxes decorated with the alphabet for use as letter building blocks for the Crusade. The literacy primer had 23 lessons, each chapter accompanied by photographs and practice exercises. It was divided into three major areas: the history and development of the Revolution; the socio-economic programmes of the Government of National Reconstruction; and civil defence and community participation. Specific lesson themes included: 'Sandino, guiding force of the Revolution'; 'Work is the right and duty of every citizen'; 'Spend little, save resources, and produce a lot - that is Revolution'.

A separate teacher's manual for volunteers provided step-by-step instructions on the use of the literacy methodology with detailed back-up readings for each of the 23 theme areas. It provided the Brigadistas with the social, political and economic information necessary to generate informed discussion. Since the approach was based on reciprocal learning, the handbook also outlined a systematic set of study activities based on users' own living and teaching experience. They were to conduct a careful study of their communities and keep an analytical field diary of their life during the campaign. By the end of the Crusade all participants, students and teachers alike, were expected to have developed critical skills in oral expression and problem-solving, and a greater commitment to and understanding of the process of social transformation. The literacy students were to be able to read newspapers, simple forms, technical information pamphlets and books within their vocabulary and comprehension range. The volunteer teachers and their families were expected to have increased appreciation for and empathy with the country's poor and rural culture, and a better understanding of the challenge and problems of national development.

The Nicaraguan Crusade was designed as a learning experience for the entire country. Specifically it was aimed at the illiterate, the young and their families. Close to 600,000 Nicaraguans participated directly as students, teachers or support personnel. To encourage massive participation and to guarantee maximum involvement of the illiterate population, the Crusade required no fees, provided all learning materials free, and in most cases took place in the learner's home or place of work. A nationwide publicity and fund-raising campaign was launched under the direction of the Public Relations Division of the National Coordinating Office. The entire country became involved and informed through newspapers, radio, TV, citizens' associations, labour organisations, professional groups, student bodies, religious orders, church parishes and congregations. Bill-boards announcing the programme adorned the roads. Respected public figures praised the project. Plays, parades, debates, dances, raffles, song contests, music festivals, poetry readings, poster sales, and even simulated kidnappings of educational officials by pencil-toting students helped raise funds and create a climate of expectation and enthusiasm.

AIMS AND OBJECTIVES

The Crusade, as part of the Revolution, and the national development strategy aimed at social transformation were viewed as interwoven and inseparable processes. In Fernando Cardenal's words 'the Revolution and Literacy Crusade are one in purpose and mission... to transform the nation.' Literacy was much more than a basic human right or an isolated means to reduce poverty. The Frente Sandinista called literacy

> an apprenticeship in life because in the process the literate person learns his intrinsic value as a person, as a maker of history, as an actor of an important social role, as an individual with rights to demand and duties to fulfil.

Literacy thus conceived prepared the way for an educated, creative, socially committed populace — fundamental to the transformation of unjust political and economic structures. The aims and objectives cannot therefore be separated from those of transformation. The campaign was considered vital to

social transformation and to addressing the challenge
of poverty and inequity in attempting to provide
citizens with the basic skills necessary for their
active participation in the life of the nation. It
was seen as a beginning in the long process of
creating a more equitable society.

In the new Nicaragua, development and transformation rested on the redistribution of power and
wealth and on involvement in participatory forms of
community organisation. This required that all
aspects of society be examined and recreated. It
called for the formation of the 'new man' and the
'new woman' - a revolutionary citizenry inspired by
goals of community service rather than individual
gain, motivated by 'sacrifice, humility, love, discipline, cooperation, creativity, hard work and a
critical consciousness'. It meant creating structures
and institutions embodying permanent opportunities
for learning and equitable economic and political
participation. Adult education and literacy were thus
seen as catalysing forces for transformation and
effective citizen participation in the creation and
management of society's structures:

> A thorough reform of the objectives and content
> of national education will be undertaken so that
> a critical and liberating process of education
> can be designed and become a key factor in the
> humanist transformation of Nicaraguan society...
> a national literacy campaign will be launched...
> programs of liberating adult education will
> begin in order to allow full participation in
> the process of national reconstruction and
> development.[1]
> We are teaching the poor and disenfran-
> chised to read and write not out of charity, but
> rather so that they will be prepared both polit-
> ically and technically to become the genuine
> authors of development and the only legitimate
> owners of the Revolution.[2]

This meant enabling the poor and marginalised to
acquire skills and knowledge for leadership and for
more complex technical roles. Only then could they
become fully 'architects of their own destiny',
'protagonists of history' rather than 'spectators':

> We believe that in order to create a new nation
> we have to begin with an education that liber-
> ates people. Only through knowing their past and
> their present, only through understanding and
> analysing their reality, can people choose their

future. Only in that process can people fulfil their human destiny as makers of history and commit themselves to transforming that reality.[3]

The purpose of education was to transform reality - to help people critically understand their world in order to shape and improve it. Revolutionary education involved a frontal attack on inherited inequities and on the passivity and subservience the system had engendered. Adult education was for people recovering their sense of dignity and self-worth, taking charge of their lives as individuals and community members, learning to become knowledgeable decision-makers and responsible citizens with rights as well as obligations. Following Paulo Freire, it meant working together to acquire an understanding of society's economic, political and social forces in order to act upon and transform them for the common good. Technical skills and knowledge were also required to increase productivity and secure a solid economic foundation for development:

We need men and women who are acquainted with, have mastered and can effectively use techno- logies appropriate to the field of production so that we can generate the wealth and economic base for the revolutionary programs of social justice.[4]

Purpose and Objectives

The overall purpose of the Crusade was to help people become more effective, productive, involved and committed to social transformation and informed part- icipation in all aspects of society. The programme was designed to teach elementary skills in reading, writing, mathematics and analytical thinking, as the foundation for further technical preparation and citizen participation. In the process people would gain a basic knowledge of history and civics, an understanding of national development and emerging political and economic structures, and an apprec- iation of themselves and their culture. The campaign was intended to sensitise the general public to the problems and rights of the poor, to promote empathy and social commitment, and to prepare citizens for their responsibilities in national development. Another important function was to provide young people who had fought and suffered the traumas of the war with a positive means to channel their energies and enthusiasm. Their participation as volunteer teachers helped them make the transition from the violence of war to the challenge of transformation.

114

Specifically the campaign proposed to eliminate
illiteracy; first reducing the actual illiteracy rate
to between ten and 15 per cent; second, setting up
an extensive programme of adult education after the
Crusade; and third, expanding primary school facilities throughout the country. Eliminating illiteracy
was the most obvious goal but others were also important, since they aimed at laying the foundations for
the new society. Specific goals included: (1) to
encourage an integration and understanding between
Nicaraguans of different classes and backgrounds; (2)
to promote political awareness and a critical analysis of under-development; (3) to provide knowledge of
the nation's new development programmes and structures; (4) to nurture attitudes and skills leading to
increased creativity, productivity, cooperation,
discipline and analytical thinking; (5) to forge
national cohesion, consensus and commitment to social
service; (6) to strengthen the channels for economic
and political participation; (7) to recover, record
and disseminate the history and popular culture
suppressed by the dictatorship; and (8) to conduct
basic research necessary for future development planning. A separate series of campaigns was planned to
begin in October 1980, to provide for the special
learning needs of the Miskito, Sumo and English-
speaking populations on the Atlantic coast.

COST

The expenditures actually incurred by the Crusade
were of the order of $US10 to $US12 million. This
excludes the voluntary labour supplied by the
teaching corps and food provided by parents during
the campaign. The cost per learner, excluding
volunteer services, was approximately $25.

STYLE AND METHOD

From the beginning extensive participation by
citizens and staff alike marked all activities from
planning to implementation. The educational methods
also depended upon and promoted participation.

Strategy and Organisation
This emphasis on participation as the guiding
strategy emerged from both the philosophical principles and the practical experience of the Revolution.
The government of National Reconstruction and the
Frente were fundamentally committed to citizen
involvement. As in the insurrection, it was felt that
victory rested on active organised community

participation. Triumphing over illiteracy meant citizens learning from citizens, neighbours helping neighbours. Detailed planning and implementation depended upon the close relationship between the Crusade's coordinating office and the network of citizens and labour associations, groups which had originally been developed clandestinely for the war and now provided the organising force behind the campaign.

Planning
Planning was characterised initially by close team-work and collective problem-solving, later by extensive local participation. After acquainting itself with different literacy programmes and approaches, the national coordinating office conducted an intensive one week workshop with experts from Mexico, Colombia, Costa Rica and the United States. Here the Crusade staff, with selected government officials and citizen representatives, modified the draft proposal for the campaign, developed operational guidelines and began to define programme structures and tasks.

At national level this team approach and collective problem-solving style predominated. As the work intensified the core coordinating group of division coordinators met daily to study problems as they emerged, and to seek effective responses. The sections of the Pedagogy Division also worked very closely and collaboratively. Massive citizen participation occurred in planning and to carry out a national census. This identified potential learners and teachers and laid the basis for subsequent planning. A series of planning and evaluation conferences was held to guarantee maximum participation during the actual campaign. These originated at community level and extended through township, county and state, culminating in two nationwide congresses. It is estimated that over 100,000 people participated in the process.

Personnel and Participation
Those directly involved in the Crusade exceeded half a million, nearly a quarter of the population. Through relatives and friends, from fund-raising events to family visits, almost the entire nation participated in some way. International participation was important as well. About 1,200 Cuban teachers assigned to rural primary schools also taught literacy in the evenings. Brigades of teachers from the Dominican Republic, Costa Rica and Spain worked full-time in the Crusade, and individuals from elsewhere also took part. The national staff was joined by

international experts from Argentina, Chile, Colombia, Costa Rica, Cuba, El Salvador, Honduras, France, Mexico, Puerto Rico, Spain and the United States.

Fund Raising

Fund-raising was international as well as local. Solidarity groups in different countries around the world who had been active during the war continued their support; fund-raising events were held from Madrid to Manhattan, from Mexico to Managua. Locally people tithed one day's salary each month or contributed through the purchase of National Literacy Bonds. Children set up road blocks collecting pennies for pencils; peasants' groups held raffles and dances. The National Lottery even devoted one Sunday to the campaign. Concerts, poetry readings, plays, poster sales, buffet dinners and song fests were organised by different groups to raise funds for the Crusade.

The Teaching/Learning Process

The liberation struggle served as an inspiration in designing the materials and methodologies for the Crusade. Its lessons were pedagogical and philosophical. Educational experiences over long years of fighting and community organising had demonstrated the validity of certain teaching approaches and learning principles. Small study groups had met to analyse, plan and carry out war-related tasks; clandestine literacy efforts had been conducted as well. Learning had been based on a process of action and reflection. Lessons had direct, urgent and immediate application to reality. In pedagogical terms, these experiences had used a combination of experiential learning, dialogue, group discussions and collective problem-solving. They had proved the importance of stimulating participation, initiative and creativity. The war had also revealed the tremendous creativity and capacity for learning that existed within people regardless of their educational backgrounds, providing the pedagogical foundation for the Crusade and enriched by the ideas and practice of Paulo Freire, and the experiences of such countries as Cuba, Sao Tome, Guinea-Bissau and Peru.

It was believed, with Freire, that participation in dialogue was critical to a liberating education and that combined with a phonetics approach to teaching literacy this surpassed any other method. However, Nicaragua's unique situation called for a methodology combining those elements in the way most appropriate to the particular needs of the nation.

117

Since Nicaragua was engaging in a national literacy campaign in a context of profound social transformation, discussion themes were concerns of the society at large rather than issues of interest only to particular communities. The team considered the dialogue and its themes highly political and critical to learning, offering participants the power of the word and of history: 'by expressing their own opinions about their lives, their culture, their past and their future, people would be able to develop and strengthen their power of creativity and analysis and their understanding of themselves as creators of culture and history'.[5]

Step-by-step guidelines were prepared to help volunteers facilitate dialogue. The five-step process contained a series of suggested question formats to stimulate discussion. Questions were designed to help participants develop both analytical skills and a profound sense of social responsibility. They proceeded from the simple to the difficult, guiding the discussion in the direction of (1) describing the contents of a photograph; (2) analysing the situation portrayed; (3) relating the particular situation to the life of the learner, to the community and to the problems facing them; (4) problem-solving around issues identified by the group; and (5) engaging participants in transforming reality, committing themselves to solving the problem and becoming active in national programmes of social change. Over the course of the Crusade however, it was realised that participation in dialogue occurred both during the literacy teaching process itself and in daily living experience, and that the latter was perhaps the richer and more profound.

The programme of teacher training used a participatory educational approach which was called a pedagogy of shared responsibility. It was designed to prepare volunteers for a role of reciprocity and shared learning:

> You will be a catalyst of the teaching-learning process. Your literacy students will be people who think, create and express their ideas. Together you will form a team of mutual learning and human development... The literacy process is an act of creation in which people offer each other their thoughts, words and deeds. It is a cultural action of transformation and growth.[6]

Training therefore required all volunteers to assume new educational roles in this new pedagogy; the traditional teacher became a type of learning coordinator. Such a role involved motivating, inspiring, challenging and working with the participants who by the structure of the workshops and the new relationships were encouraged to become active problem-solvers. Participants were considered the well-spring of the process. They were to explore, research and create. Small group study, team teaching and problem-solving affirmed this new relationship. Under the coordination of two facilitators, workshop members were given a variety of educational tasks to accomplish. During the training they reflected over the group process and their progress, integrating theory and practice into their learning.

The primary purpose was to have people master the materials and methodology while developing skills necessary to solve social problems. Workshop techniques stressed experiential learning, creative thinking and participation. Methods were chosen to enhance the capacity to acquire and apply knowledge with initiative and imagination. Simulations, role-playing, group discussions, debates, murals, poetry, drawing, songs and some artistic form of expression from Nicaraguan folklore were all used. Each workshop began with an introductory exercise to acquaint participants with one another and establish a congenial dynamic learning environment. Participants were divided into working teams of about six people which stayed together throughout the workshop. Each small group chose the name of a fallen combatant as their symbol and wrote up his or her biography, hanging it on the wall for others to read. In their teams participants discussed the meaning of the Crusade and why they had decided to become volunteers, displaying their responses on large sheets of paper on the wall to present to the entire workshop. To conclude the first exercise, they were asked to create two-line rhyme-slogans which summarised their discussion, a technique with roots in the traditional culture of Nicaragua, where couplets are a popular literary expression, and used also in the war.[7]

During the workshop, the rhymes took on a life of their own. Groups used their spare time to create new and more imaginative ones. They would practise them together in a corner and in a moment of relative silence between activities shout them out with pride and enthusiasm. The effort boosted energies when work became heavy and fatiguing, serving as a measure of involvement and comprehension. If a group did not understand an exercise or a reading, invariably a humorous couplet indicating their confusion and frustration would surface. At the end of the workshop the walls were covered by summaries of group discussions and popular poetry.

A decentralised four-stage model was designed to implement the Crusade's training programme. Success depended on a multiplier effect: beginning with seven national trainers, in less than four months it was expected to prepare close to 100,000 people. From December to March workshops were held across the country. The driving force behind the training was the group of 80: forty university students and 40 teachers specially selected for two intensive weeks of preparation and one month of field experience. From these, 40 were chosen to train the next approximately 600 students and teachers. During late February the 600 prepared over 12,000 people, most of whom were teachers. They in turn conducted eight-day intensive workshops for the tens of thousands of literacy volunteers. Once the Crusade began, permanent training workshops were given for those who still wished to enter the programme. A radio show broadcast twice daily, and special Saturday seminars by technical advisors provided continuing in-service training for the volunteers.

Follow-up Programme

With the termination of the campaign, the follow-up programme became the responsibility of the new Vice-Ministry of Adult Education. The entire adult education programme rested on community participation. Those in charge of follow-up after the volunteers left were local community members, often, in the countryside, new literates. Outstanding literacy graduates or educated members of the community were chosen to continue the work of the learning groups. After basic training by the Crusade teaching supervisors, the new coordinators were provided with a carefully designed teacher's guide and follow-up reading materials which stressed collective study and action. These learning groups were supported by the network of mass citizen and labour organisations. The work of the coordinators was bolstered by selected travelling 'promotors' who provided the regional adult education offices with liaison and the community groups with encouragement, orientation and extra learning materials when available. Rounding out the transition programme, a radio show especially for the study groups was broadcast twice daily on all national channels.

ISSUES AND ANALYSIS

Clarity of Purpose

The clarity of purpose from the beginning of the campaign was perhaps unusual in such a massive national effort. Despite shifts in emphasis between priorities the overall focus on education for liberation and transformation remained clear. During the course of the campaign increased emphasis was given to the socio-political dimensions of the educational effort. Volunteers worked with community members on development projects, and in the formation of citizens' and labour associations which served as vehicles for national development and channels for participation in national decision-making. In the final month, the focus was redirected exclusively to learning literacy.

Charisma and Leadership

Father Fernando Cardenal, coordinator of the campaign, a respected and well-known university professor, exercised charisma but it did not crucially affect the funtioning of the campaign. His special presence helped in inspiring people to greater commitment and sacrifice. The most important contribution of that charisma probably involved the attitudes of parents toward the Crusade. Cardenal was known as a priest committed to the poor, a man who stood for the highest forms of self-abnegation and honesty. His unimpeachable moral character and the values he represented helped parents more readily to accept the legitimacy of the campaign and so give their children permission to participate in it. His open personal approach, which combined expansive warmth with enthusiastic faith in the Revolution, was helpful to staff in moments of discouragement and tension. There was a feeling that in cases of conflict or problems, he was available and willing to cut through nonsense and red tape. He was revered for his flexibility, common sense, and respect for people's experience and potential.

The Crusade served as a training ground both for leaders within the government structures and for citizens' and labour associations. Because the campaign depended essentially on people with no relevant previous experience, the development of leadership was crucial. To develop and practise skills, training programmes were conducted, regular staff meetings held and participation encouraged. The series of nationwide evaluation-planning congresses during the campaign involving representatives from all levels of the programme - community, county, state and national - was part of this human development process. An interamerican group of experts in literacy and adult education formed part of the national planning and coordinating team, contributing to the development of leadership through on-the-job training.

Management
There were some structural problems of leadership and
management. At state and county levels there was confusion over roles and coordination between the Literacy Commissions and the Literacy Crusade Office.
Responsibilities were not always clearly delineated
and similarly interpreted. Rotation of campaign delegates to the Commissions by their representative
organisations early on affected coherence of planning
and programming, and integration between the Pedagogy
and Organisation Divisions of the Crusade sometimes
fell short. In the rush of planning and organising
there had not been time for a common staff training
programme. The Pedagogy personnel had the most
intense preparation, ten to 15 days which included
the philosophical, educational, socio-political and
operational aspects of the campaign, while the
Organisation Division had only one- or two-day
sessions on specific technical functions. This lack
of shared foundation sometimes inhibited the development of a coherent approach.

Flexibility
An outstanding characteristic of the Crusade was its
extreme flexibility and adaptability, and its balance
of centralisation with local participation. This
unusual achievement related to a particular historic
circumstance. The Crusade was run in a completely
unique Nicaraguan fashion according to the management
model developed in the insurrection and based not on
precise long-term planning but on being able to
respond quickly to the moment. With vision of the
future only in very general terms, it drew strength
from being in touch with the immediate situation.
Since no precise long-term plan existed, reality
became the only effective available guide for
decision-making. Up-to-date feedback was constantly
solicited and staff were always on alert. Responses
to problems were provided quickly and on the whole
quite effectively, as a result. A rare model in
management, it proved highly flexible and efficient
in most circumstances because of its close ties with
the people carrying out the programme and the day-to-
day operational problems they faced. Its major weakness was in not foreseeing the effective and timely
provision of equipment to the volunteers before they
left for the mountains, which was also partly a
function of non-availability of funds to order
supplies with enough lead time. However, within a
month most of the necessary equipment such as boots
and mosquito nets had been found on the world market,
brought in by charter plane, and distributed.

The Nicaraguan Literacy Crusade

Opposition of Vested Interests
A political minority representing the richest economic interests in the country opposed the campaign,
calling it indoctrination and domestication, and
refusing to allow their children to participate.
Rumours designed to instil fear and distrust were
spread in the cities and other parents encouraged not
to give permission to take part in the Crusade.
Rumours in the countryside were also calculated to
discourage families from participating in the campaign. Death threats were common. During the Crusade
harassment of volunteers and programme participants
occurred especially along the border where Somoza's
ex-guardsmen often made incursions into Nicaraguan
territory. Houses were stoned in the middle of the
night, women brigadistas raped, and nine volunteer
staff and community assistants assassinated.

Resources
The major problem with campaign financing was that
adequate funds only arrived late. It had been decided
that the campaign would have to be financed
completely by international donations and local contributions; funds could not be allocated from the
government budget or from loans. The Ministry of
Planning also established that the Crusade should
only spend funds actually received, to avoid going
further into debt in case with a changing international situation funds promised did not material-
ise. However a national campaign of such magnitude
needed an extensive line of credit from the very
beginning of its planning efforts. As it was the
purchase of necessary equipment and the paying of
full salaries were often postponed until adequate
funds arrived. On the other hand, although the
Crusade staff were for the most part inexperienced in
literacy, adult education and management, being
recruited on the basis of their potential and commitment, they responded to the challenge with remarkable
growth and development.

Motivation of Learners
While initially motivation was a problem it was overcome principally by the enthusiastic persistence of
the volunteers. In some cases fear of reprisals by
the ex-National Guard caused resistance. Some were
simply shy and felt they were incapable of learning.
Others were tired or ill from long years of poor diet
and heavy work. Women with young children thought it
would be impossible to find quiet time for study.
Some feared communism; others were just not
interested. In general however, when people began to

see the seriousness and persistence of the volunteers, many of whom were living in their communities and often in their very homes, resistance fell away. Toward the end of the campaign, when the unconvinced began seeing the results of the programme, new applicants increased significantly. The key to motivation was this smiling persistence and a sense that the programme offered a once-in-a-lifetime opportunity to learn practical and useful skills, often without even leaving the home.

Inter-Agency Cooperation
One remarkable achievement was the formation of Literacy Commissions throughout the country for coordination and cooperation between different institutions, ministries, agencies and community organisations . These did not always function ideally but they performed well when their tasks were clearly defined. For example, their participation in mobilisation and demobilisation was crucial to getting Brigadistas out and back again, safely fed and sheltered along the several day journey. The commissions met regularly throughout the campaign and improved their functioning with experience and practice.

Follow-up
The intensity and concentration of effort in the Crusade adversely affected the transition from campaign to adult education follow-up programme. Because the organisation and scope of adult education had not been fully defined by the end of the campaign, many Crusade staff left for other organisations or ministries anxious to draw upon their rich practical experience. In the transition, the follow-up programme of adult education lost both staff and momentum.

EVALUATION AND APPRAISAL

More than half a million people participated directly in the campaign as learners - some 460,000 as students of literacy and about 95,000 who learned about the nation's problems of poverty and the challenge of development. All were students of the revolutionary process and the national programme of development. According to official statistics, of the 460,000 about 400,000 mastered elementary reading and writing. Each student was given a battery of three tests to determine progress. The final examination tested reading, writing and comprehension skills. To be considered literate participants had to: (1) write their name; (2) read aloud a short

text; (3) answer three questions based on the reading; (4) write a sentence dictated to them; and (5)
write a short composition. They were expected to be
able to read with comprehension, pronouncing words as
a whole, and not as a series of isolated syllables.
They were to write legibly, leaving appropriate
spaces between words, and to spell phonetically. With
such skill levels, it was felt, participants could
within their vocabulary range read newspapers, application forms, technical information pamphlets and
books. They had also had the opportunity to develop
analytical skills and express themselves in public
while studying history and national development
programmes.

That so many people mastered these basic skills
in five months is quite remarkable and in conventional terms alone must be considered an extra-
ordinary achievement; but the campaign involved more
than conventional literacy, being conceived as mutual
learning and human development. The teacher corps and
support staff were also learners, who to varying
degrees acquired new understanding of poverty and the
challenge of development. It is generally agreed that
the 65,000 volunteers and support staff who worked in
the rural areas gained most from the experience. From
close relationship with the peasant families many
learned to appreciate for the first time the traditional culture of the rural people: their songs,
dances and poetry; their predominant values; and
their intelligence and capacity for survival in the
face of extreme deprivation. They saw in everyday
living the effects of misery and underdevelopment.
Rural poverty touched them personally, and moved many
to deeper commitment to the Revolution and to working
with the poor. Their families were often affected in
similar ways, especially those who visited the volunteers in their teaching.

The Crusade was part of a national development
process designed to redistribute power and wealth,
and favouring the poorer half of society. Reduction
of poverty in economic terms per se was not a stated
goal of the campaign except in reference to development, but it was implicit in the larger process of
redistribution and transformation. It is difficult to
find quantitative measures to evaluate this aspect of
the campaign; overall qualitative judgements however,
give a picture of important achievements. Besides
helping people gain skills, knowledge and attitudes
conducive to transformation, the campaign had specific results which contributed to national development and helped consolidate the new balance of power
and wealth.

The Nicaraguan Literacy Crusade

During the campaign, volunteers worked with their newly adopted communities in a nationwide malaria control programme, helped in countless local development projects, and gathered valuable information for future national development planning. Literacy brigades, especially trained research brigades, conducted several surveys collecting important agricultural data. Cultural brigades recorded thousands of stories, legends and histories from the common people to be developed into educational materials; and medical brigades plotted the distribution of rural diseases to assist more accurate programming.

The Crusade profoundly affected the nation's new institutions. Through participation in the campaign the citizen and labour organisations expanded their network of affiliates and improved their operational capacities. Government agencies were able to design corrective strategies for bottlenecks discovered, making their services more responsible to the community.

People involved in the Crusade can give the most articulate assessment of the experience. As to the purpose:

> literacy is fundamental to achieving progress and it is essential to the building of a democratic society where people can participate consciously and critically in national decision-making. You learn to read and write so you can identify the reality in which you live so that you can become a protagonist of history rather than a spectator.
>
> Fernando Cardenal S.J.
> National Coordinator of Crusade

As to skills and attitudes from learning literacy and from dialogue:

> Dona Auxiliadora, what does ignorance mean to you?
> Ignorance means that I don't know anything about who I really am or very much about this world that I live in.
> Why do you want to learn to read and write?
> Well... to wake up my mind.
> And you, Asuncion?
> Learning to read and write... we're going to be able to participate more in the benefits of agriculture. Now we're going to have the tactics, that's what I call them anyway, the tactics to work the land better. Somoza never

taught us to read - it really was ungrateful of
him, wasn't it? He knew that if he taught the
peasants to read we would claim our rights.
Literacy Discussion, May 1980
Crusade class in Masaya

Do you know I am not ignorant any more. I know
how to read now. Not perfectly, you understand,
but I know how. And do you know, your son isn't
ignorant any more either. Now he knows how we
live, what we eat, how we work and he knows the
life of the mountains. Your son, maam, has
learned to read from our book.
don Jose, a peasant farmworker
speaking to the mother of his
literacy teacher, July 1980

What was learned from teaching literacy and living in
the country?

It's difficult sometimes. Tomasita is smart and
wants to study but her baby cries a lot and she
can't put him down. I visit her three times a
day just on the chance she'll be free but...
she's only on lesson 4... Camilo doesn't seem to
assimilate his sounds very well. Of course he
does need glasses. He's 67... Socorro and
Joaquina are way ahead on lesson 14 but Julio
left to pick coffee and Catalina's in bed with
malaria... Cicente has improved incredibly since
he fell off his mule. He was really a lazy bum
before. But now, with his broken arm, he's quite
serious and dedicated, even though he's had to
learn to write all over again with his left
hand.
Guadalupe, age 16
Enoc Ortez Brigade

We take our malaria medicine twice a week and
we're supposed to use our water purifying
tablets... The sicknesses among the children are
many. Eight children in the next valley died
last month of measles, three from the same
family. It's unbelievable the inhuman conditions
these people live under. I feel indignation and
rage at not being a doctor.
Brigadista from Atlantic Coast

As brigadistas we were constantly faced with new
challenges. We were actors, masters of cere-
monies, folkloric dancers, sign painters, survey
takers and public speakers. We made rice punch

for a hundred people and planned a day of children's games where children had never before been brought together in their own honor. We learned how to make decisions about how to do all these things. We learned to challenge each other when traditional sex-roles were defended (who should cook the rice for the punch) when tasks were carried out haphazardly and when some people got bossy or offensive.

Woman Brigadista

Lessons were learned by parents and programme supervisors:

The Literacy Crusade taught us two things. One, what our own children are capable of doing and of becoming. Two, what our country is like and how gentle and how poor our people are in the countryside.

Mother of three literacy volunteers

The Crusade quickly involved a significant sector of the population directly in a programme specifically aimed at restructuring power relationships. By providing the poorest and most abandoned members of society with literacy skills, ability to express themselves and a special awareness of their own potential, the campaign prepared people for the new economic and political structures being formed. The campaign also enhanced the organisational capacity of some of these structures, in favour of the poorer sectors of society. The follow-up programme, while consolidating skills and attitudes, gave these sectors specific leadership roles in which to use their newly developed abilities. Also significant was the development of the young people participating in the campaign. Their understanding of poverty and commitment to the poor increased the likelihood of their future involvement in the revolutionary process as public servants, professionals and workers.

However, certain undesired but natural consequences occurred which could prove problematic in the future. The massive nature of the campaign and its successful termination spawned great expectations for continued learning opportunities to improve living situations through job advancement. The increased demand for education in the cities could not be fully met because of the already stretched government budget. Urban technical night schools were flooded by newly graduated literates. There was dissatisfaction when everyone could not be accommodated. In rural areas there was the possibility that people finishing the follow-up basic adult education programme would migrate to the city areas, increasing the already serious urban pressure for shelter, services and employment.

Nonetheless, the Literacy Crusade contributed significantly to the creation of a new, more equitable social order. How quickly and effectively it could continue to address inequities and reduce overall poverty levels would depend both on internal and on external factors. A vocal group from the private sector acted as a barrier to further economic development, slowing down production, neglecting maintenance of equipment, and attempting to transfer profits abroad. Ex-National Guardsmen continued to attack border regions, killing and looting along the frontier with Honduras. The hostility and economic reprisals of the USA Government were clearly intended to undermine the process. Vested interests against structural change were strong, but the advances made by the Crusade made a promising beginning for the new nation.

CONCLUSIONS AND IMPLICATIONS

The effectiveness and success of the Nicaraguan Literacy Crusade depended upon a unique set of circumstances. It was not a programme to be replicated easily elsewhere. The campaign emerged from a liberation struggle in which large sectors of the population took part. This massive participation and ultimate triumph forged a sense of national unity and pride unknown previously. The high loss of life instilled in survivors a profound sense of responsibility and commitment to the dead. People wanted to begin their lives again by working to build a better nation. The new leaders shared this feeling, and a belief that citizens needed to be educated and become actively involved in the changing society. The war taught respect for people's capacity to learn and respond to difficult challenges. Out of this context the campaign emerged. The strong government commitment, their faith in people, and the creative energy of the citizenry released by the struggle, were key factors in the effectiveness of the Crusade.

The conclusions derived from the Nicaraguan literacy programme seem very obvious. When adult education programmes address the structural roots of poverty - the system of inequitable power relationships - they inevitably create tensions and provoke reactions from the dominant elites. If these strong interests hold the ultimate power, programmes will be

limited and distorted. Under these circumstances
improved living conditions for small isolated sectors
of the population may be possible in the short run,
but because the underlying causes of poverty remain
untouched, such gains will probably not be long-
lasting and certainly not spread to other needy
sectors. Only when a nation - a government and a
people - is willing to battle the root causes of
poverty, the disparities of power and wealth, can
adult education programmes really be effective in
ameliorating these conditions. When such efforts form
an integral part of social transformation aimed to
benefit and empower the poor, they can contribute
significantly to reducing disparities. Before that
moment, however, they can still play an important
part by providing basic education to some of those
who will eventually take a lead in the changes
necessary to forge a more equitable society.

NOTES

1. First Proclamation of the Government of
National Reconstruction.
2. Sergio Ramirez, Junta member.
3. Fernando Cardenal.
4. Bayardo Arce, member of the Frente Sandinista
Board of Directors, in a speech on education and the
Revolution.
5. Fernando Cardenal.
6. First training materials for volunteer
literacy teachers.
7. During the years of struggle short chants
which synthesised and captured the spirit of popular
demands and aspirations had been used to animate
demonstrations and harass the guard.

INTRODUCTION

The third Latin American subject in this volume, the Chilean unidades operativas educationales, sharply contrasts with the Nicaraguan, yet harmonises with it. The educational operative units, developed in the late sixties, were put forward for government support under Allende in 1972. Marcela Gajardo examines these units in one of the poorest regions, and traces their diminishing fortunes under the authoritarian regime which succeeded Allende. There was some vagueness in their conceptualisation and objectives, which perhaps proved convenient in the difficult political climate. Initial demand for basic education progressively gave way to a demand for training in manual and technical skills - a shift towards perceived functionality. Gajardo suggests that initial interest was in the prospect of certification as regular courses for further study by the Ministry of Education; although the Ministry withdrew from this as early as 1974, it was still an aspiration expressed by most participants interviewed in 1978.[1] There was also a tendency, noted in other studies reported here, towards traditional class-room relations and teaching methods, which undercut the intended participatory approach. This as well as the unfavourable political environment militated against a true community development result.

In terms of impact on the reduction of poverty, Gajardo records that on the whole those taking part were the less badly off in terms of educational attainment and, contrary to intentions, mainly urban participants and women rather than rural men. Although there were some modest economic gains at the individual and family level, the education of the units proved largely irrelevant to the formal labour market. The case study gives no details of budgets, access to which was denied. Gajardo has indicated separately that resources for field workers were minimal: participants or teachers brought their own materials as necessary for the class; resources of both the state and the Organisation of American States failed to reach the local teams, being consumed in costly central administration. Despite this autonomy and lack of support, paradoxically those taking part felt very dependent on the project for continuation of any activity on their own part.

Can it be said that such a project reduced poverty, or held out prospect of doing so, in any sense? Directly speaking, only in the most marginal way. Indirectly however, 'under the present conditions of the poorer groups in Chilean society', 'rather than a programme oriented towards improving life and working conditions' its latent objective was to maintain 'a certain level of organization within the poorer groups and support to the survival strategies designed by such groups to face the social, political and economic conditions imposed by... the ruling elements of present society'. Gajardo concludes that the continuity of some kind of group and organisation among the workers in the units was not insignificant; like the Rural Information (radio and press) Programme about which she writes elsewhere, it maybe sowed some seeds for the future.[2]

The profound change which affected Chile in 1973 dramatically limited the possibilities of adult education; that the project continued to operate at all was remarkable. Even so, despite a 'careful line and a low profile' it was eventually terminated. As one worker put it: 'By 1974, community organisations were banned. Then we had to be very careful concerning the groups with which we were to work. We had to provide continuous explanations of what we were doing... we had to work with those groups which are officially recognised, officially established... It is very difficult to do this job now. It is for this reason that I have temporarily retired myself from the community... My imprisonment was quite problematic. In spite of the fact that I was working under the coordination of a military authority things happened as they happened.'[3] The shift to an urban clientele was because peasant participation in any form of community or local development was totally banned from 1973. In the urban areas 'organizations had not been banned but leaders changed'; 'but, at least, participants were the lower classes in urban settings, marginal or poor population, which kept a minimal organization alive... there was a possibility to keep these organizations working together supporting what came to be known, up to now, as "survival strategies"'.[4] Gajardo's general conclusion is that, anyway, nonformal (and other) education cannot of itself improve living and working conditions of the poor, although it may be an instrument of improvement in a wider development strategy. In this stress upon organisation, giving potential for mobilisation, one can discern similarities to comments about the importance of organisation and mobilisation by the Brazilian and Indian authors and, indeed, congruence with post-liberation Nicaragua as described by Miller.

NOTES

1. Personal correspondence, Marcela Gajardo, October 1982.

2. 'Chile: an Experiment in nonformal Education in Rural Areas', Prospects, XII, 1, 1983, pp.83-94.
3. Quoted in Gajardo, M., 'Ruptura y Permanencia: dos Dimensiones de la Educacion de Adultos en la Sociedad Chilena', Revista Estudios Socialies, 26, 1980, pp.111-130.
4. Personal correspondence, October 1982.

Chapter Six

THE EDUCATIONAL OPERATIVE UNITS: A CHILEAN CASE STUDY

Marcela Gajardo

SUMMARY

Unidades operativas educacionales (EOUs) were conceived in Chile in the late sixties, put into effect
in the early seventies and are evaluated here as they
functioned in the economically poor province of
Nuble. The EOUs were intended to link to socio-
economic development and indirectly to assist the
reduction of poverty. Data were gathered from
learners and adult educators by questionnaire and
interview. Lack of clarity about the EOU's conceptualisation and purpose was further confounded by
political circumstances which prevented direct
economic action or community mobilisation. This
evaluation of participation in 1978 revealed that
participants, though poor, were not drawn from the
poorest sectors of society; participation reflected
the nature of the organisation through which participants were engaged, and the majority of those surveyed were women outside the wage-earning sector. Manual
skills intended to have economic utility predominated
over general and social education parts of the
curriculum. The education thus did not reach the
educationally and economically most disadvantaged;
though there were some economic gains these were not
in the main related to formal employment resulting
from participation. Some shortcomings in the work and
evaluation resulted from limited experience of the
adult educators, yet much was achieved through
people's efforts with meagre human and material
resources. Given the practical constraints on what
education could attempt in Chile at this time, and
despite dependency on adult educators and organisers
for continuing existence in the main, the project did
not fail completely, especially in its creation of a
basic group with future capacity for diffusion of
knowledge and skills. It suggests lessons for the
integration of adult education efforts as a
supporting mechanism for organising deprived groups.

The Educational Operative Units: A Chilean Case Study

GENERAL CONTEXT

This project was initiated in Chile in the early seventies and carried out throughout that decade. Closely related to national policies and development programmes in the field of education, it aimed at providing adult learners with basic reading, writing and mathematical skills. An important part of its objectives was to enable the rural and urban poor to participate in social and economic life. Although the seventies were particularly conflictual for Chile the underlying values, assumptions and ideologies remained unchanged; the main objective remained social participation and amelioration of the life and working conditions of poor groups.

Part of an integrated programme of adult education, the project was originally linked to regional socio-economic development and known as unidades operativas educacionales, or educational operative units. The activities were first conceived as an element in a simultaneous process of educational action and social participation, and initially planned in both northern and southern communities at the end of the sixties. It was not until 1972 that they were put forward as a government project. By this time adult education was being conceived within the perspective of lifelong education. It was seen as a means of achieving more rational and equitable distribution of educational resources and opportunities between young people and adults, and between different social groups, also of ensuring a better understanding of social and economic phenomena as well as greater participation in political, social and economic life. International and national agencies strengthened their cooperation towards these purposes, on both a bilateral and a multilateral basis, with a view to promoting the development of adult education through new methods and educational strategies. As a consequence, by 1975 the programme of integrated adult education, and within it the educational operative units, became a multi-national project using the theoretical framework of lifelong education and the policies of interamerican cooperation of the Organisation of American States (OAS). Such a programme, as a whole, did not only pursue experimental activities in the field of adult education; it also sought regular exchanges of information and documentation on structures, strategies and research as well as producing materials and training adult educators and personnel for technical assistance programmes. We here consider only the educational operative units, on the ground that such units were the means whereby the programme engaged with the rural and urban poor, in designing an educational and methodological strategy capable of developing awareness, motivation and skills which could serve as a basis for social participation and amelioration of life and working conditions.

This analysis is based on a major study[1] which evaluated the action of all those educational operative units whose action was ensured through the financial and technical cooperation of the integrated programme of adult education, and which functioned in Chile's Eighth Region, mainly in the province of Nuble. This is one of the poorest regions in the country. Its four provinces account for 14 per cent of the country's population. Most of its inhabitants are occupied in agricultural activities in rural areas. The economically active labour force represented, by 1976, 45 per cent of the population in the region and 43 per cent in the province; 7.2 per cent were unemployed in the region and 10.3 per cent in the province under study. Unemployment rates were higher in the rural sector at twelve per cent of the labour force. The educational level of the population was very low: 54.2 per cent had not completed basic education and illiteracy stood at 20.4 per cent. Only 22.6 per cent had completed secondary education. Agriculture absorbed 48.7 per cent of the occupied population. Workers or craftsmen comprised 10.8 per cent of the labour force. No data were available on income at the time, but the province was one of the poorest in Chile.

The intention in observing the units, programmes, participants and their characteristics as well as the utility of the knowledge acquired, was to draw lessons from the innovations introduced through an experimental programme. Innovation in educational processes does not occur with the diffusion of new concepts and ideas alone. Innovations occur when new contents, methods and techniques are effectively incorporated into educational practice by means of generalised action. It was mainly for this reason that a combination of quantitative and qualitative techniques was used in the study. Quantitative information provided the structure while qualitative data provided insight into educational practice as perceived and applied by both participants and adult educators.

A questionnaire was administered to all adult learners; it inquired about personal factors as well as those related to participation, and to utility of the knowledge and skills acquired. In addition, there was a number of interviews based on a sample of the different educational activities within the units. The sample included both participants and those acting as adult educators at different levels of operation of the project. Each interview was treated as a case study trying to reproduce, as precisely as possible, the way in which the actors conceptualised their experience and participated in decision-making at all levels of the learning processes. Interviews emphasised a number of relationships and themes implicit or explicit in the theory and methodology on which the units based their action.

ORGANISATIONAL CONTEXT

The Model in Theory

The programme lacked explicit objectives at the time of the research. Units functioned by means of an agreement between OAS and the Chilean Ministerio de Educacion. Activities were inserted into what was understood as an adult education structure of formal and nonformal activities. Formal education emphasised in both basic and continuing education programmes the educational needs of groups lacking access to the education system. Nonformal activities were centred on acquisition of basic skills and training for participation in social and economic life.

In spite of insertion in such a structure it is not clear how the units were conceptualised. In part the definition was closely related to the overall integrated adult education project scheme, aiming at the organisation of an adult education system based on the needs and interests of adult learners and making effective use of experiences derived from their participation in community and productive life. Theoretically such a scheme or model assumed that:

1. educational activities should be based on participants' needs and experiences in social and economic life and enlist their participation at all stages of the educational process;
2. educational activities should include skills and branches of knowledge having direct and immediate application, and be adapted to everyday life and work, taking into account the personal characteristics of adult learners – age, sex, occupation and social background;
3. educational activities should be flexible in organisation and operation and recog-

nise, as an integral part of the educational process, forms of collective organisation established with a view to solving
problems of daily life;

4. participation of adult learners, groups
and communities in decision-making should
occur at all stages including determination
of needs, curriculum development, programme
implementation and evaluation. Rational and
efficient use of existing human and
material resources should be important
elements in community, social and economic
development.

These principles were translated into a pedagogical,
administrative and evaluative model which served as
the frame of reference for designing an outline
including curriculum planning, programme implementation and evaluation of educational activities. Pedagogically, an integrated curriculum design was set
up as the axis of educational activities. Curriculum
development was to be based on participants' needs
and interests, and on their knowledge, skills and
experience from social and economic life. It was
meant to be flexible, adapting all content to the
learning abilities and rhythm of adult learners.
Problems in the organisation of social and productive
life were to serve as a means of enhancing competence
in skills and branches of knowledge relevant to day-
to-day problem-solving.

In administrative terms, two elements characterised the programme: (1) rationalisation of existing
resources; and (2) a scheme that would guarantee
centralised planning and decentralised administration:

(1) Educational activities were not to be
carried out in a special building but in
the working or living place of adult
learners. To link knowledge and skills with
daily life, the work was to be organised
and placed within the learners' social and
economic environment. Human and material
resources should come from the community
itself and from existing institutions in
the project area. Priority should be given
to interdisciplinary work and inter-
institutional coordination, making full
use of available educational facilities
at local level and avoiding competition
and duplication.

(2) The administrative structure was planned
     for autonomous execution by each unit
     within centralised and coordinated plan-
     ning, by means of the following levels of
     operation:
     (i)   a central team in charge of
            designing policies and strategies
            for the functioning of each educa-
            tional operative unit and coordin-
            ation of the programme as a whole;
     (ii)   a local executive secretariat in
            charge of policy design and coordin-
            ation at regional level;
     (iii) a local technical team in charge
            of implementation and consequent
            supervision of the development of
            educational activities at the
            units;
     (iv)   the unit coordinator in charge of
            obtaining adequate human and
            material resources and providing
            adult educators with technical
            assistance;
     (v)   a team of adult educators in charge
            of the various educational activ-
            ities of the units, meant to be
            chosen from existing resources in
            the community or from institutions
            in the area.

Finally, evaluation was to provide systematic information on the way the experience evolved. Based on the
guiding principles it was to be assumed collectively,
stimulate and sustain adult learners' interest and
motivation, strengthen their self-reliance and
provide a self-corrective mechanism within a perspective of collective advancement. Both learning
processes and outcome were to be the subject of
continuous analysis, providing feedback on the
development of educational activities.

      The interrelation of pedagogical, administrative
and evaluative components was at the heart of the
method designed for the operation of the units. The
different stages included diagnosis, planning, execution and evaluation at regional and local level, as
shown in figure 6.1. Diagnosis and determination of
existing problems indicated skills and knowledge
needed by groups and individuals, leading in turn to
curriculum development, educational planning and
consequent pedagogical preparation, including content
and methods, to attain the proposed goals. Once
resources were available and the activities carried

Figure 6.1

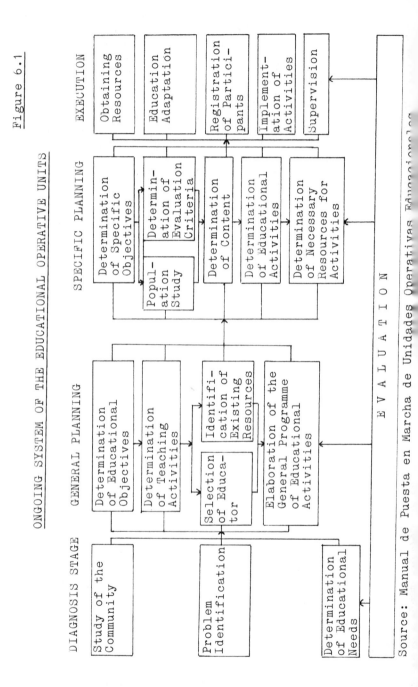

ONGOING SYSTEM OF THE EDUCATIONAL OPERATIVE UNITS

DIAGNOSIS STAGE   GENERAL PLANNING   SPECIFIC PLANNING   EXECUTION

Study of the Community

Determination of Educational Objectives

Determination of Teaching Activities

Identification of Existing Resources

Selection of Educator

Problem Identification

Elaboration of the General Programme of Educational Activities

Determination of Educational Needs

Determination of Specific Objectives

Determination of Evaluation Criteria

Population Study

Determination of Content

Determination of Educational Activities

Determination of Necessary Resources for Activities

Obtaining Resources

Education Adaptation

Registration of Participants

Implementation of Activities

Supervision

E V A L U A T I O N

Source: Manual de Puesta en Marcha de Unidades Operativas Educacionales

140

out, the evaluation should determine the extent to which initial educational or societal goals had been achieved through the unit's action. A methodological handbook, Manual de Puesta en Marcha de las Unidades Operativas, which included instruments to be used at the various stages, was to serve as a guide for the action of local teams.

The Model in Practice

The units' action began in the mid-seventies. Assumptions and method remained almost unchanged to 1978. By then various exploratory studies had been carried out to record aspects of project development and to obtain feedback. They showed field action in the Eighth Region by 1974 by 38 educational operative units, with a total of 2,038 participants. There was a steady decrease to 1977, with reductions by 1975 mainly due to financial restrictions. By 1977 there were only 17 units left, with a total registration of 1,820 participants in identifiable activities. By 1978 only ten units were still operating in the area, with 968 participants.

Important changes in educational activities were found. Initial interest in literacy and basic education gave way to an increasing demand for training in technical skills. Traditional methods of teaching predominated, revealing a deficiency in both supervisors' and adult educators' teaching experience. As a result special courses and seminars were organised to reinforce diffusion of project principles and goals and to elaborate on the handbook which, besides supporting the units' action, was supposed to strengthen the purpose underlying their operation. The handbook was intended for use collectively in constituting the unit and in educational planning and evaluation. Different instruments were designed for social diagnosis, setting of problem priorities, searching for joint solutions, registering community needs and demands, and identifying existing material and human resources. Activities were to be planned in accordance with local social and economic reality, and educational programmes to satisfy needs and demands established through accurate communal diagnosis. A special instrument supported specific educational planning, allowing pedagogical design for each determined activity. A pedagogical sequence was established prior to execution and supervision of activities. A final evaluative instrument measured achievement and gave feedback for control of the whole educational process.

This outline explains how the programme accumulated a significant amount of experience. A number of changes occurred by the time this research took place. Previous data were part of the frame of reference for exploring what happened in practice, and the extent to which the units were achieving their initial goals and thereby showing how effectively to change existing practices in adult education and community development.

THE PROGRAMME IN OPERATION

At the time of this research eight educational units were operating in Chile's Eighth Region, two in rural areas and six in urban. Six based their action on Centros de Madres, a communal organisation, gathering female householders. A sport and youth association, based on a neighbourhood league and a rehabilitation centre for alcoholic people, served as the bases for the other two units. This is important insofar as it determined the participants' characteristics, the type of activities attempted and their utility for the participants. Educational activities could be classified as regular, consisting of systematic courses in different areas of skills and knowledge including general, social and vocational education; and vocational training, including manual skills, agricultural and general technologies (see Table 6.1).

There were sporadic as well as regular activities at the units, mainly lectures on educational, nutritional and health topics, and general considerations of community development and basic needs. Some human resources for regular and sporadic activities were part of the project; others came from other local institutions and a quarter were community volunteers. More than 50 per cent of adult educators involved in the experience had already completed secondary education, denoting a certain preparedness to cope with the requirements of a project aimed at involving community organisations in the educational processes and through this at promoting social and economic development. Three hundred and eighty five adult learners participated in these educational activities during 1978. The number is low because previously the same learners participating in different activities had been counted more than once. Demographic, educational and organisational characteristics of the participants are summarised in Table 6.2.

Partly because of the character of the community organisations on which action was based, 80 per cent of the participants were female householders. Although some goals were achieved, this suggests a series of questions. First, the educational level of adult learners. Almost 60 per cent had either

142

Table 6.1

Regular Activities and Enrolment
at the Educational Operative Units *

Type of Activity	Number of Participants N	Total Enrolment N	%
General Education		27	3.9
Elementary mathematics	27		
Social Education		38	5.5
Social organisation	38		
Vocational Education			
(a) Agricultural techniques		26	3.8
- familiar vegetable garden	8		
- fruit-tree pruning	18		
(b) General technologies		85	12.4
- electricity	30		
- car mechanics	25		
- carpentry	30		
(c) Manual skills		512	74.4
- tailoring, knitting and embroidery	233		
- various handi-crafts	194		
- hairdressing	65		
- household education	20		
TOTAL	688	688	100.0

* There were 688 enrolments but fewer participants, since most adult learners participated in more than one educational activity.

Table 6.2

Demographic, Educational and Occupational Characteristics of Participants

	Percentage
SEX:	
Male	16.0
Female	80.0
AGE:	
Less than 19 years	12.6
20 to 29 years	22.1
30 to 39 years	20.2
40 to 49 years	16.7
50 years and more	21.1
EDUCATIONAL LEVEL:	
Primary Education	37.2
Secondary Education	55.2
Vocational Education	4.1
Higher Education	
OCCUPATION:	
Female Householder	70.0
Students	7.9
Remunerated Workers	17.4

Note: Sum of percentages in each variable does not total 100 as no-answer data were not included in the summary.

Source: Gajardo, M.; De Andraca, A.M.; Op. cit. 1978.

completed or commenced secondary education, support-ing a familiar adult education research finding: that those who have already attained higher educational levels benefit more from further educational oppor-unities. Most of those involved lived in urban areas and were relatively well educated, whereas the intention was to concentrate mainly on rural folk with minimal education occupied mainly in agri-culture. This suggests the inadequacy of the pro-gramme to engage with development priorities. Secondly, it is often stated that adults are highly motivated towards educational activities of immediate economic or social benefit, as suggested by data in

144

The Educational Operative Units: A Chilean Case Study

Table 6.1. Besides serving an urban population,
courses offering manual skills accounted for two
thirds of participants; only 4.9 per cent were
enrolled in general education, and 5.5 per cent in
social education. This concentration on manual skills
suggests that there was little or no interest in an
integrated curriculum approach, but high motivation
towards skills and instrumental knowledge leading to
remunerated work either at home or through the labour
market. This is not surprising, looking at the social
and economic deprivation of the region, but it raises
serious doubts about the project's premises when we
observe the extent to which participation was useful
to those involved in it. Table 6.3 shows that only
1.6 per cent of participants had access to the labour
market; most of them described their participation as
useful rather than in other terms.

Table 6.3

Usefulness of Participation in UOE

	%*	%**
Useful in terms of reducing expenses in family budget	80.5	19.2
Useful in terms of obtaining a temporary job to be carried out at home	42.9	57.1
Useful in terms of obtaining a temporary job in the labour market	14.8	85.2
Useful in terms of obtaining a permanent job in the labour market	1.6	98.4

* Percentage of participants who identified the
specific usefulness of UOE.
** Participants who did not identify the specific
usefulness of UOE and no-data cases.

STYLE AND METHODS

The method adopted was supposed to differentiate this
from other adult education programmes. What was the
methodology in practice?
    Local technical staff, adult educators and part-
icipants were interviewed, and educational practice
observed in the field. The sample was chosen to
include different educational activities. Type of
activity was considered, as well as importance in
terms of enrolment. Basic and social education,
agricultural techniques and general technologies were

represented by one unit in each case. Four manual skills activities were included in the sample by enrolment. Selection of activity automatically determined which adult educator and participants would be interviewed.

The data revealed that the stages of diagnosis, general planning, specific or educational planning, execution and evaluation did occur, but at different levels of operation. Diagnosis and general planning by unit coordinators were supervised by local technical teams. Although these stages were completed in most of the units, planning related partly to information collected and mostly to demands emerging from the annual programmes of communal organisation and to the demand for paid jobs. Most adult educators and participants knew very little about diagnosis itself, or about the needs which led to educational activity and the problems to be solved through it. Different units tended to implement those activities which were easy to carry out with the available human resources. Most material resources were provided by participants themselves, and some by adult educators. Economic deprivation caused activities to be based upon the lowest cost and highest benefit. Hence in part the predominance of manual skill activities.

Specific pedagogical planning was the adult educators' responsibility. Curriculum planning as proposed implied a high level of participation of both educators and participants. Nevertheless no general planning pattern in the different areas of knowledge could be discerned. It depended on the educator's experience and training; curriculum planning might be flexible or traditional in the same type of activity. Likewise with teaching methods: despite the fact that manual skills and technological knowledge lend themselves to a combination of theory and practice, traditional methods often predominated. This, added to adult educators' perception of their action, shows that the initial conception of an integrated curriculum design was not achieved. Integration of different areas of knowledge through a single activity did not occur. Instead, participants worked on isolated contents directly related to objectives as set by the adult educator. In spite of this, the evaluative process in the units appeared to accord with the initial assumptions. Different evaluative techniques were used by adult educators and participants depending on the nature of the activities. Generally evaluation occurred throughout the educational process, and educators tended to solve problems as they occurred through individual work. While there were strengths and weaknesses about

application of the stages as planned, in the end they
occurred as separate actions at different levels of
operation. Adult learners had little or no participation in diagnosis or curriculum planning. Likewise
for adult educators as regards diagnosis and determination of educational priorities. This lack of
participation militated against support of community
organisation and mobilisation of productive resources
for significant local or regional development.

Lack of resources was a major obstacle. The
local team in charge of the organisation and technical support of educational activities worked
through the central team to obtain financial resources. The concept of centralised planning and
decentralised administration was in practice a myth.
Local teams worked basically with existing resources
in their respective areas. In most of the activities
observed it was mainly the participants' creativity
and their organisational situation which made things
possible. The other element which contributed to the
achievement of some of the units' goals was the sense
of responsibility and dedication of local teams.
Although information is lacking about the budget and
costs of the programme, it became clear that such
projects must have the financial means to guarantee
amelioration in participants' living and working
conditions. Their linkage to national or regional
projects of development then becomes essential. This
aspect was progressively lost from sight. By the time
of the research, institutional coordination relied
mainly on adult educators' personal contacts. Moreover, those still participating in the units were
those who had been working since the very beginning.
No matter how big the effort, under such conditions
it appeared improbable that the programme could, in
the long run, afford an effective alternative means
for adult education action.

ANALYSIS OF THE PROGRAMME

Analysis of the problems besetting the adult education projects suggests that the experience evolved in
accordance with major changes occurring in Chilean
society. Clarity of purpose was affected, and objectives no longer made explicit, once social participation was restricted by the mid-seventies, as a result
of political changes at that time.

The units were effectively attended by adults
over 18 years old who had no access to or had not
completed school education. Nevertheless, and despite
the initial premises, the units tended to produce
social gaps by reinforcing existing educational

inequalities, as those participating had relatively high levels of education and were looking to obtain a diploma certifying completion of basic education, or for training programmes which could enable access to the labour market. Besides this, although purposes and steps were defined, the project was implemented poorly, due to poor comprehension of the premises by adult educators and, especially, from the nature of the participation and the lack of subsequent incorporation into the labour market. Local coordinators, asked what they understood as an educational operative unit, gave different definitions, stating that they were 'a group of persons gathered together with teaching and learning purposes', 'a second school', 'a way to support community development and to teach those adults who are interested in learning' and 'a new way of teaching adults and a place where people do what they want and learn what they need'.

Despite confusion and lack of clarity of purpose, the action of the units was not a complete failure. As a theoretical and practical attempt at community development it gives effect to a set of premises which have seldom been implemented in adult education programmes. The problems derived not from the units' conception but from the way they were put into practice. The isolation of the stages (diagnosis, planning, execution and evaluation), the absence of knowledge or low level of integration of skills and branches of knowledge in curriculum planning, and the consequent concentration of participants in manual skills: these problems could have been overcome through adequate training and technical assistance. Access to the labour market was extremely restricted in the region, and educational activities should have related to existing labour force needs or to the possibilities of constituting autonomous economic organisations capable of applying skills and knowledge effectively to increasing income or improving working conditions. This occurred only in a single unit, where participants had been able to use educational activities in support of their productive practice.

It is easy to see in principle how better methods might have been adopted; but in terms of promoting organised activities by community groups, the problems were formidable. It had already been accepted in community development strategies that education served mainly as an element in larger social and economic processes. Participation in determining needs, planning curricula, implementing programmes and evaluation, enables the acquisition of knowledge and skills, and provides decision-making

The Educational Operative Units: A Chilean Case Study

experience which can be transferred to daily life.
This implies that in a community development perspective goals should tend towards either better
distribution of educational opportunities or training
of groups and individuals to incorporate them into
social and economic life. Amelioration of living and
working conditions of community members should also
be kept in mind. The educational operative units were
in fact conceived thus. Nevertheless the implementation of various strategies for national development
seriously affected their practice. Most of the
communities and groups originally involved in the
experience remained socially and economically
deprived. Collective action was drastically curtailed
and it became difficult to promote activity which
might develop groups' self-esteem and a positive
sense of their own identity. There were obstacles to
linking educational processes with social reality and
to participants' experience in community and productive life. Transfer of the educational project to
community organisations became difficult, once their
activities had been restricted. The process of comp-
rehending, evaluating and implementing a series of
steps that might help to overcome existing limitations does not necessarily give control of
educational processes, unless both conditions and
political decisions make this possible. Similarly
with generalisation of the experience and its incorporation into the social system as alternative adult
education practice.

At least during 1978, the educational operative
units acted as isolated educational components. As
such, despite the problems, their success lay in
their capability of maintaining, through educational
activities, the existence of organisations which were
still seeking collective solutions to problems of
daily life. Seen as a mechanism for community
development, the units were obviously restricted in
spite of the fact that, both theoretically and
methodologically, they sought adult participation
in social and economic life. All this refers to the
political problems of Chilean society.

As to motivation, participants in the units
spoke of their activities as a way of doing something
about increased needs and decreased resources. There
was clear motivation to acquire new knowledge and
skills. Most important was the motivation to use
learning as a way of reducing poverty. Participants
sought to make economies in the family budget by
applying the knowledge acquired. Less frequently
there were aspirations to obtain paid jobs in the
labour market. Some participants, especially a group

149

from the rural areas, saw in the activities also a possibility of enhancing their social life and making new and better friends. Applicability of learning to real life is illustrated by the following comments of participants:

> We have earned some money with embroidery and knitting and we also work for our homes and children.

> We sell our works among friends and through an annual exposition. Many of us have thought of the creation of a workshop. It would be a labour workshop. We have a sewing machine and we should start by sewing. We know a lady who bought a TV set by selling her sewing. And a lady who did not want to participate started once learning how to paint on handkerchiefs. By the end of the month she had sold a dozen handkerchiefs. This helps to relieve the family budget.

> We work in the organisation of 'huertos' and learn to cultivate basic products for our organisation and homes. With these products we have given lunch to our children and those who come to the open dining-room in our organisation. Necessities have grown and resources have gone. We have to do something for ourselves and this is the way of doing it.

Much of this resulted from the activity of regional and local coordinators who were charged with obtaining the human resources necessary to the educational plan. Much of the success depended on their leadership and dedication. The same may be said of the adult educators and, particularly, the volunteers from different groups and communities. Material resources were frequently provided by them. It was generally agreed that without both local coordinators and adult educators the unit would disappear. In fact, none of the units considered itself able to conduct educational activities on its own, which cast doubt on their permanence over time; lack of support from the educational apparatus would mean the end of activity.

REVIEW AND SUMMING UP

Three hundred and eighty five adults were participating as learners in 1978, when the last overall evaluation was carried out (a number lower than in other evaluations, in which double counting occurred). What may be important was the existence of a group which kept a permanent relation with the project, participating in different activities, for three years or more: this basic group with a permanent link to the programme might eventually be able to assume diffusion of the knowledge and skills acquired. Although successful in maintaining a basic group in operation, the programme did not reach those for whom it was originally intended, and it did not cover the different areas of knowledge originally planned. It worked principally with women's organisations in urban settings, failing to reach peasant organisations and other communitarian groups. A high percentage were female learners, householders not part of the economically active population. Although all were adults and economically poor, they were not from the lowest educational levels. This raises a number of questions about the extent to which these projects do constitute an educational alternative for adults lacking access to the education system. As to content, emphasis was placed on manual skills. Only four per cent participated in other education related to social or general aspects. Yet the programme was intended to link, in one process, basic education, training and education for social participation. The failure may be partly attributed to the political restrictions existing in Chile.

Did the work help to reduce poverty? Although this was not an explicit objective, in the event there was some contribution towards amelioration of living conditions, and small but important effects in reducing expenses in individual and family budgets. It gave little or no access to permanent remunerated jobs, a fact to be understood by reference to the social and economic circumstances of the country and region. In spite of high unemployment there were no intentions of creating new posts or implementing major development processes requiring trained personnel. In summary, the programme had limited objectives relative to reduction of poverty, and these were partly met.

An important aspect is the extent to which activities were well rationalised to maximise yield from scarce resources. This economy, together with the efforts of coordinators, adult educators and organisations involved in the experience, was important in the success in attending to the educational needs identified; but along with the groups' need to obtain the resources to carry out an educational activity or to develop collective processes of local benefit there was a high level of dependency upon technical staff. The programme did not succeed in promoting an autonomous organisation or a local capacity to cope with social and economic problems, except for one case where technical assistance was transferred to a non-governmental agency of agricultural extension. By the time of this evaluation no new solution had been detected to help the different ongoing activities based on their own local resources, or on those of groups or agencies already occupied in providing poor groups with resources for their own development. In fact, amelioration was the only possible action at this time, in that any effort to tackle the political and economic causes of poverty would mean the immediate end of the programme and dismissal of its participants.

This observation of the way in which the educational operative units functioned does not allow generalisations about the use of such an approach as a model to be applied in other settings. The programme was a mixture of failure and success: a failure in terms of the social, political and economic context insofar as it is not possible for a participatory experience to function in an authoritarian society like that of Chile at the time; a success in terms of survival of the work based on local organisation and resources. Social and economic deprivation is not peculiar to Chile. Rather it is a consequence of a structural transformation in a capitalist and dependent society with an authoritarian style of social and political development which does not allow participation of deprived groups in political decision-making or enable these groups to participate in adequate policies of health, education, nutrition, dwelling and water supplies, excluding them from the benefits of employment and economic growth.

Overcoming or reducing poverty implies for such a society structural changes towards satisfaction of the basic needs of the urban and rural poor as well as encouraging the organisation of these groups to participate in political life. In this context adult education programmes can operate only as a support to the organisational processes of deprived groups. Literacy, continuing education, training, social and political education should then be understood as a means towards achieving a democratic and participative society, based on the social interests of less-well-off groups: workers, peasants and indigenous populations, the so-called marginal people in such societies. Only in these terms can these programmes contribute to the reduction of poverty and

amelioration of life and working conditions for the
poor. Consequently failure and success can be determined only in these terms. A programme might be
highly successful when oriented towards social and
political change, even in authoritarian societies
such as the Chilean. On the other hand, a programme,
though technically successful, may be a failure when
seen as an end in itself, unconnected with other
social, economic and political processes. Such is the
lesson of this evaluation.

NOTES

1. This paper is based on research work carried
out at the Programa Interdisciplinario de Invest-
igaciones en Educacion (PIIE). Originally published
as Gajardo, M., De Andraca, A.M., et al. 'Unidades
Operativas Educacionales: Antecedentes y function-
amiento de una experiencia en al campo de la educacion de Adultos'. Mimeographed, 1978.

REFERENCES

Acevedo, R., De Andraca A.M., Plan de Teleeducacion
    de Television Nacional de Chile. Estudio des-
    criptivo y analisis de la publacion inscrita,
    CIDE-PIIE, 1976.
De Andraca, A.M., Gajardo, M., Un proceso de
    aprendizaje colectivo. El Programa de Difusion
    Campesina de ICECOOP, ICECOOP, Marzo, 1979.
CPEIP/PEIA, 'Evaluacion Experimental de las Unidades
    Operativas', in Educacion de Adultos, 6,
    May/June 1975.
CPEIP/MINEDUC, Seminario de Educacion Integrada de
    Adultos, Documento 8037, 1970.
Duke, C. (ed.), Adult Education, International Aid
    and Poverty, CCE, ANU, Canberra, 1980.
Gajardo, M., Egana, L., La educacion de adultos en
    Chile: un analisis de su desarrollo, PIIE
    Estudios, 1977.
Gajardo, M., 'Ruptura y Permanencia: dos dimensiones
    de la educacion de adultos en la sociedad
    chilena', Revista Estudios Sociales, 26, 1980,
    pp.111-130.
MINEDUC/CPEIP/OEA, Informe. Proyecto Multinacional
    de Educacion Integrada de Adultos. Anos 1974-
    1977, Documento 17.119, Lo Barnechea, Chile,
    1978.
MINEDUC/CPEIP/PEIA, Funciones y responsabilidades
    por niveles, Mimeo, 1977.
MINEDUC/CPEIP/PEIA, 'Manual para la puesta en marcha
    de las Unidades Operativas', Documento de
    Trabajo, n/d.

The Educational Operative Units: A Chilean Case Study

Chapter Seven - SAEMAUL EDUCATION

INTRODUCTION

Dr Cheong's account of Saemaul Education within the national Saemaul Undong Movement of the Republic of Korea prompts questions both about its character and success and about approaches to reducing poverty. Note that the Movement was created in a directive, centralised and top-down manner by an authoritarian government to address the problem of inequality between rural and urban areas and the threat to security and stability - in a highly security conscious country - which rural disadvantage was thought to represent. As an 'integrated rural development programme Saemaul Undong must be judged a considerable success, as Cheong briefly indicates and other studies of the Movement explain more fully.[1] If it is accepted that the leadership training programme described here, and the village-level problem-oriented applications to which trained leaders' energies were applied, were an essential element in the Movement's success, as Cheong persuasively argues, then it follows that the success of the Movement was a success for education applied to the reduction of poverty.

The next question, however, is whether poverty has been satisfactorily reduced in South Korea. Here the evidence is mixed. Cheong points out that the poorest and most in need resented the programmes most and benefited least, probably in any direct sense not at all. The 'green revolution' phenomenon appears again: rural and agricultural modernisation benefits those with economic resources and with confidence generated by success behind them; the net result is to widen the gap within rural areas between the more and the least prosperous. Thus Saemaul Education may claim significantly to have contributed to reducing the poverty of rural Korea, but not to have helped those in greatest need. Economists might say that such general modernisation and increased prosperity, bringing rural areas on average at least up to a par with the urban, inevitably ends up by benefiting all who reside in the country. Cheong virtually says as much in describing the enhanced rural service and economic infrastructures. If one can accept the ethical as well as practical arguments for trickle-down development, Saemaul Education is a success in reducing poverty; if this sticks in the gullet one must conclude, as indeed the author appears to, that it has not been successful so far as the lot of the mostly needy is concerned.

The study also echoes the paradox sounded lightly in Bekele's Kenya account, that a programme

155

depending heavily on voluntary and collective community action but intended to promote national development through individual advancement, runs into difficulties born of its very success: as farmers and their families learn and gain from Saemaul education and development projects, they become more motivated to increase profits and prosperity, and less willing to put time into collective village and district enterprises. Thus both the more affluent and the most needy tend to opt out or stay out.

The study may leave some adult education readers discomfited by the authoritarianism evident in the programme, and perhaps by the implicit purpose of enhancing national security through ideological training. Cheong however, suggests that the education, while much in need of more professional andragogical guidance, nonetheless helped prevent Saemaul Undong from sliding into totalitarianism.[2] For readers in the western liberal tradition the overt and somewhat Spartan moral, spiritual, or ideological training well described in this chapter may appear improper; one might pause and ponder on such unease, asking whether other, more secure, societies do not merely practise socialisation and inculcation of national values in more subtle ways. On the positive side, the congruity between message and means within the socially equalising training courses must be acknowledged, as well as the valuing of rural and manual working experience implied in the account.

One reader of this study concluded that it would be difficult to replicate because of its highly centralised and top-down approach: it requires the full support of government to provide material support and the infrastructure for developing and implementing the programme. It is true that such a programme could not be initiated on a small-scale experimental basis and that some governments would feel unwilling or be unable to make and carry through such a decision. However, there are many strong and authoritarian governments of both left and right which can and might exercise the political will for such a development programme with a strong educational component. One should separate discomfort with overt government directiveness (for character-formation as well as economic development) felt by those brought up in the liberal democracies from an estimation of probability of replication. What certainly could not be replicated is the particular cultural and historical circumstances of the Republic of Korea, which combine to explain Saemaul Undong.

Saemaul Education - Introduction

NOTES

    1. See further reading at the end of this volume.

    2. Note however the fear, which proved unfounded, that the assassination of President Park, founder and patron of the Movement, would spell its demise.

Chapter Seven

SAEMAUL EDUCATION AND THE REDUCTION OF POVERTY

Ji Woong Cheong

SUMMARY

The Saemaul Undong (New Community Movement), a
nationwide Korean community development movement
initiated in 1971, has contributed much to the rapid
transformation of rural settings and even of people's
attitudes to development. Rural poverty was widespread, and discontent had increased by the end of
the 1960s when the discrepancy between rural and
urban communities grew as a result of urban industrialisation. The Saemaul Movement, which began as an
attempt to balance rural development and urban
industrialisation, has considerably reduced rural
poverty and the rural/urban gap; rural people in
Korea are no longer poverty-stricken in an absolute
sense.
        Saemaul education, a nationwide adult nonformal
education programme to promote the Saemaul Movement,
has played an integral and pivotal role in every
aspect of the Movement. Most of the village leaders
called Saemaul leaders and many high-ranking officials and intellectuals have undergone Saemaul education programmes at national or local level. Most
Saemaul education programmes have been pursued not on
a voluntary basis but through bureaucratic channels.
However, village-based and small community-based
Saemaul education not imposed by the authorities has
also been undertaken in many villages by enthusiastic
village leaders to mobilise residents. These projects
seem to have been more successful and to have reduced
poverty to a great extent.
        This study deals with the process and substance
of Saemaul education in general and with a model
village. Saemaul education is analysed generally and
in terms of its contribution to the reduction of
poverty. A field survey was conducted in a model
village (Chilwon-Ri) where Saemaul education played

an indispensable role in rapid reduction of poverty.
Data gathered through interviews and observation are
analysed and presented descriptively.
  Saemaul education, like the overall Saemaul
Movement, was not specially designed to benefit the
rural poor, but gave an impetus from which the poor
as well as all others might be able to benefit.
Village leaders, including Saemaul leaders taught
especially at the Saemaul Leaders' Training Institute, have been influential in motivating and mobilising villagers, rich and poor, to work together for
the development of their communities. The model
village reveals that the Saemaul leaders who emphasised farmer education could better achieve development goals and contribute to the reduction of poverty
of all villagers.

GENERAL CONTEXT OF THE SAEMAUL EDUCATION PROGRAMME

Origins of Saemaul Education

'Saemaul Education' (New Community Education) origin-
ates from the Saemaul Undong (New Community Movement), a nationwide community development movement in
Korea elaborated in 1970 and fully supported since
1971 by the President and Government. The main focus
has been rural development, neglected in the 1960s
during rapid industrialisation when the record high
annual economic growth rate was concentrated in
cities and the gap between rural and urban communities became a most serious problem.
  The late President Park first advocated the term
'Saemaul' in a speech to a meeting of provincial
governors on 22 April 1970 and suggested it as a
movement to narrow the rural/urban discrapancy. The
Ministry of Home Affairs thereupon planned a nationwide development programme based on the Saemaul
Undong idea, to be administered through its local
bureaucratic channels; this was approved in October
1970. The programme was immediately implemented in
1971 by providing all 35,000 rural villages with 335
sacks of cement and rods of reinforcing steel, and by
encouraging villagers to improve their roads and
other infrastructure through cooperative work, which
involved most farmers in the Saemaul Movement. By the
winter of 1971/72, major progress was made in
environmental improvements: road expansion, small
bridge construction, thatched roof replacement with
tile, metal or composition, and the like.
  Because of unrelenting pressure from the top,
bureaucratic efforts to achieve the movement's goals
at the level of local government were intense, and
Saemaul became the main focus of activity for all

local administrative agencies. Most farmers distrusted the motives of the authorities and resented their constant interference in village affairs. Other problems were due to lack of leaders and agents to mobilise villagers and resources fully to develop the villages.

To overcome such problems the government recognised a need for adult nonformal education for Saemaul leaders and change agents, including ranking officials and intellectuals, and promoted 'Saemaul Education' in 1972 through the Ministry of Home Affairs (MOHA) and Ministry of Education (MOE). MOE used the terms to strengthen previous community school activities including public school adult nonformal education, while MOHA promoted its own unique Saemaul education as an integral part of the Saemaul Training Institutes assigned by MOHA to undertake adult nonformal education for Saemaul leaders and the socially influential. MOHA categorised MOE Saemaul education as school-centred. Both are still using the same term to represent the different concepts. Saemaul Education supported by MOHA has played a key role both in the Saemaul Movement and in adult education for real development, while MOE has focussed more on formal education usually for children at school level. The term 'Saemaul Education' refers here to all adult nonformal education activities in line with the Saemaul Movement, undertaken mainly by the Saemaul Training Institutes and partly by the public schools.

Structure and Functions

The Movement, which was directly controlled and coordinated by the President's Office through local administrative structures of the Ministry of Home Affairs, now has four phases: rural Saemaul, urban Saemaul, factory Saemaul and school Saemaul. Other ministries such as Agriculture and Fisheries (MAF), Health and Social Affairs (MHSA), Commerce and Industry (MCI), Education (MOE), and Culture and Public Information (MCPI), are related to the Movement in their respective fields as follows:

MAF: Saemaul income-generation project of farmers through agricultural extension work of the Office of Rural Development (ORD).

MHSA: Saemaul medical service through local hospitals and health centres.

MCI: Factory Saemaul Project in which all kinds of factories undertake Saemaul education for their workers and take part in the Movement, and Saemaul factories are built in remote rural areas to mobilise local labour.

MOE: School Saemaul in which all levels of schools participate in the Movement through community school activities, including adult nonformal education. For example, Standing Saemaul Schools were open several times a year at most agricultural high schools.

MCPI: Saemaul Broadcasting (radio and TV) Programme in which all kinds of media broadcast Saemaul information and news for some hours a week. Weekly/monthly Saemaul Magazines describe Saemaul information and progress and Saemaul Stories are distributed to existing print media, newspapers, weekly Farmers' Newspaper, etc.

All non-government organisations particularly related to rural development and adult education are inevitably involved in the Movement in some way. Voluntary agencies for the development of rural communities have to harmonise their projects with the Saemaul projects being carried out everywhere. Otherwise conflict or contradiction between non-governmental organisation projects and Saemaul would occur and frustrate the voluntary efforts. Many non-governmental nonformal education agencies became Saemaul Education Institutions where business workers and members of voluntary agencies are asked to undergo Saemaul training. In every aspect and phase of the Saemaul Movement education has been integral; emphasis on Saemaul education is the key to the success of the Movement. If the Movement is now weaker at grassroots level, it may be because Saemaul education is inappropriately rigid and no longer motivates trainees actively to participate in the Movement.

Most of the people - agents and leaders, men and women, intellectuals, workers, farmers, higher ranking officials, top business managers, local officials and staff - have undergone Saemaul education in institutes such as the Public Officials' Training Institutes at different ministries and non-governmental training centres assigned by the MHA as Saemaul Training Institutions under its supervision. Participants' expenses are supported by their respective companies and organisations.

There are 85 Saemaul education institutes around the country identified by the Ministry of Home Affairs, 49 governmental and 36 non-governmental. Three, including one public facility, were established exclusively for Saemaul training. The others provide Saemaul education in addition to their original training programmes, such as in-service training for public officials and business agents. The training is organised to influence certain people, to modify their behaviour for better attainment of social and organisational goals. It is supposed to offer not only managerial and technical training but also social education, mobilisation of political and social supports and cultural change in rural communities. It stresses aspects of both spiritual enlightenment which stimulates and encourages the desire for participation, and techniques that provide practical directions for projects. To nourish the spiritual aspect, such subjects as ideology, leadership, the scientific way of living, directions for economic development, the directions of the Movement, the people's attitude, the national policy of reunification of the nation, and national history are taught. For technical aspects, such subjects as general farm management, cash crop production, animal husbandry, silkworm culture, swine breeding, afforestation, erosion control, agricultural civil engineering, construction and farm machinery are taught.

At the village level, some Saemaul leaders who participate in Saemaul education have voluntarily provided villagers with a similar but shorter Saemaul education and tried to motivate them actively to participate in community-based Saemaul works. During the winter off-farm season extension workers also undertake winter farmer education which might be called Saemaul education, in which farmers are taught about new rice varieties and other farming techniques. Likewise, in a company or agency one who has undergone Saemaul education usually briefs other staff or workers about the experience, and may lead the group to organise institutional Saemaul activities.

Chilwon-Ri - a Model Village
Chilwon-Ri is a village in Song-Tan Eup, Pyung-Taek County in Southern Kyung-gi Province, four kilometres northeast of Pyung-Taek Township. The village is proud of achieving integrated Saemaul projects and has been named a Saemaul Model Village to promote Saemaul information to outside visitors. Originally, the village was very poor, with many problems; as a model village it has certainly impressed those who knew it years ago.

There are 70 households with a total population of 328; seventy-one percent of the households are engaged in farming, on 24.9 hectares of paddy and 28.4 of upland. The rice paddy fields are almost all irrigated. The average size of cultivated land per household is 1.4 hectares which is above the national average but about the same as the provincial average. The major sources of farmers' income are dairy products, rice, cattle beef and other livestock (chicken and swine). The average income per household in 1979 was nearly 4.6 million won (roughly $8,000) which is equivalent to $US1,600 per capita - higher than the national average and 2.5 times that of the average farm household. This was more than ten times the average for 1971 when Saemaul was launched, and implies revolutionary changes as a result of the villagers' cooperative efforts under the flag of Saemaul Undong. Exposure to mass media and cultural level are very high, as is the educational level. Out of 70 households, 51 have television sets, 70 have radios and there are two telephones, 16 refrigerators and six electric washers. There are seven college graduates, 25 senior high school graduates and 31 junior high school graduates.

Under the strong leadership of the 46-year-old Saemaul leader the village rapidly developed from almost nothing in early 1972 to prosperity, following the model of a Danish rural community. The concept of integrated rural development guided improvements in environment, production and income, education, applied nutrition and women's activity, elders' and children's welfare and other areas. The villagers also benefited from outside influences, notably a big company construction nearby, the government's interest in building a Saemaul model village, and a good marketing structure for the sale of dairy products.

When the Saemaul projects started in 1971 with cement and other materials provided by the local government, the villagers repaired the community well with a sanitary holder and drainage canals, and built a small monument for the community to encourage cooperative community work. They began a partial cooperative farming system in planting trees, applying insecticides, planting medicinal herbs for cash income and so on. In 1972, they replaced all thatched roofs with tile or tin, built or improved roads in and near the village, installed a methane gas system (which is not popular as yet), created an arch at the entrance of the village, a flag pole and a community bell, organised a water supply system and continued to finish a drainage system. They reorganised the cooperative farming group and continued their cooperative income-raising farming. The Saemaul leader received a presidential award.

In 1973, Saemaul projects included house improvement, with a water supply system and toilet repair, electrification, a Saemaul School operation, construction of an applied nutrition house and equipment and of a grain dryer, purchase of village farm machines and tools, installation of a loudspeaker and other information materials including a tape recorder and camera, planting of trees and a nursery, expansion of soil composting, acquisition of additional Korean cows and creation of a wedding preparation committee. Next year the villagers began dairy farming, building a dairy farm house and purchasing milk cows. They introduced and expanded other income-boosting projects like beef cattle and cultivation of medicinal herbs and some environmental improvement projects like kitchen and roof repair. In 1975, dairy farming was expanded by developing pasture meadows and building ensilage. An improved fence project and a drainage repair project were implemented and communal estate land purchased. In 1976, a village warehouse was built, a cooperative store opened by the women's club, a joint work place developed, fences for some dairy farm houses put up and cooperative farming organised for such activities as pesticide work. In 1977, the villagers built a small reservoir and canals to supply water to the paddies during drought, paved roads near the village and planted nut trees on the mountainside. In recognition of the great number of successful Saemaul projects the village leader was awarded the 'Cooperation Order' by the President. Since 1977 this has been a Saemaul Model Village and entertained a flood of Korean and overseas visitors. The Saemaul leader and other villagers have been so busy briefing visitors they have had little time for new work.

After 1978, the local government paid serious attention to the village not only because of pressure from the top but also because of County Office pride in it. Taking out loans to cover 60 per cent of the construction expenses, most of the villagers built new houses. Agricultural and livestock cooperatives helped with special loans and technical assistance. The Dong-A Motor Company, which built a large factory near the village, has helped to complete the paved road to link the village with nearby towns on condition that they pay back part of the expenses in future years. Now the village owns tens of million won of community property. There are 17 dairy farm houses with 143 dairy cows; 14 cattle houses with 16 Korean cows and 39 head of beef cattle; pigs, chickens and rabbits. The problem is that livestock prices in the domestic market are neither stable nor profitable. The villagers are now building a welfare centre for elders and one for children. The women's club is also very active. As incomes increase and people get busier than ever with individual farming and other work, however, they cannot but pay less attention to community work than they did in the mid-1970s.

Consequence for the Reduction of Poverty

The Saemaul Movement is generally recognised in Korea as a key to the successful integrated rural development of the 1970s. It is difficult to measure what Saemaul education has contributed, but it is said to be one of the most influential factors in making the Movement successful. Farmers' average annual household income increased between 1970 and 1976 from 255,800 won to 1,156,300 won, and that of urban wage workers from 381,200 won to 1,151,800 won.[1] Absolute poverty seems to have disappeared. Rural poverty in particular appears generally to be greatly reduced However, wealthier farmers benefited more from the Movement than the poorer. It has been assumed that the 15 to 20 per cent of rural people who are still poor would have their standard of living raised by the trickle-down of general economic prosperity. The poor, less able to spare time from work, have had less opportunity for Saemaul education. Saemaul projects directed solely at the poorest of the poor in both rural and urban areas, such as employment creation and medical service, have been few in number and slight in their effect on problems of poverty.

THE WORK OF SAEMAUL EDUCATION

From the beginning of the Saemaul Movement the government provided full administrative and financial support. Its scale and complex nature required well-organised project selection, planning, implementation and coordination, processes considered part of the training and education of villagers.[2] The Ministry of Home Affairs has a section which coordinates Saemaul education and information. There is also a Saemaul Education/Information Section in each provincial capital, and at the lower levels, the Saemaul section of the Gun (county) and Myon (subcounty) Office deals with related affairs. The Movement is intended to train the villagers from the beginning of project selection to the final stage of project completion. Accordingly, Saemaul education is an integral part of the Saemaul Movement.

Saemaul Leaders' Training Institute

By 1979, 40,539 people had passed through the central institution, the Saemaul Leaders' Training Institute

(SLTI), opened in 1972: 15,996 Saemaul leaders, 8,156 women Saemaul leaders, 9,802 leaders of society's top echelon, 1,517 student leaders and 5,068 staff members of agricultural and fisheries organisations.[3] There is no bar of age or educational level, but priority is given to those recommended by government authorities or other experts. Saemaul lecturers range from university professors to village leaders with only primary school education who have, however, extensive practical experience, valuable ideas and insights.

The main activities of the Institute are: (1) training through sharing experience of trainees and staff members lodging together; (2) cultivating the Saemaul Jungshin through actual practice; (3) fostering mutual learning through group discussions and presentation of successful cases of Saemaul activities; and (4) providing follow-up service for the graduates. The curriculum of Saemaul training is as follows:

Lectures	Hours	(Percentage)
-Saemaul Jungshin	20	(19.4)
-National Security and Economy	7	(6.8)
-Saemaul Projects Planning and Implementation	27	(26.2)
Group Discussion	18	(17.5)
Case Study	14	(13.6)
Field Trip and Others	17	(16.5)
Total	103	(100.0)[4]

The 92 well-organised staff members of the Institute, thirty-seven of them teaching staff, have effectively managed the training programme as well as the miscellaneous work of the Institute. Cooperation between the five departments under the Director's strong leadership is regarded as indispensable to its successful operation.

Saemaul Education at Village Level

Most village leaders including Saemaul leaders have been trained in the Institute. In Chilwon-Ri the head, Haksoon Park, was trained there in 1972. On returning to the village he played a leading role in implementing the Saemaul project, and recommended others in the village for the Institute. At first many were sceptical, and not interested in the leaders' efforts for village development. As villagers began to recognise the leaders' practical orientation, village leaders succeeded in getting

Saemaul Education and the Reduction of Poverty

cooperation and support. Being directly provided for
the villagers, the education plays an important part
in improving the village environment and increasing
farmers' income.
     Saemaul education at this level is provided both
by village leaders and by experts from various organisations, including agricultural extension agents.
Most village leaders who play a major role in
teaching their villagers have been trained at Saemaul
education organisations outside. Both the Saemaul
leader and the village head at Chilwon-Ri were
trained in the Saemaul Leaders' Training Institute.
Haksoon Park, the village head, also participated
in various education programmes including dairy
farming at the office of Rural Development, before
teaching fellow villagers at the Saemaul Village
Centre. For specialised problems as with dairy
farming and veterinary care, experts including
extension agents were invited to give necessary
information and technical education.
     Saemaul education has enabled farmers to align
their different interests with the efforts of government in implementing the Saemaul Movement for nationwide socio-economic development. In general, the
education assists individual farmers to change their
attitudes and update their technical know-how, while
the Movement takes the form of group efforts for
communal works. Accordingly, the education plays a
principal part in economic results with respect to
motivation and improvement of farming skills. The
effects become apparent over time, enabling the
educated individual to perform his job more effectively; those who put emphasis on education are
leading farmers in income-boosting and public work
activities. Of course, factors other than education
also influence agriculture and other development.
Price policy, marketing structure and weather
conditions have a direct influence on farming, but
education at village level enables farmers to prepare
well for their jobs, to improve the present situation
and to take advantage of new scientific knowledge and
skills.
     Such education is provided mainly in Saemaul
Village Centres. The Centre at Chilwon-Ri was built
in 1972 mainly for education. Other education facilities there include a nutrition house, a broadcasting
room for the village community, a village library and
a nursery school. The content of Saemaul education at
the village level is as follows: Saemaul Spirit
Training; Agricultural Technical Training; Rural
Saving Campaign; Saemaul Credit; Saemaul Women's Club
Activities; Village Library Activities; Saemaul

Education for public officers and people outside the village; Applied Nutrition Improvement. Although some villages emphasise adult education for their development, most do not. The Saemaul education system at village level is not therefore yet institutionalised.

AIMS AND OBJECTIVES
The basic philosophy of Saemaul education may be deduced from that of the Saemaul Movement. First it seeks to modernise Korean society on the basis of its socio-cultural traditions, aimed at not only material improvements but also spiritual enlightenment. Secondly, it is directed toward improvement of living standards for individuals, communities and the whole nation. Thirdly, it is a movement towards spiritual reforms led by government to establish new values and human relations congenial to national development.[5]

Saemaul education, as a major component of the Saemaul Undong and the educational input for rural development, is intended to maximise the social functions of education and the educational functions of society,[6] achieving not only managerial and technical training but also social education, mobilisation of political and social support, and cultural change in rural communities.[7] There is an educational flow from the training institutes through Saemaul village leaders to the villagers. The importance of the Saemaul leader cannot be overemphasised: development of rural leadership is a major factor in effective implementation of the Saemaul Movement.

At the central Saemaul Leaders' Training Institute in Suweon, the objectives are to train a vanguard corps for the Saemaul Undong; to support the Saemaul leaders as catalysts for the movement; and to contribute to the nationwide creation of the Saemaul spirit of diligence, self-help and cooperation.[8] Three life principles are stressed in the training course from the time trainees get up until the time they sleep: to have a lofty ideal for modest living; to stay out of debt and take pride in thrift and saving; and to prefer a life of substance to one of appearance.[9] The Institute trains village leaders rather than ordinary villagers, and emphasises spiritual education to arm them with the Saemaul spirit.

On the other hand, Saemaul education at village level caters to villagers' different needs. Content may vary according to the problems facing the village. Various information from outside comes into the villages and the education is likely to be given an integrated form. Saemaul education is needed to motivate villagers to participate in Saemaul projects for village development, and to enable them to tackle problems related not only to agricultural production but also to home management. With the exception of technical subjects requiring qualified experts, most education is by local officials, knowledgeable Community Committee members, or other capable villagers.

At the beginning of the Saemaul Movement, non-formal education at village level was to mobilise villagers for the Saemaul projects. The education programme tried to create socio-economic and psychological incentives for villagers' participation and to induce cooperative efforts for communal projects. As a result of successful communal projects, villagers have developed an infrastructure which has improved living conditions. Although applied nutrition training has improved individual villagers' daily life, other projects requiring group efforts' sometimes meet with the opposition of the lower class of the village. Because their livelihood is based on daily wages, it is difficult to provide free labour for village communal work. They take little interest in training which puts emphasis on group efforts, but are enthusiastic about educational activities such as applied nutrition programmes which are directed to their own better living.

The objectives of Saemaul education at village level can be summarised as follows: to establish values directed towards development; to equip villagers with the Saemaul spirit of diligence, self-help and cooperation; to motivate them to participate actively in village communal projects; to meet villagers' particular needs in farming; to enable villagers to tackle problems related not only to agriculture but also to the home; and to help villagers understand the government policy related to social progress and rural development.

COST AND EFFECTIVENESS

Various institutions provide just Saemaul education, whereas others provide it as a part of their own programmes. This decentralised implementation makes it difficult to calculate the costs of what is strictly Saemaul education. The annual budget of the Saemaul Leaders' Training Institute in 1979 totalled 322,095,000 won, comprising: educational expenses – 154,674,000; current expenditure – 103,259,000; facility expenditure – 64,162,000. The cost of Saemaul education per head ranges from 22,000 to

Table 7.1

Per Capita Cost of Training,

Saemaul Leaders' Training Institute (1979)

Course	Training Period (Days)	The Cost of Training					
		Total (won)	Meals	Clothing	Materials for Study	Inspection Trip	Other
Saemaul Leaders	11	32,165	9,000	5,500	800	323	16,539
Special Course for Saemaul Leaders	14	40,025	11,700	5,500	800	1,495	20,530
Women Leaders	7	28,933	5,300	5,300	700	210	17,323
Social Leaders	7	22,000	5,400	-	700	213	15,687

about 40,000 won, all supported by the government (Table 7.1).

Park, the head of Chilwon-Ri, was aided by his village to participate in training. Although belonging to a richer segment of the village, the villagers gave him money for his training expenses to express their respect for his contribution to the village development. A cooperative relationship is thus established between leaders and the other villagers, showing also recognition of self-sacrificing effort for village development and trust in a leader. Leaders' participation in the training is thus regarded as for the villagers as a whole. There is a minimal charge to participants and maximum support from the Institute, which is financed and managed by the government.

The cost effectiveness of education is seldom calculated exactly. Nonformal adult education at village level would be most difficult to measure in these terms. Saemaul education in Chilwon-Ri takes various forms. Educational activities, except for those requiring qualified experts, use the voluntary service of village leaders, and communal facilities are freely used for educational purposes. Materials for teaching are provided without exact calculation of the cost, which in any case is small: the villagers participate without financial cost, receive information from lecturers and apply what they learn to their daily life. In the applied nutrition training programme, for instance, the villagers need not pay for materials because they bring what is needed with them from their own farms. Sometimes however, they pay a fee for lectures by outsiders.

The leaders, like the villagers, are not very conscious of the cost of educational activities. As the living standard of the village rises educational activities become more important to their daily lives, and villagers spend more on educational activities, but they are apparently not conscious of the increased cost. On the other hand there is sometimes opposition from those with low incomes to spending time in education instead of working for their living. An increase in indirect costs of education at village level, except for such cases as applied nutrition programmes, might thus increase the alienation of those of low income.

TEACHING AT SLTI AND AT VILLAGE LEVEL

Saemaul education in SLTI and other Saemaul training organisations consists of sets of courses, but educa-tion at the village level is generally informal in style and method.

Saemaul Education and the Reduction of Poverty

Saemaul Leaders' Training Institute

SLTI has three main courses: for Saemaul leaders, for women leaders and for social leaders. In any course of training three specific features are commonly stressed.

Firstly, presentation of the experience of successful village Saemaul leaders (case studies) is a very effective and persuasive means of educating other Saemaul and social leaders. For a member of the social elite who makes policies for others to implement, the story of a poverty-stricken village woman who, with no formal education, finally managed by dint of hard work to extricate herself from poverty, and is now helping other villagers to live better, makes a longlasting impression and makes him feel that the village woman is perhaps contributing much more to society than he is. By listening to such stories, the prominent person reevaluates his past life style and begins sincerely to respect the village Saemaul leaders, and therefore becomes better able to offer as much support to the village leaders as possible.

Secondly, the training emphasises 'doing' rather than 'talking'. Every trainee lives under the same conditions, eats the same food, makes his own bed and cleans his living quarters. Every session starts exactly on time and ends on time. Every trainee participates in the two km morning jogging and uses the stairs when going from the classroom on the ground floor to the living quarters on the ninth. No one expects or receives special treatment. Everyone is treated equally. A thrifty life is practised with no alcohol, coffee or tea but only a simple diet composed mainly of coarse grains. Through such practices, the trainees learn that 'doing' is much more difficult than talking, and that the farmer's rough hands covered with calluses are equally as beautiful as the slim and pale hands of the talker.

Thirdly, self-evaluation through group discussion makes the trainee evaluate his past life style. The evaluation focusses on what he has done in the past and what he should do in the future (1) as a person, (2) as the head of a family, (3) as the head of an office and (4) as a leader in society...[10]

172

The training period and content are said to be rather flexible in accordance with the specific needs of trainees and suggestions of institutions related to the Saemaul Movement. However, there is some uniformity in subject matter, discipline, case presentation, group discussion, meditation and other methods of training. Usually training for Saemaul leaders is for two weeks and training for other leaders of society requires one week. In every course, emphasis is on practical experience to promote attitudinal and behavioural change. For instance the lecture 'The Saemaul Movement and National Development', usually given by Joon Kim, director of SLTI, is one prerequisite for all kinds of Saemaul training. It describes the Saemaul spirit as the firm foundation of the Saemaul Movement and extols the so-called 'rural mind' or 'agricultural spirit', which means a humble rational way of thinking based on a belief in cause and effect and natural law. Trainees should learn that a man in farmer's clothes or labourer's outfit is as respect-able as an urbanite in city attire. As to the qualifications of a Saemaul leader, Joon Kim emphasises trust and service. Trust is a result of consonance between talking and action and a sense of service: like the farmer engaged in food production for people, all have to sacrifice themselves for community and national development which will lead to individual prosperity. Such a sense of service is produced not by talking but by hard work guided by a broader ambition. There is great need for cooperation, implying a basic collective social order which can be realised only by following a common purpose. To establish a new order is the purpose of the Saemaul Movement, which it is believed will contribute greatly to modernisation and prosperity.

The contents of each training course are the philosophy and spirit of Saemaul, the direction of the Movement for the specific year, national security and the international situation, introduction to economic development, conservation, energy-saving, public ethics and morality, successful case studies, a study tour to model project villages, and panel discussion. Several additional subjects are offered to meet the needs of specific groups of trainees, mainly technical, focussing on income-boosting projects for rural leaders. Urban people learn how to improve business management and neighbourhood rela-tions and women leaders usually learn child care, health care and alternatives for economical daily living. Some institutes undertake special short-term Saemaul training for those who cannot afford a long absence. Two or three day refresher training is also provided for alumni to renew friendships and rearm themselves with a fresher Saemaul spirit.[11]

Manee Lee, MOHA Education and Information Section Chief, explains the unique training methodology as follows:

> Trainees are collected at the campus with no connection nor communication with outside permitted. Trainees and trainers lodge together, eating at the same table, using the same facilities, and treating each other on just the same level. Both sides cultivate a blood-tied relationship to which they dedicate themselves in order to find the ideal way of life based upon truth, good and beauty.
>
> Saemaul Training won't emphasize sophisticated theories of research, instead, it calls for the steady and sincere practice and experiencing of what one thinks should be done. Each trainee gets up early in the morning, cleaning his own bed, saluting to the national flag, singing the national anthem together, jogging a few miles together, practising physical exercise together, carrying and cleaning his own dishes, meditating by himself under the broadcast of a mild voice awakening the tainted people, listening to lectures presented by earnest instructors including poor and ill-educated living heroes from the bottom class of the society exchanging humble experiences with group or panel members, visiting the real sites of touching struggle against hardships, and above all fighting against himself so as to lead himself to an inner sanctuary remodelling himself into a dedicated contributor to the common welfare.
>
> Success stories presented by community leaders in the local peasant tongue used to move most of the trainees, well-educated and ill-educated, young and old, men or women. Some stories are presented in movies or slide shows.[12]

Evaluation and follow-up.[13]
Evaluation is in three stages: needs assessment; intermediate monitoring; and assessment of training accomplishment. Trainees' needs are assessed upon their arrival at the Institute on Sunday afternoon in terms of background, knowledge of and attitude toward the Saemaul Movement, and needs and expectations of their prospective training. The results are

analysed that night and reflected in guidelines for
training and in slightly adjusting the subject
matter, during the instructors' meeting on Monday
morning. Intermediate monitoring and evaluation are
performed by trainers who stay with trainees in the
same dormitory and are in charge of different
discussion groups. Before going to bed they exchange
information and views about the trainees' attitudes.
The problems encountered are then adjusted if necessary at a meeting which may be called as late as mid-
night. At the final session just before the closing
ceremony, trainees are asked to fill out a questionnaire with two main items: what the Saemaul Movement
is; and what has changed in their way of thinking, if
anything. The results of the group discussion are
also analysed to assess the training effect.

On the basis that the crucial effect of training
depends upon real life behaviour, four kinds of
follow-up activity are considered important. First
is communication through letter and publications.
In addition to answering all letters from trainees,
the director and trainers send them several letters a
year encouraging them to write about what they are
doing and describe problems they may have encountered. The Institute has published a quarterly communication booklet since 1974 entitled Saemaul Undong to
send to trainees, mainly conveying successful cases
and letters from and between trainees. Secondly,
trainers visit trainees' homes all over the country
during non-training periods. Trainees welcome the
trainers and seem more enthusiastic when they meet
them in their own remote rural areas. The third
follow-up action is a local one day session convened
by the Institute to encourage trainees to keep
informed of Saemaul projects in other areas and to
solve the problems they have encountered. Finally
trainers can take part in an alumni meeting. This is
voluntary and held either with room-mates (16) or
with session-mates (20 rooms) in good friendship.

Saemaul Education at Village Level

Saemaul leaders trained in the Suweon Institute
return to their villages and resume educational
activities, playing an educational role in selecting,
planning and conducting village projects. The
educational influence of the Saemaul Movement supported by administrative power makes it possible for
leaders to motivate villagers to participate in
Saemaul projects. Nonformal education is crucial to
village development at every stage. It varies in
style and method, but is usually given in village
meetings and in the form of personal communication.

Saemaul education led by the village leaders is generally connected with farming techniques during farming seasons; in the off-farming season it is concerned with the general affairs of the village, family and personal life. It may be epitomised as on-the-spot and problem-oriented, closely linked with villagers' real life.

Saemaul education at Chilwon-Ri divides into two kinds: that usually undertaken by the Saemaul leader to promote the village Saemaul project; and that undertaken by outside service agencies like the Office of Rural Development (Country Rural Guidance Office) to meet specific needs. In the case of Saemaul education for common village work, the Saemaul leader as well as the village head plays a leading educative role. As the standard of living rises more opportunities present themselves for increasing income. Villagers are also provided with more educational opportunities than before, but tend to be less willing to participate in educational activities than previously, preferring to spend time on their own income-earning activities.

A village leader promoting participation must mobilise the villagers and try to persuade any who respond negatively. In most cases this appears successful, but some poorer villagers complain that the community projects do not help them economically. In reality they are experiencing an improved living environment, whether or not they are conscious of it. However, almost complete attendance is common with the nutrition programmes. The programmes use demonstration methods to show the advantages of applied nutrition.

Although the basic infrastructure of the village has been developed to some degree and the villagers are more interested in education which can help them increase their farming income and improve their living conditions, Korea's material development not-withstanding, spiritual education is still considered to be as important as technical education. Political circumstances and changes, especially, demand new consciousness for a new political structure. This means strengthening spiritual education. The spirit-ual parts of Saemaul education still depend on the traditional leadership of village leaders developed during the past decade.

SOME IMPORTANT ISSUES

Is there Clarity of Purpose?

Saemaul education has been used to implement the Saemaul Movement for the past decade. During this period, the purpose of the Movement has been firmly asserted and it is now stronger than ever. It is reflected in Saemaul education. Based on the Saemaul spirit of diligence, self-help and cooperation, the Saemaul Movement has attempted to achieve (1) spiritual reform (human development), (2) economic development and (3) social development which will make it possible to modernise the country. President Chun's regime continues to support the Saemaul Movement as a national movement to realise social welfare in Korea.

Saemaul education at the central training Institute has a close relation with the Five-Year Plan for socio-economic development. Its purpose is clearly evident in the interaction between educational and administrative factors. Village level Saemaul education takes place where the government's top-down policy contacts and interacts with bottom-up needs. The Saemaul Movement to develop each village as a whole sometimes conflicts with people's own interests and can then be misunderstood. A major point of confusion is whether centrally directed Saemaul education aims at developing individuals through the development of the whole village, or whether education at village level is pushed to develop the village through the individuals' development. Such conflicts can however easily be solved if democratic activities and participatory planning are employed.

The Role of Leadership

SLTI stresses developing village leaders; despite the short period of training it appears successful in raising their pride and improving their leadership. When they return to the villages they encourage others to get training in turn. At Chilwon-Ri Mr Park, the village head, who has had many opportunities for training, emphasises training and education especially for young men.

In Korea, traditional and modern factors combine in the exercise of village leadership. In the transition from traditional to modern society, education is regarded as a channel to improved social status, so being trained outside the village is respected by most villagers. In some cases leaders exercise charismatic leadership with traditional authority but this does not last for long, and democratic succession of potentially good new leaders is sought.

Competition between villages has been employed in implementing the Saemaul Movement: villagers are to be united under their village leaders, and external competition has stimulated internal solidarity of the village. Development is very dependent on village leaders' implementation of the Movement. At Chilwon-Ri, most villagers think that their village has reached its present stage by dint of their leaders' efforts, and village leaders feel strongly committed to village development. As the Saemaul programmes at village level diversify, responsibility is divided among such leaders as the Saemaul leader, women's leader and village head.

The Political Context

The Saemaul Movement was initiated under President Park's powerful leadership. After his death in October 1979 many who had criticised his government expected the Movement to be rapidly phased out. Many Saemaul village leaders were worried for the future of the Movement. Such apprehension disappeared before long as the Movement began to resume its activity under the more powerful leadership of the new administration. Saemaul education has however, now contributed not only to developing rural leadership but also to informing farmers of the government's policies. In addition to improving living conditions in rural areas, it functions as a channel of information from government to farmers, which renders it sensitive to political change. Thus political manipulation of the Movement seems possible. As the Movement is not for the political benefit of a particular administration but for the farmers themselves, it ought to be perpetuated for rural development. Most villagers at Chilwon-Ri seem to think this way, especially about Saemaul education which has contributed to modernising their perspectives.

A serious problem for Saemaul education at national and local levels is that it is too rigid and doctrinaire to bring about voluntary change in the behaviour of trainees who are tired of being passively disciplined. New techniques in nonformal adult education might usefully now be adopted and employed.

Resource Development and Motivation

Most achievements in the Saemaul Movement are through the development of human resources by means of Saemaul education. Its institutions have mostly tried to develop leaders as generalists. As a village advances many kinds of work require experts or semi-experts. This need can be met by technical training. Thus Mr Park at Chilwon-Ri obtained a first-class certified licence to teach dairy farming techniques, taught the villagers what he had learned of dairy farm techniques and had a great impact on their economic life. Now the village has become a model dairy farm community, and in terms of material resources has enjoyed external support from local government and other sources. A mini-library was started, for instance, by village leaders with outside help. Since being selected as a model village the village has benefited from many other sources. Mr Kim, the Saemaul leader at Chilwon-Ri, considers the natural environment of the village the best resource to be developed, and has inspired villagers to cultivate unused barren land as a communal culti-vated area.

While village leaders are well motivated, low income villagers are less keen to participate. In general, rich farmers take pride in going it alone, while the poorer farmers think the Saemaul Movement does not benefit them directly. In fact Saemaul has been implemented through positive participation by middle class farmers, by women rather than men, and by youths rather than older men.[14] In the case of communal projects village leaders have to think how to mobilise the low-income class, for whom foregoing income-earning labour to contribute labour for community work is extremely difficult.

The Trainers and their Methods

In most Saemaul training institutes, the trainers feel strongly that they have to sacrifice themselves, even to the point of poor health and a disrupted family life because of continuous residence at the training centre. They are also short in number and in quality. Most are not trained as professional trainers and have only had experience in adminis-tration. They are not cognisant of new adult education techniques and seldom try to learn them. Such techniques are introduced via overseas institu-tions which they occasionally visit. This suggests the importance of appropriate professional develop-ment in adult nonformal education.

Several other issues detract from effective nonformal Saemaul education. First, all levels of training are uniform and no linkage exists between them either horizontally or vertically. Most of the programmes are too strict and disciplined to be flexible; they are more like military training. Secondly, most of the Saemaul training has too many trainees at one time. They are not selected on a voluntary basis but are usually forced to undergo the training, so that its effect, while radical, is not intrinsically pleasurable. Sometimes trainees are evasive when they should more frankly evaluate

the results of the training and criticise it.
Thirdly, most of the subject matter and methodology
is already fixed when the training begins, so that
trainees' needs and individual differences are not
fully catered for. On the one hand the trainees'
uniform is intended to suggest equal treatment,
despite the differing status among trainees, but on
the other hand, it may be taken as indicating a
failure to recognise individual differences. Such
problems are all related to adult nonformal education
methodology. This should be developed adequately and
with variety, and employed throughout all Saemaul
education as soon as possible.

OVERALL APPRAISAL OF SAEMAUL EDUCATION

Although Saemaul education has played an important
part in combatting poverty in rural areas, it is
extremely difficult to isolate and measure directly
its impact on rural poverty. Factors other than the
educational are also associated with improving the
standard of living and reducing poverty; they
influence each other and are interwoven. Since the
Saemaul Movement is an integrated rural development
project, the impact of its education on rural poverty
is in association with the impact of other aspects
of the Movement and the project.
     From its inception the Movement has been imple-
mented through bureaucratic channels. Centralised
power has exerted strong direction in its implementation. Most striking, educational activities have
been initiated in the Movement through bureaucratic
channels yet have prevented the Movement from becoming totalitarian. The educational processes of
selecting, planning and carrying out village Saemaul
projects hold the administrative power in check,
however strong this power is at village level. Educational factors make it possible to check the administrative power and to harmonise with villagers' needs.
In addition, villagers have made efforts to realise
their own interests in close collaboration with the
government's policy. Recognition of the potential
benefits has provided the incentive to participate.
Likewise the government wants to make farmers effectively aware of rural development policy and the
Saemaul Movement through the Saemaul education
programme.
     Saemaul education provides farmers with an
opportunity to review the government's rural
development policy. As the Saemaul Movement was
initiated from above, not from the community, the
authorities concerned with the Movement urgently

required the Saemaul leaders to inform people of rural development policy. Saemaul education has contributed much to motivating village leaders and other villagers to participate in the Movement and projects. Most leaders have participated in Saemaul training. Saemaul education can motivate leaders to participate both in training programmes and in the Saemaul Movement.

In that Saemaul education made it possible to propel the Movement to the present stage it has been very successful, although there is room for further improvement. It has contributed to changing villagers' orientation to the past into an orientation to the future. Under the influence of Confucianism, deep-rooted in the society, Koreans have had a past-orientation central to traditional worship of their ancestors. This presented many difficulties for rural development, and Saemaul education has been successful in inspiring a modernised consciousness.

Saemaul leaders who have undergone Saemaul training with social leaders including high-ranking officials (even government ministers) and intellectuals are proud of their invaluable experience and upon returning from the training try enthusiastically to transmit what they have learned and felt to other villagers, and to persuade them to work together for village Saemaul projects. Village leaders' ability to mobilise villagers in the Saemaul projects is attributed to the training institutes. In short, Saemaul education has played a most crucial role in village development and the improved standard of villagers' lives, as the case of Chilwon-Ri well demonstrates. Saemaul education at village level is, however, sometimes faced with difficulties due to individual differences in incomes. Rich farmers with a high level of income can easily find ways in which they can apply the practices learned. Poorer farmers cannot take such risks. Accordingly, special programmes should be prepared for low-income farmers.

Also Saemaul education tends to be dependent on administrative power. Excessive involvement of the government in Saemaul education may threaten its future. Educational activities should be strengthened, and administrative intervention reduced. It would be desirable for the Saemaul Movement to be more civic-oriented, based on the needs of the villagers while still striving to harmonise their needs with government efforts for further development. The foundation of Saemaul education with emphasis on voluntary participation and on special consideration of the poor may be the key to the future success of the Saemaul Movement, as well as of Saemaul education.

CONCLUSION AND IMPLICATIONS

The Saemaul Movement is indigenous to Korea in method and style. It was initiated in all 35,000 villages in the country; at the initial stage all the villages were almost equally financed by the government. Most village leaders were trained in Saemaul education institutes at various levels.

Saemaul education is one of the most indispensable components of the Saemaul Movement, bringing up pioneers at the central level who can vigorously implement village Saemaul projects. It has contributed much to upgrading the social function of education in rural areas, where most people are not well educated to adapt to the changing society. At village level it has been responsive to needs and problems, action-oriented, enabling villagers in the process of sharing experiences to modernise.

Saemaul tries to provide equal educational opportunities to all. However, villages differ in the extent of development as well as in emphasis of education. The same Movement has been introduced into all villages, but the village leadership functions as a crucial factor in education and development. Differences of leadership influence the extent to which collective attitude change occurs. The leader who gets along well with villagers and motivates them to learn can more efficiently develop the community.

Saemaul education within the Movement is an educational approach to integrated rural development. Administrative power is often used excessively to accelerate development, due to the ambition of those in power, and to demonstrable successes for the rapid transformation of poverty to prosperity. Nevertheless, the educational factor is intrinsic to the Movement, motivating people for voluntary participation in it. Educational and administrative power interact dialectically for the reduction of poverty.

Saemaul education is conducted in many villages in spite of the socio-economic differences between them. This suggests that similar education might prove successful in the rural development programmes in other countries. The socio-economic situation facing each country should however be carefully considered before replicating this education in a different culture. One reason for the success of the Saemaul Movement and Saemaul education so far must be that Korean people, though cantankerous, are yet readily supportive of government policy. Even though most villagers have had little chance to undergo education in Saemaul training institutes they have experienced it indirectly from Saemaul leaders who influence their neighbours.

Saemaul education has contributed much to reducing rural poverty in general. It is also true that Saemaul education, like the overall Saemaul Movement, has components not directly designed to benefit the rural poor, but designed to give them the opportunity to benefit. The case study of a model village reveals that Saemaul leaders who emphasised adult education were better able to achieve their development targets and greatly contribute to reduction of poverty of the whole village. However, ten households out of a total of 70 are still, relatively speaking, very poor. In the process of rapid economic development of the villages, the most poor experienced less benefit from Saemaul education and the Saemaul Movement. Clearly the Movement and its education have not yet fully succeeded where needs are greatest.

NOTES

1. In 1970-1976 $US1.00 = roughly 500 won and in 1981, 690 won.
2. Choe Yang-Boo, ed., The Korean Model of Rural Saemaul Undong: Its Structure, Strategy and Performance, Korea Rural Economic Institute, Seoul, Korea 1978, p.47.
3. Data from Saemaul Leaders' Training Institute, 1980.
4. Source: Saemaul Leaders' Training Institute, Guide to the Training Program for Saemaul Leaders, 1977.
5. Jong-Chol Kim, et al., The Saemaul Education in the Republic of Korea, The Korean Society for the Study of Education, 1974, p.206.
6. Unesco Regional Office for Education in Asia and Oceania, Administering Education for Rural Development: Report of the Second Advanced-Level Workshop on Education for Rural Development, Tehran, 9-18 September 1978. Bangkok, 1979, p.8.
7. Jong Whang, 'Training Strategies for Integrated Rural Development: Search for Alternatives', Journal of Rural Development 1:1 (November 1978) pp.111-131.
8. Ministry of Home Affairs, Saemaul Undong, Republic of Korea, 1980, p.604.
9. Saemaul Leaders Training Institute, Guide to the Training Program for Saemaul Leaders.
10. Ministry of Home Affairs, SAEMAUL UNDONG, Republic of Korea, 1980, pp.37-38.

        11.   Manee   Lee,   'Education and Training on the
SAEMAUL   UNDONG',   presented   at the Regional SAEMAUL
UNDONG   Study   Seminar,   9-22 June 1980, Seoul, Korea,
p.38.
        12.   Ibid., pp.11-13 (revised). A further account
is   provided   by   Soon-Jong   Kwon,   'SAEMAUL   Leaders
Training   Programs   in Korea',   paper presented at the
Consultative Meeting on Monitoring and the Evaluation
of   Social   Development   Programmes, Manila, February
1978, see Appendix.
        13.   See   Soon-Jong Kwon, loc.cit., 1978, pp.25-
30, 18-20.
        14. Dae Hwan Kim and Yoo-Hyun Kim, 'Universality
and   Particularity   of the Saemaul Movement', in Man-
Gap   Lee,   ed.,   Toward   a   New   Community: Report of
International   Research-Seminar   on   the   Saemaul
Movement,   1980.   12.   8-13,   Seoul,   Korea,   Seoul:
Institute   of   Saemaul Undong Studies, Seoul National
University, 1981, p.584.

APPENDIX

Daily   Training Regime at SLTI, Soon-Jong Kwon, Chief
of   Planning   and   Evaluation   Division,   SLTI, 1978,
pp.12-14.
        The trainees chosen among Saemaul leaders arrive
at   the   institute   on Sunday afternoon from all over
the   country   and register upon arrival. After registration, daily necessities such as a uniform and text
materials are supplied. Then the trainees are divided
into   groups   of 18 trainees each per room, and shown
the   dormitory   where   they   will   live   during the
training   period.   The   trainees   settle   into their
accommodation and change into uniforms.
        They   are   then   shown to classrooms to answer a
background   questionnaire   and write a brief essay on
what   they   feel   about   the training. The results of
the   background   questionnaire   are   then   carefully
analysed   and taken into consideration in formulating
the training course.
        Once   these   entry procedures are completed, the
trainees   are   invited   to   the cafeteria for dinner.
Here,   they   learn   table   etiquette,   particularly
related   to   group   eating.   The   meals   are   served
cafeteria style with the trainees waiting in line for
their   food.   After   the   meal they carry their trays
and plates   to   the   designated   place   for   proper
disposition.
        After   dinner, trainees gather in the auditorium
for an orientation session on what they should expect
during   the   training   period. The instructors, all of
whom live with the trainees, are introduced.

Next, a film strip is used to introduce the curriculum and daily schedule. Then the dormitory supervisor explains the training life in detail. Preparing them thus to make mutual concessions for a conductive cooperative living, the trainees are able to step into the 'training through living together'. Finally, the trainees join in singing wholesome and joyful songs under the music instructor's direction.

The day ends with a roll call at 22:00. This roll call checks that everything is in order at the end of the first busy day.

For the remainder of the training programme of one to two weeks, the daily schedule is very tight. The Saemaul songs wake the trainees at 5:50 every morning and shortly thereafter they assemble outside. After a brief morning roll call, they jog around the lake in front of the institute and then undertake physical exercises.

Following their return to the dormitory, they wash and clean up the facilities until breakfast at 7:00. At 8:00 all the trainees gather in the auditorium, where they meditate and sing the Saemaul songs together and then a volunteer among the trainees presents his or her experiences on the Saemaul programmes of their village. Morning classes start at 9:00 and last four hours.

The trainees are allowed one and a half hours for lunch and relaxation. This is followed by afternoon classes ending at 18:00.

After dinner, the trainees meet again to participate in group discussions for three hours until 22:00. This is immediately followed by a brief evening roll call with the trainees retiring at 22:30, unless further discussion is required.

INTRODUCTION

Ariyaratne is one of the world's great contemporary charismatic leaders, and one of the few to make education and human development his life work. Wijetunga, author of this account of Ariyaratne's Sarvodaya Shramadana, enjoys in full measure the authority of other contributors to this volume: he writes from within the movement and with long experience of its work. One strength of his account is its unfolding of the story of the movement from the particular circumstances of its birth and within the particular social and cultural circumstances of Sri Lanka. Sarvodaya Shramadana is committed to education for development in all aspects of living and being: a rare example both of a 'learning organisation' and of a very large-scale bottom-up and non-governmental adult education programme.

Despite its size and influence - active in 3,500 of Sri Lanka's 24,000 villages - the movement has kept itself apart from conventional national politics, as Wijetunga explains, though not without difficulty, for Ariyaratne is both courted and feared by those in power. One source of strength is the congruence between the philosophy and the lifestyle and practices of the army of volunteers who are the backbone of Sarvodaya. The scale of voluntary effort makes accurate calculation of costs impossible, although the amount of direct support, most of it from sources external to Sri Lanka, can be identified. This raises two more general matters about studies such as this. The first is the evident futility of trying to calculate accurately and completely the cost of such adult nonformal education programmes. Many large governmental programmes, as well as non-governmental programmes, rely heavily on contributions in kind and in time. The Brazilian authors raise the problem first in this volume, indicating also how simple conversion, eg. into US dollars, can seriously mislead; and other studies have shown the important but immeasurable part played by unpaid effort and resources, be it in the EOUs of Chile, through Kenya's harambee spirit, or in Korea's Saemaul Undong villages. The case for adult nonformal education as a means of reducing poverty needs foundations other than estimated cost-efficiency.

The second matter concerns comparability between government and non-government programmes, and replicability from country to country. It is a fallacy that only non-governmental organisation can mobilise voluntary efforts, as these and other studies demonstrate. The degree of identification and voluntary effort will however vary as a function of people's perception of the integrity and purposes of the government; and some educational and social change objectives under some political systems cannot effectively be pursued other than through non-governmental channels.[1] One reader has suggested that Sarvodaya Shramadana may not be replicable without external sources of aid (noting that 95 per cent of this movement's cash comes from abroad). The question may not be about the source of the relatively modest amounts of cash which the movement uses but about how to persuade those with funds, national or international, governmental or other, that this is a good way to deploy them.

A more serious questioning of replicability of Sarvodaya relates to its clearly religious character, which is specific to one culture and society. Wijetunga argues persuasively for generalisability to other cultural and religious traditions, providing of course that trouble is taken to anchor and relate it appropriately, as Ariyaratne did for Sri Lanka. It seems plausible that countries experiencing Islamic reawakening, for example, could adopt the spiritual and moral approach to development indicated here; nor would this seem to sit strangely with Catholic socialist Nicaragua. To the reservation that this is not a 'quick-fix' approach to development and abolition of poverty, a genuine solution which does not engender undesirable and unintended consequences of the 'green revolution' variety is surely worth the longer road. Indeed the challenge here is that poverty is a product of attitudes and of wealth (echoing the MOBRAL study), its ultimate resolution only accessible by confronting the human, non-economic, causes in the realm of values. Only thus may the cycle of poverty be broken. One practical test is to ask who benefits from the programme: although Wijetunga does not describe very fully the effects of the programme at village level he is clear that the energies are successfully directed to and do reach the poorest and most needy, a claim which perhaps only Nicaragua among the countries included here could match.

NOTES

1. See in particular the studies of small non-governmental adult education programmes directed towards conscientisation, political mobilisation and/or greater economic self-reliance, commissioned as part of this same inquiry and to be published as a separate volume.

Chapter Eight

SRI LANKA'S SARVODAYA SHRAMADANA MOVEMENT

W.M.K. Wijetunga

THE SRI LANKA CONTEXT

Sri Lanka, 25,000 square miles in area, is a developing, in other words a poor, country, deficient in
mineral resources and with a very low per capita
income. The 1981 census recorded a population of over
14.8 million people. More than 75 per cent live in
24,000 villages, some of them primarily extensive tea
and rubber plantations. In relation to cultivable and
habitable land the population density in most parts
of the country is very high indeed. Those living in
the rural areas have a much lower standard of living
than the urban population, other than the urban poor
who are perhaps even worse off, and suffer geographical isolation, landlessness, sub-standard housing,
unemployment or under-employment, malnutrition,
inadequate health-care, indebtedness and general
poverty.
     The great majority of the people are Sinhalese;
the largest ethnic minority are Tamils. Both adhere
to their own peculiar caste social systems. Over the
years much change has taken place in these, with a
moderating effect on traditional inequities, discrim-
inatory practices and social relationships. However
isolated and socially ostracised groups belonging to
the lowest of the so-called lower castes are still
neglected or ignored, and left to languish in
poverty, illiteracy and destitution.

GENESIS OF THE LANKA SARVODAYA SHRAMADANA MOVEMENT (SSM)[1]

In 1958 a small band of teachers and students, members of the Social Service League of Nalanda College,
Colombo, a leading government Buddhist boys' school,
and a few other volunteers, pioneered a service
project in the village of Kanatholuwa, about 70 miles
from Colombo in the Kurunegala District. A.T.
Ariyaratne,[2] a teacher, led this initial group,

and has remained the leading light and pioneering spirit of the SSM. This initial project took place hardly two years after the many radical changes brought about by the new Mahajana Eksath Peramuna Government (People's United Front) of S.W.R.D. Bandaranaike in 1956. There was promise of change in the air, and expectations ran high.

Nalanda College was not the only NGO active in the field of community development. However, Nalanda volunteers were specially blessed by Bandaranaike for their pioneering spirit and effort. Thus, it was a very opportune.time for such a project, not only as an exercise in voluntary service but also as a learning exchange between urban groups and the rural poor - an opportunity to 'learn from the village and then to utilize the knowledge gained to improve rural life', and to 'give the urban elite an insight into the real living conditions of some of their low-caste fellow country men in the rural areas'.

Kanatholuwa is predominantly a village of depressed Rodiya caste people. Though not 'untouchables' as such, the Rodiyas have been shunned by the rest of the society, including other so-called lower castes, and forced to eke out a living by begging or engaging in menial tasks. There were many felt needs in Kanatholuwa at the time: wells for drinking water, child and maternity care, personal hygiene, basic educational facilities and a place of religious worship. The volunteers had been exposed to prior training in village work, and tackled immediate tasks such as sinking wells, digging latrine pits, cleaning home gardens, inaugurating a formal education programme, organising adult literacy classes, conducting classes in health, child and maternity care, and engaging in cultural and religious activities, including a place for Buddhist worship. The last of these had been anathema to the caste-conscious local Buddhist clergy. What took place was for the most part voluntary social service: a dedicated and enthusiastic urban group coming to a depressed rural community to lend them a hand to improve their living conditions. As with many similar groups of the time, the main motivation was service or shramadana. It was not a participatory exercise in community development. Now was consciousness-raising or 'awakening', as it came to be called later, a main objective. However, it proved a worthwhile experience which motivated the group to engage in many similar efforts in other parts of the country among the most depressed and deprived rural communities during the next few years.

As this 'shramadana' movement grew its leader realised that it was not an end in itself, and looked round for that essential element which would make it endure and sustain itself, once the initial euphoria and enthusiasm in shramadana itself had dissipated. In this quest Ariyaratne was drawn to India, which has profoundly influenced the history and culture of Sri Lanka. He sought inspiration from Mahatma Gandhi and his spiritual successor Vinoba Bhave, both of whom had extolled the virtues of 'Sarvodaya' or 'awakening or welfare of all'. 'Sarvodaya' as originally conceived by Gandhi was a constructive programme of rural and national reconstruction through non-violent self-realisation and selfless action which increasingly stressed its spiritual overtones and began to lose social, economic and political relevance. It became an end in itself. Ariyaratne perceived these limitations, but at the same time appreciated the potential for rural and national rejuvenation. He deliberated on the benefits of fusion of 'Sarvodaya' and 'Shramadana', the former signifying a thought and the latter its implementation. This would mean sharing one's time, possessions, thought and energy for the awakening of all: a process of perpetual interaction, 'Shramadana' leading to 'Sarvodaya', 'Sarvodaya' to 'Shramadana'. Ever-widening horizons of thought, activity and achievement would begin with the awakening of the individual (paurashodaya) and reach the group or village (gramodaya) and thence the community or the nation (deshodaya), leading finally to the awakening of the total community of nations (vishvodaya). Unlike the 'mandala' theory of the ancient Arthasastras, a theory of conquest, conflict, acquisition and universal sovereignty, this would be a concept of integration, self-realisation and harmonious development of a total personality, in terms of both the individual and the whole world community.

Finding 'Sarvodaya' and wedding it to 'Shramadana' was only the beginning of the quest. Having looked outwards, now it was time to turn inwards for indigenous roots and meanings, to relate to local conditions and to identify with the social and cultural milieu of the people. This new quest took Ariyaratne to the Buddhist culture of Sri Lanka: 'while the word 'Sarvodaya' with its literal meaning was adopted from India, the interpretation of its deep meaning as relevant to our own Sinhala Buddhist culture and national population is completely our own. We have our own indigenous character both in thought and action so far as the Ceylon movement is concerned'. However, the 'Sarvodaya philosophy of the Movement is a synthetic ideology and a universal concept. All forms of creative altruism and evolutionary humanism, be it from Marxian aim of material integration, Rousseau's option of social integration or Asoka's endeavour of moral integration, just to give a few examples, are inherent in the Sarvodaya philosophy practised by us, for ours is an attempt to bring about total human integration. The philosophy that influenced us most in evolving our Sarvodaya concept in Sri Lanka is Lord Buddha's teachings.'[3]

GROWTH OF THE MOVEMENT

'In geographical spread, as in programmatic scope and public visibility, Sarvodaya is one of the rare alternative development strategies which has become truly nationwide.'[4] SSM has had phenomenal growth and expansion, not only in numerical terms and in terms of people's participation; it has also matured tremendously in development thought and action, evolving a distinctive and challenging philosophy and thought processes. It has also grown in dynamism, in ability and agility to adjust to new situations without losing identity or compromising its commitment to non-violent social and economic change in the framework of cultural and moral stability and national integration.

There have been four stages of development: (1) formative; (2) consolidation; (3) expansion; and (4) mandated.[5] The initial volunteers formed themselves into a Kanatholuwa Development Education Extension and Community Service Camp, an on-going rural development programme which generated another 36 Shramadana Camps in 26 other villages within the next three years. This success and its immediate impact brought government recognition. The programme was accorded the status of an approved charity in 1965. In the meantime 'Shramadana' became a household word. Other volunteer agencies adopted the term and its strategies for their own community development projects. The government also launched its own National Shramadana Service under the Land Development Department. All this created confusion, competition and even conflict. In 1966 Ariyaratne and his colleagues were compelled to give their movement a separate identity and a distinctive name. Thus was born the lengthy name - Lanka Jathika Sarvodaya Shramadana Sangamaya.

Till 1966 the SSM grew without organisational structure, programmatic approach or specific development goals, a movement without regular and secure funds, depending on meagre voluntary contributions and occasional material and financial help from the government. In 1966 the government withheld its support and the movement was suddenly faced with either drastically curtailing and reshaping its activities or seeking substantial support from external sources. In fact the withdrawal of government support proved propitious: in November 1967, SSM successfully approached foreign individuals and organisations for support, and was able to plan a more coordinated three year development programme intended to reach 100 villages, selected as evenly as possible from the 22 Administrative Districts of the time. Selection was on the basis that the weakest villages deserved the highest priority. The 100 Village Development Scheme required as its main strategy setting up a Gramodaya (Village Reawakening) Programme in each selected village to dissemine the basic development principles of the movement in a more systematic manner than before. By 1968 the Movement had spread to 125 villages, with more than 25,000 volunteers active in the field and ready to respond to its call for any further efforts.

How did the SSM select the 100 villages? To find those qualified the Movement's headquarters gave much publicity to the Scheme, and called for nominations or applications from prospective villages. Those were furnished with special sheets to obtain preliminary data. Villages which provided this information were then visited by teams of volunteers from the SSM, to conduct further surveys and initiate a dialogue with the villagers. On the basis of reports and further data supplied by these teams the Executive Council of the SSM decided on the final selection.

The next step was to launch the development work under the direction of experienced Shramadana organisers. A series of Shramadana Camps met those most urgent felt needs of the villages which could be satisfied with Shramadana and with a minimum outlay of capital expenditure. Teams of urban volunteers worked closely with those drawn from the selected villages. Outside initiative and inputs were invariably matched with local effort, participation and material contributions. The SSM set targets for each year of action. The first year of the Scheme was expected:

(1) to complete projects started with the first Shramadana camp, such as the improvement of water supply for agricultural purposes, communications, agricultural and housing facilities;

(2) to inculcate higher individual and social values, elementary scientific and technical skills and know-how, and the capacity to participate actively and intelligently in group and community programmes;

(3) to identify a group of young and intelligent village leaders and train them in SSM methods of community development to be village level Sarvodaya extension workers;

(4) to combine existing village leadership with new blood to form a common village planning body;

(5) to link the village development scheme with an educational or similar institution in close proximity, to train young people drawn from the latter and to obtain their active and voluntary participation in village projects;

(6) to conduct a thorough house to house survey and data-collection of village households with a view to assessing their economic, social, educational and cultural life, their need for health and medical services and expectations with regard to the latter;

(7) to provide an opportunity to three national-level Sarvodaya workers (preferably university graduates) to gain a thorough understanding of the conditions prevailing in the village and the trends of future changes, as part of a proposed 3,000-strong cadre of rural reconstruction resource personnel drawn from the 100 villages;

(8) to form for each village project a link with one foreign community group or welfare agency for mutual help and understanding;

(9) to form for each village project a link with one private local voluntary body and/or supporting agency with financial resources to assist the Scheme.

With data collected and evaluation of work accomplished during the first year, and a realistic assessment of available local resources, outside support, villagers' motivation and the degree of participation, it was thought possible to plan and implement a three-year programme. However after four years, success was neither uniform nor entirely satisfactory in all 100 villages, mainly due to inadequate financial resources and lack of adequately trained full-time workers. This led to analysis, and the formulation of fresh strategies. Fund-raising was more vigorously pursued; an entirely new Development Education Programme launched to meet training needs; and at village level an equally novel scheme of participation was introduced through Gramodaya Mandalayas (Village Re-awakening Councils), and diverse groups or 'haulas', organised by age or special interests. In 1969 Ariyaratne was selected for the coveted Ramon Magsaysay Award for Community Leadership; this gave a much-needed boost in the international sphere, in the search for influential friends and benefactors. (He was also awarded the King Baudouin International Development Prize in 1982.)

The development of an educational philosophy and appropriate strategies, and the promotion of educational activities, were synonymous with the development of the Movement. SSM has been consistently critical of the nature and objectives of the formal school system: education, prescribed by age, set syllabuses, teachers, timetables, examinations, schools, universities and other formal institutions, seems to spawn more problems rather than helping to solve them. Education to be meaningful should directly relate to life and living experience, and to the environment. It should not only impart knowledge but also develop useful life skills, instil good moral, cultural and psychological attitudes, generate a spirit of service and a feeling for humanity, awaken people to their full potential as individuals and as groups, and thereby help develop a total personality, leading to the development of a total society.

How can this be achieved in practice? First, new strategies should be designed to integrate the different segments of the population. Objectives should be redefined to relate not only to the material well-being of the few but to the material and psychological well-being of all. This should lead to a total living experience, to awareness of the universality of problems faced in modern times, and to ways to solve them. New initiatives involving all groups (haulas), new strategies such as Shramadana, and new institutions like the Development Education Centres in Sarvodaya, should play a vital role in this proposed new scheme of things.

The last decade has seen much growth of SSM: consolidation and expansion of the Development Education Programme with support from the World Assembly of Youth (1970); incorporation of the SSM by Act of Parliament in 1972, followed annually by very substantial financial support from the Netherlands Organisation for International Development

Cooperation (NOVIB): inauguration of the Agricultural
and Development Education Institute at Tanmalwila in
1972; inauguration of the Bhikku[6] Training Centre
in 1974 with assistance from the West German
Friedrich Naumann Stiftung; launching of the three
year 1,000 Village Development Scheme in 1976;
opening of new Headquarters (Damsak Mandira) at
Moratuwa, in close proximity to Colombo, in 1978; and
setting up of the Sarvodaya Research Institute. The
seventies was a period of unprecedented expansion of
the Movement, but also a period of unrest in the
country and of considerable tension and distrust
between SSM and the government, particularly between
1975 and 1977. Since 1977 relations between SSM and
the government have been more harmonious, with close
collaboration in various development activities. This
has caused some apprehension, and is not without its
critics.[7] Ariyaratne has tried to dispel these
fears: 'Sarvodaya theory is deeply wedded to politics
although it has no direct relationship with party and
power politics. Sarvodaya works aloof from all
political ideologies, excluding all those involved in
party politics from being members of the active
formulation of policy and putting it into action; yet
Sarvodaya is deeply committed to politics in the
sense that it hopes to make people conscious of their
rights. This in turn involves the technique of
increasing the participation of the people in the
decision-making processes as well as the implementation of decisions thus arrived. Sarvodaya hopes to
secure the maximum participation of the people in
their own affairs and believes in the inalienable
goodness of human life and the right of man to enjoy
equally and fully all that life could provide. In
this sense one could say that Sarvodaya theory is
highly political; but beyond this Sarvodaya does not
hope either today or tomorrow to get itself involved
in any battle to secure the reins of political power
into its hands.'[8]
     SSM has become massive, active in more than
3,500 villages with nearly 6,000 full-time workers
and hundreds of thousands of unpaid volunteers; it
touches the lives of more than a million people. It
has spread from backward village communities to other
rural areas and to the urban sector, composed mainly
of people of South Indian origin. It maintains links
with numerous international agencies and organisations, and provides frequent familiarisation visits,
seminars and training programmes for overseas participants. In 1981 SSM sponsored the second Sarvodaya
International Conference in the Netherlands,
following which a Sarvodaya Shramadana International

was founded, incorporated in the Netherlands but with
its headquarters in Sri Lanka.

THE DEVELOPMENT PHILOSOPHY OF SSM
Ariyaratne claims that Sarvodaya Shramadana is a
synthetic ideology, with possibilities of universal
application. In the Sri Lankan context it had to draw
its inspiration from the dominant Buddhist culture
and philosophy to be easily understood by the people,
most of whom are Buddhists. If it is to succeed elsewhere it will have to identify itself with the
dominant social and cultural milieu in that country,
which could be Hindu, Christian or Muslim. SSM has
followed very closely the Buddha's analysis of the
problems besetting man and his environment. According
to the Buddha craving or tanha is the root cause of
all human suffering. The solution can only be found
within the individual, since all actions are conditioned by the mind. In making the mind and thought
free of evil, defilement and craving, and raising
them to a state of purity and sublimity, one can
bring about cessation of suffering. The SSM bases its
development philosophy on the individual as its main
element, and expects to change perceptions and
attitudes. Programmes are designed to develop in each
person an insight into the true nature of things and
thereby relieve his or her suffering. 'One cannot go
very far as an agent bringing about effective social
change unless one's ideological conditioning is non-
fragmentary and embraces harmoniously one's own welfare with the welfare of others'.[9] As in Buddhist
meditation one starts with thoughts on one's own
well-being, and goes on to extend the same thoughts
to the welfare and well-being of others, close as
well as remote. There is assumed an inherent need for
two-fold liberation for true awakening: 'first within
one's own mind or thinking process there are certain
defilements one has to recognise and strive to
cleanse. Second, one has to recognise that there are
unjust and immoral social and economic chains which
keep the vast majority of people enslaved. Thus a
dual revolution pertaining to an individual's mental
make-up, and to the social environment in which he
lives is kept foremost in Sarvodaya Shramadana
workers' mind and behaviour.'[10]
      How can one awaken one's personality according
to the Sarvodaya Shramadana philosophy? According
to the Buddha, one should cultivate four sublime
abodes of Satara Brahma Vihara:
          metta - respect for all life, or practising
                  loving kindness to oneself and to all
                  other living beings.

> Karuna - practising compassion, and doing only compassionate deeds.
>
> Muditha - having dispassionate or altruistic joy, and
>
> Upekkha - maintaining equanimity or a balanced state of mind.

These four states of mind should provide an answer to all the problems that arise from social contacts, and the right way to conduct oneself towards one's own self and towards others. 'They are the great removers of tension, the great peace makers in social conflict, the great healers of wounds suffered in the struggle of existence. They are called abodes (viharas), because they should become mind's constant dwelling places where our minds feel at home; they should not remain merely places of rare and short visits, soon forgotten.'[11]

'The Sarvodaya Shramadana Movement adopted these Brahma Viharas to explain why from a spiritual point of view a human being should help another human being or work for one's fellow beings. It leads to one's own personality awakening or self-fulfilment or "Yava Nirvana Pattiya" - the final goal of attaining uncon- ditioned supreme happiness or Nirvana. On the other hand such self-sacrificing and dedicated individuals are indispensable to bring about social development in a village setting or national level. Thus the Movement made a deliberate attempt to harmonize an accepted and existing spiritual concept with a necessary social action process.'[12] A Sarvodaya Shramadana Camp will be automatically transformed into 'a place where both the physical and psychological requirements are fulfilled for every individual to imbibe these qualities in him'.[13] Metta is interpreted as the motivational factor, motivating to work and to share, with loving kindness and friendliness towards all and in a spirit of ahimsa or non-violence. This identification with others leads to compassionate actions or karuna, which helps to remove the causes that make others unhappy and suffer. The immediate result of such selfless action is joy in seeing others happy, the feeling of Muditha; the long-term benefit is Upekkha, the feeling of equanimity or mental equipoise which helps one to face gain and loss, praise and blame, success and failure, all in a spirit of equal under- standing and detachment. While Metta is the motiva- tional factor, the personality-awakening factor is interpreted as Karuna. This through Shramadana would lead to the fulfilment of ten Basic Human Needs, identified as the most vital preconditions at individual, village and regional levels. They are: (1) a clean and beautiful environment; (2) a clean and adequate supply of water; (3) a minimum of clothing requirements; (4) a balanced diet; (5) basic health care; (6) a modest house to live in; (7) energy requirements; (8) basic communication facilities; (9) total education; (10) spiritual and cultural requirements. Shramadana is the means by which one tries to meet these needs in those who lack them, sharing one's time, thoughts, energy, skills and material possessions. Through compassionate actions (karuna) one imbibes the virtues of generosity, of reducing greed or tanha, radiates dispassionate joy or muditha, and cultivates a balanced state of mind or upekka.

Comparing these ten Basic Human Needs with proposals attributed to Rajni Kothari, an Indian development thinker, Kantowsky concedes that the SSM shares with Kothari the need to pool skills and resources at regional level as a development strategy, but departs from his definition of the specific social and economic situation:

> Sarvodaya does not ask what has to be done to overcome the growth crisis and the distributive problems of a national economy. Instead it begins with a Buddhist definition of man and an insight into the causes of his suffering. The illusion of permanence, craving for existence, and violent competition to realize one's identity through material acquisition are the real causes of underdevelopment, as the central Buddhist doctrine of conditioned genesis teaches:

> > When this is present, that comes to be,
> > From the arising of this, that arises.
> > When this is absent, that does not come
> >   to be,
> > On the cessation of this, that ceases.

> The ten basic needs programme of the Sarvodaya Movement in Sri Lanka is not meant to redistribute poverty or guarantee the dissatisfied rural masses who threaten the system's stability and minimum standard of living. This would be the crisis-management approach of international institutions with their elitist urban bias. Their calculations are based on how little is sufficient; Sarvodaya teaches how much is

enough. Buddhist norms tell one what is needed so that all living beings may be well and happy...

Western alternatives are based on what is needed to keep those already living below the poverty line from starving. While Sarvodaya defines a maximum necessary for the well-being of all, development technocrats measure the minimum energy input required to keep individual labour intact and craving for material acquis- itions growing. The juxtaposition shows that Sarvodaya's development concept does indeed offer an alternative. It starts with a new definition of aims, one which is made possible by reference to a value system that differs fundamentally from the world view which governs modern thinking.[14]

The following principles are recommended for the pursuit of individual and group conduct: dana or sharing, priyavachana or pleasant speech, artha- chariya or constructive activity and samanathmatha or equality. Other Buddhist and Gandhian principles that have profoundly influenced SSM are truth, non- violence and self-denial. With the awakening of the individual the next step is to awaken the group, or the village. Here both Sarvodaya concept and Shrama- dana action come into play in raising the conscious- ness of the entire village and making people appreciate their potential and value as human beings, working together in a spirit of sharing, with agree- able speech and in a sense of equality, and engaged in constructive activity. People in the village are made to identify their basic problems, analyse them and seek solutions which they themselves could adopt. Seven important steps are as follows:

(1) Laying the psychological infra-structure – done by the organisation of Shramadana in the village in which people participate by sharing their labour and resources.
(2) Laying the social infra-structure – the creation of interest groups such as children's, mothers', farmers', groups in order to establish a basis for communal, economic and social development activities.
(3) Physical infra-structure – creation of the physical infrastructure such as schools, roads, training centres, farms.
(4) Training – attempts are made to motivate the people to identify the kind of training, formal or informal, that they

desire and provide a back-stop for such training in necessary technical or functional work either in the village or outside.

(5) Credit and economic development — where the village needs some form of capital help geared to economic development, Sarvodaya takes cognisance of this and provides capital and know-how towards economic development, always emphasising the need of the people to help themselves while securing maximum participation of the people in their own affairs.

(6) Integrated spiritual and cultural develop- ment — economic development alone does not result in the awakening of all. Emphasis on utilising traditional cultural and social stabilising factors and those that promote socio-cultural development encourages this awakening.

(7) Basic human needs and their satisfaction — every attempt is made to satisfy the ten basic needs while emphasising that the creation of extra needs before satisfying these needs in all results in the denial of the principle of sharing. Sarvodaya theory recognises that man's inordinate multipli- cation of needs ultimately ends in disaster; in such a process, while a few privileged go on attempting to satisfy their ever increasing needs, the majority are denied even the minimum satisfaction of their basic needs.[15]

'The uniqueness of Sarvodaya comes through most clearly here in its depth of philosophical belief and cultural integration. Most development programmes have almost totally secular values; Sarvodaya has a spiritual dimension that gives it both a history and a moral quality that sets it apart.'[16] Six integrated processes should be simultaneously awakened: the spiritual, moral, cultural, social, political and economic. This integrated approach is considered essential: the goal is not economic and material alone, but total human development. This goes beyond conventional growth models and measure- ments of growth rates, including the more recent Physical Quality of Life Index.

Spiritual development takes pride of place, in the form of developing a harmonious relationship with one's fellow beings and with other living beings, with plant life and even inanimate objects, with the total environment. One is expected to understand intellectually and experience spiritually the inter-relationship that exists between different manifest-ations of life, the biological world, and natural phenomena. Spiritual development should necessarily lead to a life of simplicity and of satisfying basic needs and minimum wants. Happiness and contentment should not be judged only in terms of material advancement and acquisitions. Moral awakening, the second component, derives from spiritual. It could take many forms such as instilling 'self-discipline, humane modes of conduct, harmonious personal relationships, practising pleasant and kind speech, abstinence from over-indulgence in sensual pleasures, cultivating simplicity, truthfulness and honesty, upholding trust and abstinence from speaking ill of others or addiction to intoxicants and drugs...'⌊17⌋ Every aspect of life and living that helps to sustain spiritual and moral awakening processes is considered as the cultural component, embracing both the material and non-material things of life which are conducive to spiritual and moral life. It also concerns life-styles, tastes and values, customs, beliefs and traditions, and what induces pleasure and joy to our senses.

Social awakening, the fourth component, is measured by progress in the following:

(1) Social consciousness on the part of the members of a family, village or urban group and the national community.
(2) The level of community participation in decision-making.
(3) The level of community organisation.
(4) The level of community education.
(5) The degree of realisation of social equality.
(6) The degree of community health conscious-ness.
(7) The degree of national integration.
(8) The level of functional enjoyment of funda-mental human rights.⌊18⌋

It is accompanied by analysis of the existing social order and delineation of the desired Sarvodaya social order:

Present Social Order	Desired Social Order
1. Lacks self-knowledge and self-reliance.	1. Strives for self-real-isation and self-reliance.

2. Blindly follows materialistic values.

2. Motivated by indigenous cultural and spiritual values. Learn to accept values etc. on the basis of experience.

3. Worships wealth, power and position and uses untruth, violence and selfishness.

3. Respects virtue, wisdom and skills and uses truth, non-violence and self-denial.

4. Organisations based on possessions and competition become strong. Capitalistic economy, bureaucratic control, power and party politics become major social forces.

4. Organisations based on sharing and cooperation become powerful. People's politics based on economic trusteeship, people's participation and party-less democracy become major social forces.

5. Evil in man is harnessed; society gets fragmented into caste, racial, religious and party political differences.

5. Good in man is harnessed; society tends to get integrated as one human family; forces that divide give way to forces that unify.

6. Economic resources are improperly utilised. Economy becomes weak. Unemployment increases.

6. Economic resources are properly combined. Production increases. Employment increases.

7. Depends on an import/export economy based on colonial inherited patterns or production of cash crops. Foreign debts increase.

7. A self-sufficient economy based on people's basic needs. An economy free from foreign debts. National self-respect and economic freedom.

8. Subjugated to large scale organisations. Human labour wasted. Corruption increases. Environment is polluted.

8. Small scale organisations. Labour intensive. Less corruption. Protection from psychological and environmental pollution.

9. Villages subserve the cities. Rural exodus, moral degeneration, social unrest.

9. Balanced village and urban awakening. Moral reconstruction.

10. Power of the laws of punishment and the state increase. Laws of righteousness and people's power weakens.

10. Laws of righteousness and the power of the people become strong. No ruling class. People's power becomes supreme. Sarvodaya is realised.[19]

Constructive non-violent action is expected to liberate from the vicious circles in which man and society are ensnared. Hence the distinctive form of people's participation through groups or haulas, and through them the Gramodaya or Village Reawakening Councils. Education and skill development, the promotion of equality, including equality before law, of physical, mental and community health, and finally of national integration, are the other essential elements in the successful social awakening processes.

The fifth component, political awakening, concerns people's politics, as opposed to partisan politics which are divisive and lead to hatred, strife, competition and violence. Political awakening should mean working with governments to attain the Sarvodaya objectives, and where possible to awaken in politicians a consciousness of greater ideals as opposed to preoccupation with self-interest and partisan politics.

The final component is economic awakening. Economic thought should not be limited to combining as efficiently as possible the classical factors of production and distribution of goods and services, land, labour, capital and entrepreneurship. SSM views economic activities in the context of harmonious interaction of the processes of nature, the human personality, the total society and knowledge. Ariyaratne furnishes the following summary:

(1) We lay a psychological infrastructure; eg, through an activity like Shramadana Camps.
(2) We lay a physical infrastructure by continuing such activities in communities.
(3) We help communities to direct their energies on a course of basic human needs satisfaction programme.
(4) We help to create a climate and institutional arrangement where a functional indigenous leadership both individual and group emerges.
(5) We create situations where appropriate technologies and training are continuously given to the above leadership.
(6) We strive to create wealth and help it multiply without intervention by the middle men or the exploiters, by an indigenous system of savings, credit and investment.
(7) Progressively we try to create non-dependency in the village economy by adopting methods like the establishment of community shops and group economic enterprises.

In other words a form of people's participatory economic regeneration process has been released in many rural areas... This type of non-dependent economic regeneration can bloom into national dimensions depending on the extent to which the economic and political policies of the country as a whole take a similar trend. Still we are not passively watching until such changes in policies take place. Within our own capacity in our villages we are putting into practice the above-mentioned principles we believe in within limits of law and resources at our command.[20]

ORGANISING SARVODAYA SHRAMADANA: TOWARDS A WORKING MANUAL

Village awakening begins with a village expressing the desire to join the Sarvodaya Village Development Scheme with a request to the SSM headquarters in Moratuwa, to a District Development Education Centre, or to a Gramodaya Centre, by one of the village elders, a religious dignitary, a youth or women's organisation, or any other such individual or group. This request is referred by the Gramodaya Division of the SSM at its headquarters in Moratuwa to the appropriate authority, either at headquarters or at a District Centre. A properly completed data sheet is expected to furnish such information as the location of the village (Grama Sevaka Division, AGA Division, Electorate, Administrative District, closest town, village boundaries, etc.); communication facilities; existing active volunteer organisations; main crops, industries or crafts; employment position and prospects; number of families and population figures; main economic, social and other problems; ways in which the community can participate in development work; names of local personnel who can be expected to join any proposed development work; and a suitable venue and date for a preliminary meeting in the village.

On receipt of the completed preliminary datasheet a team of trained Sarvodaya volunteers from either headquarters or a District Centre will visit the village, establish contact with responsive groups or individuals, engage in a dialogue on Sarvodaya philosophy and activities, and become familiar with the problems of the village. This is a further fact-finding mission in which the idea of a Shramadana camp will also be raised. The appropriate type of activity and degree of shared responsibilities will be discussed, then the implementation of the activity. SS Workers and the local volunteers who will later be forming themselves into planning, programming and implementation committees have to consider: strength of felt needs of the community; feasibility of completing the project within a specific period; availability of voluntary labour including basic skills; need to minimise capital expenditure; availability of any services and support from government agencies and of food, refreshments, medical facilities, etc. Initial projects may take the form of restoring or desilting a village tank or reservoir, clearing irrigation canals, opening up new canals, constructing motorable roads to provide access to the village, etc.

The SSM team reports on the suitability of any follow-up work such as organising Shramadana camps, to awaken the villagers as well as to test their response and degree of active participation.

Organisational structures are created to obtain the necessary facilities for organising one or more camps: physical facilities to supply the daily needs for food, water, sanitation, etc. of volunteers staying together in the village, and to store and distribute tools, general supplies, etc.; and contacts with nearby village communities and government agencies to draw on their resources. This work is handled with great care by specially trained SS camp organisers.

As the work camp takes shape and goes into action a host of other activities will also be organised, such as village gatherings during rest periods and evenings, with the focus on learning exercises and cultural exchanges. Meditation, talks on relevant topics, religious discourses, songs, dances and other entertainment, will be provided. These are called 'family gatherings', being representative of all ages and interest groups in the village. They provide a forum for discussions on the history of the village, its social and cultural setting, its needs and resources and future prospects and expectations. Village problems receive much attention. SS work is also explained and discussed. An atmosphere is thereby created for the active participation of the villagers, for natural leadership to emerge and for generating a spirit of community, sharing and commitment:

> The camp is normally inaugurated in the evening around 6 pm. A fair number of village men, women and children along with youth gather at the camp site at this time. A youth leader who is assigned to conduct proceedings invites a village elder or a village child to inaugurate the camp by lighting the traditional coconut-

oil lamp and hoisting the national and Sarvodaya flags. This is done to the chanting of 'Pirith' or religious stanzas by monks if they are present or to the singing of a Sarvodaya song.

This ceremonial opening is followed by what we call a 'family gathering'. The idea being that all the people gathered consider themselves to be the members of one family and in that spirit discuss their problems and the ways and means of solving them. A Sarvodayan elder or youth leader initiates a dialogue with the people who participate as equals. The volunteers have come to learn and not to teach; they have come to share and not for charity. All are seated on mats spread on the floor. The village elders, men, women, youth and children seated in a circle shoulder to shoulder with volunteers from outside soon feel one with them and fearlessly express their views.

A mass education programme is thus set in motion where the history of the village, their habitual customs and beliefs, their problems and aspirations are readily discussed. Relevant quotations from great religious teachers and other great men are read and explained. Song and dance items are intermixed with serious discussions regarding community, national and international problems. Family get-togethers of this nature with a total duration of about four hours a day are held daily in Shramadana camps. Hence one sees the rare sight of a university professor or a college principal seated on a mat with illiterate villagers, youth and children exchanging experiences and learning from each other.[21]

Meanwhile special teams will be active to see that everything goes smoothly, such as a medical or first-aid service. Teams will organise the supply and distribution of food and refreshments, the necessary implements and their immediate repair and maintenance, transport facilities, and will monitor and evaluate the work in progress.

The camp is concluded with a final 'family gathering', where an evaluation of the project is presented and discussed. Both achievements and short-comings are highlighted. Follow-up will be considered and, if agreed upon, a programme will be elaborated and decided on. This will be a long-term programme, interspersed with short-term projects and leading to closer collaboration and identification with the SSM.

Sri Lanka's Sarvodaya Shramadana Movement

COST AND COST-EFFECTIVENESS

The total annual budget of the SSM for 1980/81 was Rs.37,524,150/-, of which Rs.35,557,135/- came from external sources, predominantly overseas donors. Local income from diverse sources was only Rs.1,967,015/- or five per cent of the total budget. Only a very small fraction was spent directly on Shramadana work (Rs.360,527/-). The accent is on pooling and sharing resources, and on keeping capital expenditure as low as possible. Direct expenditure consists only of such items as building materials, transport and fuel, payments for highly skilled labour (where it is not available for sharing) and similar items. Even the first two items may be met by donations, depending on the initiative of the organisers and the economic circumstances of the villages and out-lying towns. Food and refreshments are invariably donated by benefactors. Since labour is always free (except skilled labour) there is no need for large amounts of money. Even with educational activities such as pre-schools, adult literacy classes, training in skills and income-generating activities, direct expenditure is kept to a minimum, and is largely dependent on the principle of sharing.

During 1980/81 2,192 work camps were held with up to 50 participants, lasting from one to more than three days. Volunteer groups of between 51 and 100 engaged in 771 camps of the same duration. Groups of over 100 took part in 474 camps of similar duration. Thus during the year 3,437 work camps were reported from various parts of the country. More camps may have gone unreported from the more remote centres. At the same time Sarvodaya workers may have joined other volunteer or village organisations and even government agencies in such developmental work, without claiming separate credit for their efforts.

The Annual Report for 1980/81 gives the following break-down in relation to the ten Basic Needs: Environment - 414; Water - 282; Clothing - 0; Food - 302; Housing - 553; Health - 155; Communications - 741; Energy - 16; Education - 409; Spiritual and Cultural - 565; Total - 3,437. In terms of man days, these activities have been calculated to be around 286,143 and the value in monetary terms to be as much as Rs.3,331,243/-. The same work would have cost many times more through normal governmental machinery, or even through the commercial sector. Other factors to be reckoned with are the quality of work and the long delay in execution by the latter agencies, whereas the satisfaction in sharing and in tangible achievements accrue to the SSM and the villagers. Work of this nature can never be measured and valued in monetary terms alone.

EVALUATION AND APPRAISAL

The SSM is perhaps unique: it is not a simple social service organisation or an organisation engaged in 'developmental' activity in any narrow sense, but a movement with distinctive development goals, philosophy and strategy. It emphasises the totality of human development, individual and group. Education, or Development Education as it is called, and Shramadana play important roles at every level and stage, and can foster balanced, closely integrated development in the political, social, economic, moral and cultural fields. Development Education and Shramadana also lend themselves to: skills development and training, promotion of income-generating activities, and running of community shops which serve producer and consumer with equal fairness; developing appropriate technologies to suit the needs and the resources of the rural areas; improving the health and nutrition of village folk and slum-dwellers; and helping to conserve and better utilise the human and other resources of rural areas. Development Education as part and parcel of Shramadana activity makes no exception as regards age, class, caste or other barriers, but tries to reach all, from the pre-school child to the most elderly: it is both life-long and total education. Between them, this education, Shramadana and the community organise to attain development goals.

SSM lays most stress on the proper infrastructure for development, not only in the narrow physical and material sense. Only through full development can people's level of consciousness be raised. Thereby they can come to lean less on governmental and other agencies, to develop self-awareness and self-reliance, and to claim their due share in decision-making, in participatory planning and implementation, in solving problems with their own resources and ingenuity. Through such transformation and organisation the process of eradicating poverty of thought, of action and of material conditions can be started and reinforced.

WIDER APPLICABILITY

The Sarvodaya Shramadana concept and plan of action can have universal application, being adaptable to the varying needs of both developing countries and affluent West. 'Sarvodaya' and 'Shramadana' should go hand in hand. 'Sarvodaya' will blend itself into different social and cultural settings, and can be interpreted in terms of their common and distinctive ideals, traditions and thought processes, while also reaching to higher ideals. 'Sarvodaya Shramadana' is not cost-intensive or capital-intensive. With the most meagre material resources but with adequate motivation and inspiration people can be mobilised to practise Sarvodaya Shramadana: 'we build the road, and the road builds us'.

NOTES

1. Many published works were consulted in preparing this case study, supplementing the author's personal experience, but special mention should be made of Ariyaratne (Vol.1, n.d.), Ariyaratne (1981), Compton (1981), Kantowsky (1980).

2. A.T. Ariyaratne has been the recipient of the coveted Ramon Magsaysay Award for Community Leadership in 1969, and an Hon. D.Litt. from the Srijayawardenepura University, Sri Lanka, in 1981.

3. Kantowsky, 1980, p.43.

4. Goulet, 1981, p.1.

5. Compton, 1981, p.6.

6. 'Bhikku' refers to a member of the Buddhist clergy or Sangha.

7. See Denis Goulet, Survival with Integrity: Sarvodaya at the Crossroads, Colombo 1981; D. Kantowsky, Sarvodaya, The Other Development, New Delhi, 1980.

8. Ariyaratne, 1981, p.31.

9. Kantowsky, 1980, p.46.

10. Kantowsky, 1980, p.46.

11. Nyanaponika Thera quoted in Kantowsky, 1980, p.47.

12. Ariyaratne, 1981, p.12.

13. Kantowsky, 1980, p.47.

14. Kantowsky, 1980, pp.179-180.

15. Ariyaratne, 1981, pp.29-30.

16. Compton, 1981, p.8.

17. Ariyaratne, 1981, p.33.

18. Ariyaratne, 1981, p.34.

19. Ariyaratne, 1981, pp.35-36.

20. Ariyaratne, 1981, pp.47-48.

21. Ariyaratne, n.d., pp.64-65.

REFERENCES

Ariyaratne, A.T., Collected Works, Vol.I, ed. N. Ratnapala, n.d.

Ariyaratne, A.T., In Search of Development, Moratuwa, 1981.

Compton, Lin, 'Sri Lanka's Sarvodaya Shramadana Movement: Promoting People's Participation in Rural Community Development', (Mimeographed), 1981.

Sri Lanka's Sarvodaya Shramadana Movement

Ethos and Work Plan, Sarvodaya, n.d.
Goulet, D., Survival with Integrity: Sarvodaya at
    Crossroads, Colombo, 1981.
Kantowsky, D., Sarvodaya, The Other Development, New
    Delhi, 1980.
Ratnapala, N., Study Service in Sarvodaya, 1958-1976,
    Sarvodaya, n.d.
Ten Basic Needs and their Satisfaction, Moratuwa,
    1978.

'GRAMODAYA' - VILLAGE RE-AWAKENING: CIRCLES OF
DEPENDENT ORIGINATION OF A DECADENT AND A
SARVODAYA VILLAGE

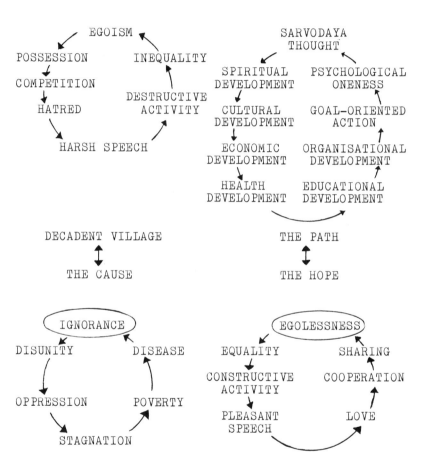

Source: Kantowsky, 1980

Appendix   <u>Figure 8.2</u>

MODEL OF SARVODAYA VILLAGE DEVELOPMENT
THROUGH DEVELOPMENT EDUCATION

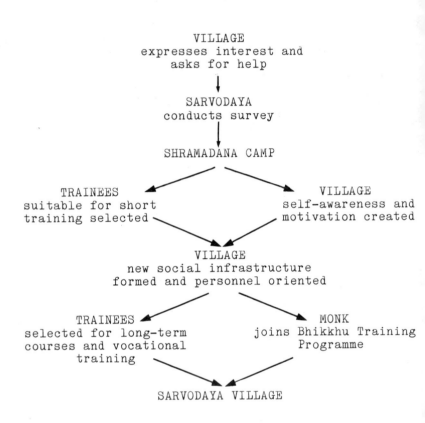

crafts and industries   new social infrastruc-
rebuilt to assure inde-   ture firmly established
pendence from outside
skills

Source: Kantowsky, 1980

Chapter Nine

HOW CAN LARGE-SCALE ADULT EDUCATION COMBAT POVERTY?

Chris Duke

There are many analyses of the causes and nature of
poverty, the causes, nature and directions of social
change, and the meaning of development. Some imply
a role for adult education. The further reading at
the end of this volume introduces some of this work.
This book sets out to suggest ways in which large-
scale adult education programmes may more or less
successfully address the scourge of poverty in
different societies. Conclusions are not clear-cut
(which at any rate suggests that the studies retain
contact with the world as it is); they give no
grounds for unbridled optimism. But they do demonstrate the utility of such comparative studies: a
number of lessons emerge, not as incontrovertible
proof about return on investment in adult education
compared with bridges, dams or agricultural R & D,
but in terms of indicating under what circumstances,
at what times and by what means, adult education may
more or less successfully contribute to the reduction
of poverty. There are lessons from failure no less
than from success; indeed it is not always clear
whether a particular programme deserves either such
description. Indirectly the studies challenge assumptions and, if it still exists, complacency among
western liberal progressive adult educators. These
mostly governmental programmes would also benefit
from comparison with the local, small-scale efforts
which are more typical than is Sarvodaya of non-
governmental agencies. Such comparison would bring
out the strengths of national and governmental programmes as well as underscoring those things which
national adult education programmes and mass literacy
campaigns are unlikely to be able to achieve.
    The potential of many Third World governments to
effect change through adult education appears considerable, given the national planning modes which
prevail. The ideology of the government, and its

willingness to address the causes of inequality, is
clearly one decisive factor in the utility of adult
education as a tool to effect changes touching the
poorest groups and classes. The countries included in
this set of studies range from the authoritarian
right to Marxist socialist, and the role assigned or
permitted adult education varies as widely: from
Chile where even the most cautious form of organisation and education of the rural poor proved practically speaking impossible, through India where fine
intentions became emasculated through the timidity of
adult education workers at levels away from the
centre, to Nicaragua where the elation of liberation
inspired one of the most successful literacy campaigns the world has known, in a context of avowed
social reconstruction towards participative social-
ism. The lessons of India may be more pertinent for
most countries than those of Nicaragua; such revolutionary moments are rare and tend to be short-lived.
Seldom are political and popular will so closely
aligned and purposeful, with adult education treated
as a means of cultural and social transformation.
Adult educators may generally feel more familiar with
the situation of their colleagues as here described
in Kenya, Brazil and the Republic of Korea: working
with government may mean feeling that one is able to
make a large-scale contribution, but of a modest
kind, and with the frustrations and shortcomings
which appear to beset large bureaucracies the world
over. Adult educators working for social change in
government systems even in planned economies of
socialist persuasion may find they must tread a
narrow path, bite their tongues and bide their time.
National government programmes generally may be
expected to make wide impact but be modest in their
objectives; India is more typical than Nicaragua. The
trade-off is the possibility of effecting modest
change quite rapidly throughout the nation; resources, though often lean, tend to be less thinly spread
than for those working in the private or non-governmental sector, often with more radical objectives and
less inhibition. Whether a national governmental programme is able to meet its objectives, even if there
is willingness and commitment, may depend in part
upon resources but more upon clarity of purpose and
capability in management. This concluding review of
the main themes and issues in the several country
studies helps to clarify where such expectations were
borne out and where, perhaps, common sense and stere-
otypical assumptions are disturbed. The following
sections follow the general structure and order of
the country studies.

How Can Large-Scale Adult Education Combat Poverty?

NATIONAL CONTEXT

The historical setting, political and economic circumstances influence the nature and outcomes of each of the programmes described in this book. Most dramatically, the Nicaraguan crusade can be fully understood only against the background of events in previous decades as well as months. The history of literacy and adult education programmes helps to explain the over-optimistic ambitions and initial targets of the Kenyan and Indian adult education programmes. Wijetunga emphasises the radical political change and sense of excitement which contributed to the birth and character-formation of Sarvodaya Shramadana. If the circumstances surrounding the origins of the educational operative units in Chile are but lightly sketched, the dramatic consequences of the fall of Allende for their work and ultimately survival are unavoidable. The particular character and strength of Saemaul education would be inexplicable without some knowledge of Saemaul Undong; that Movement in turn cannot be explained apart from the circumstances of the Republic of Korea, blessed by an urban industrial 'miracle' which possibly surpassed Japan's, and haunted by division of the country and fear of the socialist North. The Brazilian and Kenyan authors show how economic progress and the high rate of growth in the late sixties and into the seventies were instrumental in the decision to attack illiteracy in each instance.

Both political and economic circumstances are evidently important. The authoritarian and anti-participative regime in Chile severely constrained and eventually terminated the work of the units, even though they limited their own operations and shifted from a preferred rural to an urban setting. On the other hand very substantial educational efforts proved possible in Brazil and South Korea despite their anti-socialist governments, although the authors of these studies make clear the limitations which government ideologies placed upon the work, and criticise the programmes and outcomes from an adult education as well as an egalitarian perspective. Sarvodaya as a non-governmental and, in the conventional sense, apolitical programme stood apart from government, though even here there have been problems of political suspiciousness in the mid-seventies and again more recently. In India a programme couched in social transformation terms reminiscent of Nicaragua was effectively castrated, at least in the state of Tamil Nadu, by timidity at more local levels of government.

The economic context includes the broad circumstances and fortunes of the country, especially where illiteracy is seen as a barrier to modernisation and economic development, to be removed via 'human resource development', and also the specific national and more local economic circumstances which may hamper or prevent even the most successful educational programme from leading to economic improvement. In Brazil and Chile the economy simply could not provide additional jobs for the neo-literates. In South Korea those with some resources behind them were able to participate in the boom in rural development and prosperity which the integrated rural development movement, Saemaul Undong, accelerated. In India, Ramakrishnan concludes, poverty was so extreme that programmes of adult education simply could not alter the situation; basic relief appeared a prerequisite.

Thus the national context - political, economic, historical and cultural - proves generally decisive for the possibility and fortunes of one or another kind of programme. On the other hand, however, several of these studies suggest also, for better or for worse, the importance of international economic and political circumstances. The three Latin American studies each suggest something of the power of international economic forces over the fortunes of national adult education and literacy programmes. In the case of Nicaragua there is a more overt political and military aspect as well, as with Saemaul Undong and Education in Korea. The international appeal of Sarvodaya, and the capacity to raise funds from sympathetic overseas sources, may have been essential to its survival; it was also of considerable importance for the Nicaraguan crusade; and while one must look beyond the boundaries of the nation state at the role of international finance, international aid and regional politics for some relevant factors, so too it is necessary to take account of more local diversity. The Brazilian and Indian studies remind us of regional, economic and cultural diversity. Even in smaller countries like Nicaragua and Sri Lanka there is huge diversity in economic circumstances and degree of poverty, and in cultural and ethnic circumstance, which dictates what kind of adult education may be possible and fruitful.

One other international influence bears comment: that upon national programmes exercised by educational theorists and planners especially in the intergovernmental agencies. Three of the studies in this volume - Brazil, Kenya and Chile - make explicit mention of the concepts of lifelong learning and lifelong education promoted especially by Unesco, in describing the strategies and intentions behind their respective programmes, while Ramakrishnan signals this as a desirable end state rather than a viable purpose in his Indian analysis.

THE ADULT EDUCATION AGENCY AND THE PROGRAMME

Five of the programmes described here are governmental, and national in scale. The Chilean, also national in scope, was non-governmental but enjoyed the direct support of the Allende government and the reluctant temporary tolerance of its successor. Sarvodaya Shramadana has always been non-governmental; after recovering from a crisis and withdrawal of government funds, it came to rely almost entirely on external aid funds for that part of its operation which required direct cash support. Some of these programmes were clearly conceived as part of an economic or socio-economic development package: the Korean as part of the Saemaul rural development and modernisation Movement; the Chilean educational operative units intendedly part of a larger socio-economic plan for regional development; the Indian, where the intention was to integrate educational efforts with those of other development-oriented ministries to promote economic development and social transformation. One lesson of the Brazilian study is the necessity for an integrated approach directly linking adult education programmes with economic strategies and with the resources and efforts of other ministries.

Most of the programmes described in this volume are quite massive in scale, even though paucity of resources is common. Saemaul education enjoys strong government support and mobilises the resources of several major ministries in different ways. There is an unusual level of integration of effort to carry through the effects of Saemaul education with concrete and reinforcing rods, roads, factories and agricultural R and D throughout the Korean countryside. MOBRAL is a huge operation with very large resources, although even so inadequacy of resources limited what could be done by way of monitoring and support. India mobilised both central and state-level, governmental and non-governmental resources, although one failing in Tamil Nadu as Ramakrishnan describes it was caution about and low level of involvement of the non-governmental sector which is so strong in that country.

Because of their scale, most of these programmes had problems about mobilisation and management of resources. Probably for each there was some kind of ideal model whereby planning was a central function while implementation belonged and varied locally. Different central agencies are described in these chapters, associated with one major ministry and seeking to coordinate both cross-sectorally at a national level and vertically from national through regional to local levels, ideally replicating the cross-sectoral (inter-disciplinary or inter-departmental) coordination at each level down to the sub-county and the village. The different forms adopted naturally reflect different traditions and historical circumstances, from India's bureaucratic tradition developed from imperial times to Nicaragua's rapidly assembled machinery for a rapid national crusade. The different mechanisms described in these chapters reward comparative scrutiny, as do the problems of bureaucracy and centralisation which each generated. The Brazilian authors reach conclusions similar to those from the other very large country, India, and not out of accord with Cheong's personal judgement about the authoritarian and centralist aspects of Saemaul education. In Kenya, curiously, the problem as presented was of local enthusiasts imbued with the harambee spirit galloping away before the new government agency could organise and order the field. Most instructive is the different style and approach to creating a central agency and structure adopted by the large non-governmental Sri Lankan organisation. Here, relating to and growing from local needs appears to have been closely adhered to in designing and developing both agency and programme. Sarvodaya emerges from these accounts as the most successful 'learning organisation', a characteristic shared with several of the smaller non-governmental agencies to be described in a subsequent volume of case studies.

AIMS AND OBJECTIVES

The purposes with which the architects of these programmes approached their work varied considerably, and in some cases there was change of purpose or emphasis along the way. The Brazilian account for example suggests a shift from a very individualised intention to seeing education as one element in a constellation of factors, although the priority target group did not change. Sarvodaya developed its arrangements and programmes, and refined its objectives, out of the experience of the work in the villages, and through reflection upon this. Some programmes had clear and explicit objectives, with a high degree of congruence between these and what

transpired, as in Nicaragua. In Chile the EOUs' purposes were somewhat inexplicit and the main target
group was, perforce, changed. A third general observation about aims and objectives is that the correspondence between these and what transpired varies
greatly: from the close congruence in Nicaragua to
the wide gulf which Ramakrishnan described between
the fine concept of the Indian NAEP and the cautious
objectives actually adopted during implementation
within Tamil Nadu.

In practice most of the programmes here described had as adult education objectives 'literacy
plus'. The 'plus' in the first two instances was the
acquisition of attitudes, skills and habits congenial
to modernisation: basic literacy skills perhaps
leading into formal school equivalency qualifications
and equipping learners as good citizens and producers. In Kenya this included information about
government development plans, and basic functional
knowledge in health, agriculture, etc. In Brazil the
evaluation suggests that more attention to coordination with other departments and development efforts
might have been more fruitful, also that the individualistic orientation did not accord well with
collective development objectives. One of the three
objectives set for the Indian programme also concerned applications of what was learned to daily
family and productive life. In Korea the main thrust
of Saemaul Undong was towards rural (economic)
development. Gajardo notes a shift in demand on the
Chilean units from literacy and adult basic education
to training for technical skills. In Sri Lanka the
programme certainly included economic objectives, but
Wijetunga's list of forms of 'awakening' places
economic at the end, indicating quite a different set
of objectives, and a different strategy for the
attainment of a better society.

Of particular relevance for this study is
whether amelioration of the lot of the poorest
features among objectives for adult education
programmes: specifically, is the reduction of poverty
an explicit objective? Again the answer varies from
case to case, as does the relationship between intent
and apparent result. The Kenyan and Indian programmes
were explicitly intended for the most needy; in Sri
Lanka the movement set out to identify and work with
the poorest villages and the most stigmatised castes
or groups. In a more general sense the programmes of
MOBRAL and the Chilean units were intended to assist
those in greatest need, and one might reasonably
assume such a priority in the whole ideology of the
Frente in Nicaragua, which attempted a 'frontal

attack on inherited inequalities'. In South Korea it is less clear that the Saemaul leaders were concerned with inequality between individuals within and between villages: here the strategy related to rural poverty more broadly, by comparison with urban development; the outcomes as Cheong describes them both in the model village of Chilwon-Ri and generally suggest a more classic modernisation approach, with reliance on 'trickle-down' to benefit the poorest eventually, if indeed their particular needs entered the calculation at all.

Another way of looking at aims and objectives is to ask whether, overtly or implicitly, the programme was geared to the needs of particular groups and categories of individuals, or, rather, to advancement or transformation of the whole society. The question may be distasteful to those for whom only individuals can be the proper subject of education. For some even extrinsic objectives of education for the individual, much less for the collectivity, may be unacceptable. All of these programmes had some kind of social or economic purpose, some 'ulterior' purpose going beyond individual learning. Some shifted deliberately from a societal to an individual emphasis or vice versa; others remained more firmly anchored on one side or the other. The Sarvodaya philosophy most comprehensively embraces a rationale, set of purposes and strategy encompassing individual awakening and transformation and extending through the group and village to the nation and ultimately to the whole of humankind. In Chile a broad social purpose was contracted back to the more modest objective of sustaining some continuing skeleton of organisation from which socio-political action might again grow in the future. Meanwhile more individual objectives prevailed overtly: acquisition of practical skills which might relieve the family budget and reduce individual poverty. In India, for political reasons of a somewhat different kind, ambitious founding objectives were reduced towards individual acquis- ition of literacy and some safe practical knowledge. In Kenya and South Korea broad social purposes were attempted through individually-oriented programmes; in each case the success of some individuals with aspirations raised problems for the programme organisers or tended to widen the gap between those benefiting and those in greatest need. Brazil's programme was also essentially individualistic, but awareness of the need for collective transformation is evident. Thus the lesson drawn by the authors in Brazil resembles that from India. Nicaragua offers the clearest case of strong ideological purpose, in

both design and action, for societal transformation
requiring individual mobilisation and transformation
- new citizens for the new society. Organisation and
mobilisation are central and unproblematic for revolutionary Nicaragua whereas they appear unattainable
in India, and essential prerequisites for real
development in the eyes of several other authors in
this volume.

The set of studies suggests a crude spectrum of
aims and objectives, from the cautiously reformist
within conservative assumptions to the overtly
revolutionary or transformational. Basic literacy or
literacy plus 'safe' functional skills - health and
hygiene, innovations in farming, the duties of the
citizen - cluster at one end of the spectrum; at the
other end is structural transformation to create a
new, more egalitarian, society. The reader may plot
each of the programmes described here along such a
continuum, noting tendencies to move in one direction
or the other as different forces exert pressure.

COST EFFECTIVENESS AND EVALUATION

Authors of case studies were asked to address a
'common weakness of descriptions of adult education'
- 'absence of information about costs'. The
importance of this in promoting the cause of adult
education was stressed, together with the need to
consider carefully measures and conversions between
currencies and countries. Information was sought
about costs compared with those of formal education
and of other kinds of programmes, as well as about
hidden or in-kind contributions to the costs of
programmes. Most authors addressed these questions
seriously, and some sophisticated and persuasive
calculations were made, as reflected (despite con-
traction through editing) in some of the studies in
this volume. The Brazilian and Indian authors for
example made well-informed estimates of effective per
capita costs for different kinds of programmes. So
far as visible costs and payments are concerned,
Miller and Wijetunga give clear figures which can be
converted to per capita costs by simple arithmetic
where number of participants, or successfully completing participants, is known - the latter more
firmly for Nicaragua than Sri Lanka. Cheong gives per
capita training costs for Saemaul education, but the
real cost of Saemaul Undong would be substantial and
hard to calculate, given its dispersal between ministries; it does not however make complete sense to
treat Saemaul education costs in a vacuum. Gajardo
was denied access to the necessary figures even to

estimate per capita costs in Chile, but concluded
that national and American regional funds intended
for the units were not getting through to the field
where the work took place. Somewhat similar is the
conclusion in Tamil Nadu that a large proportion of
the budget was absorbed in personnel, and that the
whole idea of a mass programme planned and administered in minute detail was wrong.

Ramakrishnan is one of several authors to
suggest that resources allocated were meagre and
inadequate - despite the huge increase in government
support for adult education by contrast with the
neglect of previous years. The MOBRAL study shows
that much could not be done for lack of resources,
despite the massive scale and investment of the
Brazilian programme. Bekele describes the big
national programme in Kenya similarly, observing that
the Departmment concerned employed 'only 8,000
persons'. In Nicaragua financial impoverishment
imposed severe constraints and drove the crusade
organisers to rely on overseas funds. Here commitment
appears to have gone far to overcome lack of resources; the enthusiasm evidently communicated itself to
overseas supporters and aid agencies which were able
to mobilise the necessary funds and equipment. One
clear message from these accounts is the importance,
and non-measurability, of hidden contributions,
mainly volunteered time and use of existing community
facilities without cost. Ramakrishnan finds the
failure adequately to tap this resource disappointing
in India; in Kenya the harambee spirit of self-help
drove the programme ahead of the schedule which the
government machinery could support. The units in
Chile got by so long as they did only through the
volunteered contributions of teachers and participants. Local facilities, such as the public buildings
and private houses used for classes, were important
in Brazil. Cheong similarly emphasises the importance
of local effort and volunteered resources in Korea.
The Nicaraguan crusade was driven by the enthusiastic
energy and commitment of the host of volunteer
workers, teachers and students from the towns, who
went to remote areas and taught and worked with the
peasants. Thus it is not only Sarvodaya, the purely
non-governmental programme among those presented
here, which was able to mobilise an army of volunteers and generate energies and resources way beyond
what can be added up in terms of dedicated funds. The
lesson is that government programmes and agencies of
the right through to the far left are often able to
mobilise quite massive community resources, especially the unpaid time and efforts of various kinds of

volunteers. What some might consider the prerogative
of voluntary and private bodies, or of revolution-
ary/liberationist movements, belongs more widely.
This is not to deny that the most effective commitment and mobilisation may come from ideologically
strong and committed groups and movements.
The importance of community and volunteer
resources shows how futile it is to try to measure
and prove the cost, and relative cost-efficiency, of
nonformal adult education programmes. On the one hand
the real costs of such programmes cannot be measured
accurately. Only crude estimates are possible of the
value of unpaid time, materials and facilities used
in these programmes. Even the cost of purely governmental programmes may be almost impossible to com-
pute, where several ministries and other agencies
take part in a programme – as may be necessary for
successful development-oriented adult education. On
the other hand several authors doubt the efficacy of,
measures of success, and ipso facto of cost-
efficiency, even in the narrowest adult education or
literacy terms – witness the careful consideration of
this matter by the Brazilian and Indian authors.
Others suggest that the official figures which they
have obtained have little or no real meaning. These
reservations apply even to the cost of directly
measurable adult education attainments. How much more
tenuous is the connection when one claims to measure
the extent to which adult education has reduced the
incidence of poverty, and the cost of its reduction.
Cheong appears confident that rural poverty has significantly reduced in South Korea, and that Saemaul
education within Saemaul Undong has been indispensable in this. The lot of the poorest however is not
included in such a calculation, and it would not
appear possible to prove the value of the Saemaul
education dollar in the overall index of rural
development. Miller is reasonably confident about the
visible cost of bringing literacy to illiterate
citizens in Nicaragua, but does not attempt to demonstrate to what extent this educational effort might
be translated into the elimination of poverty – not
only because the time is too short and the political
survival and economic future of the country still all
too uncertain.
Other comments are in the same direction.
Ramakrishnan shows how little the apparent per capita
costs of achieving literacy mean, given the statistical uncertainties and varieties of possible definition of literacy, observations similar to some from
Brazil. He considers the direct impact of the work on
the reduction of poverty to be negligible; the

Brazilian conclusion is less negative but no more definite - it is not really possible to prove that income has increased as a direct result of taking part in the programmes of MOBRAL, even when students have been directly assisted to gain jobs in the formal labour market. Gajardo feels that some families have benefited economically despite lack of access to the labour market (80 per cent of her respondents recorded gains in terms of family budget and 43 per cent in terms of temporary work at home, compared with only 1.6 per cent gaining permanent access to the labour market). All authors however, tend to agree that important questions about the costs and means of reducing poverty, and about using adult education for this purpose, cannot be addressed through conventional economic measures and reliably quantified. The complexities of causality and relationship mean that the case for supporting adult education as a means of reducing inequality and addressing poverty must be made on other grounds. More positively, the studies in this volume do muster persuasive evidence that, providing the time is right and the methods well chosen, adult education has a significant contribution to make as part of a larger strategy.

IMPORTANT FEATURES OF THE PROGRAMMES

Strategies

Several points alluded to already are here drawn together. First the tension between individual education for economic advancement and societal purposes. Where relatively free market economic development is the objective, as in Brazil and Kenya, although the purpose is national economic development, the means is by equipping and motivating individuals to become economically viable and prosperous. Adult education may contribute to this objective, yet unintendedly even exacerbate poverty and widen the gap between the poorest and those enjoying benefits from the programmes. In Brazil, and possibly also in Nicaragua, a consequence may be to increase poverty for those whose aspirations are raised and expressed in the form of migration to urban areas unable to absorb additional labour.

Mass programmes as described in most of these chapters call for management ability, and the capacity to coordinate efforts between different agencies and at different levels. Sheer competence in management is important, although below a certain level inadequacy of resources may be an insuperable problem. However several of these studies suggest

that commitment, the will to succeed, can go far to
compensate for lack of material resources; one thinks
again of Nicaragua, and also Sarvodaya. Apart from
the need to conceive and then implement interdepartmental and interagency cooperation, large programmes
mean centrally directing a programme which must
desirably (to win motivation and commitment, often
prerequisites for success) be implemented in a
diverse and decentralised way. This appeared a
problem in Brazil, India and Korea, perhaps also in
Kenya. Ramakrishnan goes so far as to suggest that it
was in principle mistaken to try to plan and orches-
trate a mass movement in minute detail, even if the
resources, abilities and will to risk change had been
there. A conclusion from the MOBRAL study is that
decentralisation and debureaucratisation must be
achieved somehow.

Personnel and Training

There are different approaches to preparing literacy
teachers, trainers or instructors for their work.
Nicaragua adopted, with evident success, a 'cascade'
strategy whereby a small group of highly committed
planners and campaign managers passed on their skills
and presumably their commitment to a particular kind
of facilitation first to 80, thence to 600, then
12,000 and then to the tens of thousands who were the
engine of the crusade: 'the traditional teacher
became a type of learning coordinator'. The strength
of teacher preparation in Nicaragua lay in the clear
choice of a Freirean methodology wedding phonetics
through a liberationist approach to the realities of
life as it was encountered in different villages and
regions - and through the content of what was studied
to the ideology and triumph of the revolution as well
as the continuing realities of malaria, poverty and
inequality. In India Ramakrishnan shows through
informal inquiry and by questionnaires how lack of
confidence and of ideological commitment among
literacy teachers undercut the grand intentions for
structural transformation of the NAEP: some tutors
actually became more conservative through the experience, adopting the view that poverty and illiteracy
were the fault of the poor and the illiterate, who
failed through sloth and lack of motivation. (Only
the Brazilian authors explicitly call for destigma-
tisating illiteracy as part of the necessary transformation of attitudes.) In several countries the
rhetoric of facilitation, group work and participation proved inadequate to resist the pressure -
among students and teachers alike - towards a
familiar school model. Teachers adopted traditional

instructional roles, and students behaved depend-
ently, in Brazil, Kenya and India, possibly also in
Korea and certainly in Chile, according to these
accounts. In Sri Lanka as in Nicaragua, it appears
that the philosophical commitment of the leaders was
strong enough to hold to the preferred facilitative
and participative mode. The Korean stress upon
leadership training in the context of an authoritarian and directive programme presumably militated
in this direction, even though the somewhat rigid and
authoritarian design of the workshops had built into
it an egalitarian, maybe deliberately humbling,
character.

Volunteers are important in large-scale programmes, governmental as well as private. Their
orientation and training is crucial and problematic,
as is the provision of advice, supervision and ongoing support systems. Ironically in Nicaragua the
adult education work scheduled to follow the main
crusade was hampered by loss of experienced crusade
leaders to other areas of administration. Here the
usual phenomenon was reversed: it is more common for
adult educators to find themselves marginal to the
mainstream of government effort than courted for
their skills and experience. Adult education is an
uncertain profession. Like other helping professions
it has impossible hopes and expectations placed upon
it, usually receives meagre resources, and finds it
impossible to demonstrate objectively and in quantitative terms what it has achieved. Even when adult
educators are well placed and well regarded within
government - MOBRAL in Brazil, Macharia and Bordia in
Kenya and India - their situation still tends towards
the marginal and vulnerable. In Korea the situation
could be still more ticklish, and in Chile a programme nominally supported by government had to adopt
a very low profile which yet did not protect its
workers from gaol. Even in Nicaragua, where adult
educators came to power with and through the
revolutionary government, and in Sri Lanka where a
different kind of authority was won through poor
people irrespective of government, one can discern
difficulties inherent in the role of 'professional'
adult educator. At least in Nicaragua, as in contemporary China, the question is not whether adult
education may work for a better social order and the
end of poverty but how best this might be achieved;
there will still be differences about means, and the
values of adult educators will not always hold sway.

In the west it is more usual for adult educators
to be an out-group, fringe-dwellers working to effect
reform or more radical change usually against the

academic-industrial-political elite. The exception tends to be those in labour market training and retraining who often dissociate themselves from and are regarded with disdain by those who call themselves adult educators. Studies in this volume show adult educators working within systems of government, often critical of those in power, bending their efforts to being about tangible, albeit modest, changes. In this they challenge those adult educators in the western industrialised world who might prefer the purity and marginality of working 'outside the system' to the tensions and compromises which accompany working from within.

Teaching Methods

There is almost complete harmony in these accounts over the value placed upon participative methods. In several countries, however, the reality differed sharply: teacher preparation was too brief and slight to override the pull of tradition; the image of schooling which teachers and learners brought into the classroom with them too powerful, converting informal settings like homes and church halls into formal instructional settings. The problem of trying to ensure minimal standards with teachers of low formal education and little teaching materials naturally pressed towards standardisation: if some basic teacher training can be given and some minimal teacher's handbook and learners' manual provided, there is a hope that at least minimal literacy will be achieved. On the other hand the range of languages of instruction employed in Kenya is impressive, as is the attempt, for all that it fell short, in most places to employ participative group methods, gear teaching to perceived needs, diversify content for different local circumstances, and encourage participants to share responsibility for evaluation, application and follow-up. What comes through time and again is the importance of shared values and commitment to the core purposes of the programme. Where these exist, as among the Nicaraguan Brigadistas, and probably many of the Chilean workers as well as the Sri Lankan volunteers, there appears to have been firm adherence to the spirit, purpose and process of participatory planning and learning. Where there was ambivalence and nervousness, as in Tamil Nadu's adult education centres, the gap between precept and practice became wide. Most striking is the sense of congruence between values and practice not only in Nicaragua but also in Sri Lanka and - for all that Cheong calls for more knowledge and practice of andragogy in Saemaul education - in the work in

Korea. In each of these it appears that the teachers, paid or volunteer, understood and believed in their work, and set out to create a learning environment in which those taking part adopted roles as co-learners in a common cause. In Nicaragua and Sri Lanka this appears to embrace crusade and Sarvodaya volunteers as well as the villagers they were teaching and from whom they learned; the difference in Saemaul education is the more distant, directive and didactic role of teaching staff who, though they live and work with the (conscripted) participants, appear to be more separate.

In summary, participation appears the first principle of adult education across the very diverse circumstances represented here. Is it the infusing principle of planning, reflection and action, or is it honoured rather in the breach? This varies partly as a function of the posture and complexion of government and of the extent to which government interests itself in the activities of adult education. In some instances there is a high level of congruence between principle and practice; in others the dissonance is equally strident, and Freire either ignored or coopted.

Motivation

The practice of participation from the point of view of the student relates closely to motivation. There appears to be a correspondence in these studies between the extent to which principles of participation could be given effect in planning and teaching, and the motivation displayed by those for whom programmes were intended. In South Korea participation was apparently mandatory; according to Cheong it was therefore not intrinsically pleasurable, but nonetheless appeared successful in achieving its rural development objectives through equipping and motivating Saemaul leaders. The integrated concept of curriculum design and implementation in the Chilean units was not put into effect: different actions came to belong at different levels, and participation was consequently low, although some women evidently remained motivated to learn and to apply what they learned to the family struggle for survival. Women were similarly well motivated and active in Kenya where, as for many Korean villagers, the programme seemed relevant to their daily life. In Brazil literacy was valued for the prospects of job mobility which it appeared to offer, although it was not directly functional for and in rural areas. The accounts of work in Sri Lanka and Nicaragua suggest that motivation was not a problem, other than among those ideologically opposed to the Sandinistas; however the Sarvodaya method of selection of villages could mean that some in need but unable to express interest in participating were bypassed. Certainly the methods employed in the Sarvodaya movement appear to have created and sustained motivation. Ramakrishnan's Indian study reveals low motivation, measured by low enrolment and high dropout, which he credits to the failure to adapt to diverse local needs as well as the (inevitable) failure actually to address and alter the root causes of poverty.

Respect for Indigenous Skills and Culture

An important principle of the participatory research network promoted by the International Council for Adult Education, and one long held in the social change tradition in adult education, is that people are not so much ignorant and stupid as frequently abused and exploited. Many traditional ways which planners and economists see as standing in the way of modernisation and 'progress' are well founded in experience and indigenous science. Local people are commonly the most expert in what is good for them, what works in their particular environment. Modern education and urban culture often have the effect of disabling and discrediting such knowledge and wisdom, defining the unlettered as ignorant and blaming their poverty on traditional attitudes and ways.

Several of the programmes described in this book have a commitment to development and some kind of modernisation, but this does not automatically mean hostility or lack of respect for traditional institutions and knowledge. Indeed, perhaps surprisingly, the more radical programmes tend to place greater value upon the wisdom and traditions of the people, even while they seek the more fundamental changes. Nor does respect for indigenous skills and culture automatically correspond with a conventional left-right spectrum in political terms. Although the literacy drive of MOBRAL was launched to remove what was perceived as an obstacle to national economic development, the Brazilian authors favour destigmatising illiteracy. Kenya's modernisation-oriented adult education programme makes use of traditional barazas. More fundamentally, the whole Sarvodaya Shramadana philosophy is anchored in Buddhism and derives a programme of awakening and action which is fundamentally anti-modern in terms of conventional views of progress and prosperity, yet claims to have a viable solution to the world's desperate problems of poverty and inequity. In MOBRAL it is acknowledged that collective productivity might be increased through forgotten indigenous technologies. Kenya's use of many indigenous languages for literacy implies another kind of respect for tradition, since crude modernisation tends to favour one lingua franca.

Then there is the valuing of indigenous village experience and its under-pinning philosophy as expressed in the Korean, Nicaraguan and Sri Lankan studies. One intention of the Korean pedagogy is to (re-)introduce urban intellectuals and bureaucrats to the philosophy and folk-ways of village leaders, in the process teaching that the horny hands of the labourer are no less beautiful than the manicured hands of the senior government official. This echoes in Miller's account of how middle class urban volunteers worked with and for, and learned from, rural folk. Each suggests a remaking of the middle classes, a restoration of deeper and simpler values drawn from the wellspring of the people of almost Rousseauesque optimism. In the case of the Nicaraguan crusade the traditional couplet form was used, as well as the more subtle and fundamental kinds of learning which Miller conveys in the concluding vignettes. In Sri Lanka again value is placed upon senior intellectuals sitting side by side with simple peasants and learning in equality, with mutual respect and lack of dominating status. Perception of and respect for indigenous knowledge appears a litmus test for the potency of adult education for development and one measure, perhaps, of their potential for touching and altering the conditions which sustain poverty.

CONCLUSIONS

Did these large-scale, mainly governmental, adult education programmes reach those most in need - the poorest of the poor? The answer varies from place to place. In Chile, in Tamil Nadu and in the Republic of Korea they did not. In Brazil and Kenya, and probably also in Nicaragua and Sri Lanka, the opposite is true. Evidently there is no simple correlation along a socialist-capitalist or authoritarian-liberal political spectrum. It seems that a combination of circumstances is required: those responsible for fashioning and leading a programme need to be clear, and clearly committed to structural change in the interests of the most disadvantaged; and the government must either be positively committed to such transformation or at least willing to allow and support programmes in this direction. In Chile the government changed and a benevolent climate became a highly inhospitable one. In India the success of leading adult educators in conceiving and winning

support for the NAEP at Union level did not carry
through in conviction and commitment against
entrenched interests at more local levels in that
huge and complex country, even without a change of
central government which further hampered prospects
for a while. In Korea classic modernisation, well
laced with concerns for national security, meant that
general rural uplift mattered more than particular
individuals, so long as these seemed politically
irrelevant.
    In Brazil, despite the criticism which radical
adult educators habitually level at the land which
exiled Paulo Freire, and at MOBRAL as the state
instrument of adult education, programmes did succeed
in reaching the poorest provinces and districts.
Somehow the large resources of MOBRAL did in the main
reach the poorest rural areas, although the intention
was to concentrate more on urban areas, an interesting difference between intention and take-up. In
Kenya girls and women were perceived as heavily
disadvantaged educationally, socially and economically, but the much greater take-up among women than
men became in turn cause for concern about lop-sided
development. Bekele is confident, however, that the
programme was reaching the poorest and most in need -
and that it tangibly improved their incomes and
living conditions. Nicaragua's and Sri Lanka's programmes, one official, the other non-governmental,
focussed on group and national needs rather than on
individuals per se, but in the process appeared to
reach the most needy classes and regions.
    Large-scale programmes can then in certain
circumstances reach and influence the circumstances
of the poorest of the poor. The complexion and role
of government however, proves critical. Authoritarian
modernising regimes may allow gains to reach the
poorer groups, so long as this does not threaten
political and economic stability. There is however, a
tendency for priority in large government programmes
of whatever political complexion, other than the
exuberantly liberationist like Nicaragua of the
Frente, to go to what are seen as the best bets for
national economic progress. If this means equipping
citizens to be competent producers and consumers it
may still mean concentrating on those in greatest
need. If it is seen as raising productivity, economists' arguments about efficiency of investment and
returns are likely to outweigh equity arguments. Even
a quite socialist government, like that of India, may
prove unable to communicate its commitment to a radi-
cally conceived conscientisation, mobilisation and
education programme - which the NAEP was - with

sufficient conviction to carry along officials at all levels from the capital to the village, and so to reach those in greatest need.

Among the studies here Sarvodaya appeared able to sustain a commitment to radical social transforma-tion and to avoid becoming embroiled in and destroyed by formal politics, despite the deeply political import of what it was doing. Nicaragua, celebrating a unique historical moment, bent the energies of the new regime to remaking society and its members, with rare commitment and unit of purpose. At a lower level Kenya and Brazil provided official support to pro-grammes with prospect of ameliorating the lot of the poor, but only in ways not fundamentally disruptive of the status quo. In Korea the reins were firmly held, and in Chile even the modest low profile efforts of the units in the mid and later seventies proved too disturbing for that regime to countenance. The most that the unit workers could hope for was to sustain some kind of survival organisation as a base for mobilisation as conditions eased in the future. While the regimes and the attitudes of governments as described here varied widely, the adult educator authors appear closely in sympathy one with another as they draw implications for the capacity of adult education to contribute to the reduction of poverty. In most, if not all, conscientisation or awakening, organisation and mobilisation, are seen as necessary for real change in the social structure. Programmes of other than revolutionary governments are inhibited by caution and bureaucratic procedures. They need to allow far more decentralisation and diversification if they are to amplify the modest benefits which, admittedly, they bring to those in greatest need.

The general conclusion is that political will and commitment exercises an often decisive influence. The timing and circumstances of programmes may also be crucial. Agencies and systems lacking the compet-ence to organise and deliver will fall down even if there is a willingness to effect change; on the other hand, liberationary commitment and voluntary fervour can go far to make amends for lack of resources, and even for shortness in managerial experience. Problems of overcoming schoolish authoritarian-dependency attitudes are formidable. Traditional skills, know-ledge and wisdom appear quite widely respected, pointing to a possible easing of the dichotomy between tradition and 'modernisation'. Participation is everywhere valued rhetorically, but there is a wide gulf between precept and practice, which makes the cases of congruence shine out the more by contrast. Political and economic power can intrude and interfere at district and local levels and also from the international arena, as well as at national level. Inter-agency cooperation is almost essential for adult education programmes effectively to address poverty; yet problems of interdepartmental cooperation appear almost universal, with the possible exception of very new revolutionary regimes. There may be strength in the arguments for a trickle-down approach to development and the gradual reduction of poverty, but there are severe ethical questions to be considered. Moreover the experience of very affluent free market societies, so far as extremes of wealth and poverty are concerned, is not encouraging; there is no reason to suppose that some hidden hand will ensure that all will eventually share in greater productivity and prosperity.

All in all these studies caution against expecting too much of adult education, especially acting alone, in the war against poverty. As the Brazilian study concludes, 'reduction in poverty is above all a political matter'. 'It is necessary to act concomitantly'; unless there are economic opportunities, and arrangements such as easily available loan funds and genuine economic prospects for neo-literates, relapse is likely and anyway poverty will not be significantly diminished. Ramakrishnan sees a prior 'need to redistribute non-labour productive resources', providing the resource base for economic take-off. Absolute poverty he considers must first be alleviated by direct relief, and opportunities provided for income augmentation, before programmes like the NAEP can have serious prospect of success. Ironically, while most authors conclude that adult education can be only a means to reduction of poverty as part of a wider strategy and set of programmes, Ramakrishnan suggests that it makes more sense to think of it as an end – a desired state in societies which have abolished absolute poverty. Thus he comes around full circle to the position of liberal individualists, though for rather different reasons: the 'reduction of poverty seems to be a prerequisite to educational activities becoming relevant'.

The last word is reserved for the author of the last case study. Wijetunga, like Sarvodaya Shramadana, addresses the debate about adult education and poverty at a deeper level. If greed, craving, or tanha is the cause of human suffering (poverty a product of wealth) then an approach to its resolution different from that of the 'international institutions with their elite urban bias' is needed: 'their calculations are based on how little is sufficient; Sarvodaya teaches how much is enough'. The Sarvodaya hierarchy of awakening and development gives pride of place to the spiritual, then the moral, cultural, social and political, with economic awakening as the final component. If motivation and inspiration are there, only meagre material resources are necessary: 'we build the road and the road builds us'.

ABBREVIATIONS

AEC	Adult Education Centre
AEP	Adult Education Programme
ANDEN	Nicaraguan Educators' Association
ATC	Farmworkers' Association (Nicaragua)
COMUN	Municipal Commission (Brazil)
DAEO	District Adult Education Officer
DNAE	Department of Nonformal Adult Education
DVV	Deutscher Volkshochschul-Verband (German Adult Education Association)
EOU	Educational Operative Units (Unidades Operativas Educacionales)
EPA	Popular Literacy Army (Nicaragua)
Frente	Sandinista National Liberation Army (Frente Sandinista de Liberacion Nacional)
GUAS	Urban Literacy Guerillas (Nicaragua)
ICAE	International Council for Adult Education
K.Sh.	Kenyan shillings
MAC	Peasants' Literacy Militia (Nicaragua)
MAF	Ministry of Agriculture and Forestries
MCI	Ministry of Commerce and Industry
MCPI	Ministry of Culture and Public Information
MHA	Ministry of Home Affairs
MHSA	Ministry of Health and Social Affairs
MOE	Ministry of Education
MOBRAL	Brazilian Literacy Movement
NAEP	National Adult Education Programme
PAF	Functional Literacy Programme of Brazil
RFLP	Rural Functional Literacy Programme
Rs	rupees
SAEP	State Adult Education Programme
SLTI	Saemaul Leaders' Training Institute
SSM	Sarvodaya Shramadana Movement
YMCA	Young Men's Christian Association

CONTRIBUTORS

Dr Chris Duke

Director, Centre for Continuing Education, Australian National University
Secretary-General, Asian and South Pacific Bureau of Adult Education
Associate Secretary-General and Coordinator, Adult Education and Poverty Project, International Council for Adult Education

Hugo Rodolfo Lovisolo   (Coordinator)
Luna Azulay Steinbruch   (Assistant)
Terezinho Catarina
  Pereira Ramos   (Assistant)
Isabel de Orleans e
  Braganca   (Editor)
Anne-Marie Milon
  Oliveira   (Editor)
Staff of the Brazil Literacy Movement Foundation – MOBRAL

Ms Fekenu Bekele

Research Associate, African Training and Research Centre for Women, United Nations Economic Commission for Africa, Addis Ababa

K. Ramakrishnan

Chief, Adult Education Evaluation Unit, Madras Institute of Development Studies

Valerie Miller

Fellow of the Center for International Education, University of Massachusetts and a Planning Advisor of the Literacy Crusade

Contributors

Marcela Gajardo	Formerly Associate Researcher, Facultad Latinoamericana de Ciencias Sociales (FLACSO) and at the Programa Interdisciplinario de Investigaciones en Educacion (PIIE), Santiago; Inter American Institute for Cooperation on Agriculture (IICA), Rio de Janeiro
Dr Ji Woong Cheong	Associate Director, Institute of Saemaul Undong Studies, Seoul National University Secretary-General, Korean Association of Adult and Youth Education
Dr W.M.K. Wijetunga	Department of History, Srijawawardenapura University Secretary, Region 1, Asian and South Pacific Bureau of Adult Education Executive Member, International Council for Adult Education

FURTHER READING

(With acknowledgement to Karen Kotchka for a number of the references on Brazil, Kenya, Korea and Sri Lanka.)

BRAZIL - THE WORK OF MOBRAL

Development Education Centre, Toronto, Canada, 'MOBRAL: Un Modelo para la Educacion de Adultos?' Convergence, 7, 1, 1974, pp.61-70. Discusses the role of MOBRAL as part of an economic growth plan. Questions are raised about the stress of MOBRAL on the economic function of the students and a need for a humanist perspective is mentioned.

Fletcher, Phillip R., 'Literacy Training and the Brazilian Political Economy', US Educational Resources Information Center, ERIC Document ED 070 121, 1972. An annotated bibliography in essay form of sources concerning MOBRAL and its implications for the country's economy.

Lopes-Correa, Arlindo, 'MOBRAL: Participation-Reading in Brazil', Journal of Reading, 19, 7, April 1976. Describes the methodology used in teaching people in the MOBRAL programme to read through the use of generative words.

MOBRAL, 'MOBRAL: Final Report', US Educational Resources Information Center, ERIC Document ED 089 091, 1973. Outlines the substance of a report on MOBRAL at the MOBRAL Inter-American Seminar on Adult Education. Subjects discussed are MOBRAL's structure, administration, resources, mobilisation and technical aspects in the context of trends in adult education in Latin America.

MOBRAL, Project for training literacy instructors by radio, MOBRAL, Rio de Janeiro, Brazil, 1975. This booklet describes a project for training additional literacy instructors through the medium of radio. It gives the goals and requirements of the project, the plan of action and an evaluation of the programme.

Further Reading

Moreira, C. 'Planning Literacy and Post-Literacy for the Implementation of Basic Education' in <u>International Literacy Workshop Papers</u>, IIEP and Unesco, Madras, 1982, pp.236-267.

Pereira da Costa, Lamartine, 'Workshop Organization and Management in Adult Education: Case Study of the MOBRAL System', US Educational Resources Information Center, ERIC Document ED 131 242, 1974. A case study of the organisational structure of MOBRAL and various organisational changes made as a large-scale programme developed. It talks about the relative merits of open and closed organisational systems.

Salles, Marlise S.M., 'Adult Education and Inequalities - Brazil', in Adiseshiah, Malcolm S., (ed.) <u>Adult Education Faces Inequalities</u>, Sangam, 1981, pp.249-272.

UNESCO Regional Office for Education in Latin America and the Caribbean, 'MOBRAL: The Brazilian Adult Literacy Experiment', UNESCO, 1975. Outlines the problem of illiteracy in Brazil in the context of its present stage of development and describes the conceptual bases of MOBRAL, the strategies adopted by the programme, the organisational relationships and the participants. It concludes with a very positive and glowing report of Brazil's efforts.

KENYA - THE NAEP IN KENYA

Abbott, Susan, 'Women's Importance for Kenyan Rural Development', <u>Community Development Journal</u>, 10, 3, 1975. Suggests that more emphasis be placed on women in farmer education because they are generally responsible for the farming in the family.

Bhola, H.S., 'A Comparative Study of the Mass Literacy Campaigns of Tanzania and Kenya', US Educational Resources Information Center, ERIC Document ED 208 200, 1981. Proposes the theory that the prevailing ideology of a country will determine how a literacy campaign is run in terms of objectives, organisational structures and incentive systems. It concludes that socialist countries are more successful because they can better articulate an ideological position on literacy which can be accepted by all.

Godfrey, E.M. & G.C.M. Mutiso, 'The Political Economy of Self-Help: Kenya's Harambee Institutes of Technology', <u>Canadian Journal of African Studies</u>, 8, 1, 1974, pp.109-135. Traces how the institutes of technology emerged from political and economic trends. As the educational

explosion flooded the market with those merely
academically qualified, the institutes of technology became attractive alternatives to secondary school.

Kalweo, J.I. and David Macharia, 'Kenya's Literacy
Program: from the 1960s to the 1980s', in H.S.
Bhola, et al, The Promise of Literacy, Nomos,
1983, pp.117-133.

Kebathi, Joyce, 'Decentralization of Educational
Administration for Literacy Programmes' in
International Literacy Workshop Papers, Madras,
IIEP and Unesco, 1982, pp.190-210.

Keller, Edmond J., 'Harambee! Educational Policy,
Inequality and the Political Economy of Rural
Community Self-Help in Kenya', Journal of
African Studies, 4, 1, Spring 1977. Proposes
that the harambee movement for secondary schools
has contributed to an increase in the disparity
in the quality of education between government-
aided and self-help schools and exacerbated
ethnic, regional and class imbalances in educational opportunity.

INDIA - THE NAEP

Bhan, Susheela, 'Adult Education and Inequalities -
India', in Adiseshiah, Malcolm S., (ed.) Adult
Education Faces Inequalities, Sangam, 1981,
pp.144-154.

Bordia, A., 'Planning and Management of Post-Literacy
Programmes', in IIEP and Unesco, International
Literacy Workshop Papers, Madras, 1982, pp.369-
393.

Gomez, R., 'State Resource Centre for Non-formal
Education (SRC) in Tamil Nadu' in IIEP and
Unesco, International Literacy Workshop Papers,
Madras, 1982, pp.554-569.

Indian Journal of Adult Education, Indian Adult
Education Association, New Delhi.

Jayagopal, R., Village Case Studies in Literacy Programmes, DACE, U. of Madras, 1981.

Madras Institute of Development Studies, National
Adult Education Programme: An Appraisal of the
Role of Voluntary Agencies in Tamil Nadu, MIDS,
1980, especially Ch.3, on methodology.

Pillai, K. Sivadasan, 'Income Generation, Better
Living and Literacy - Three Stories from India',
Adult Education and Development, 22, 1984,
pp.73-77.

Ramakrishnan, K. 'Social Change Through Education',
Madras Institute of Development Studies (Paper
for Research Methodology Workshop), 1982.

Further Reading

Shah, A.B., and Susheela Bahn (eds.), Non-formal Education and the NAEP, Oxford UP, New Delhi, 1980.

Sharma, D.V. et al, 'Adult Literacy in India: History, Current Status and Future Directions', in H.S. Bhola, et al, The Promise of Literacy, Nomos, 1983, pp.173-184.

Venkatachari, R., 'The Weaker Sections on the Road to Progress', in IIEP and Unesco, International Literary Workshop Papers, Madras, 1982, pp.598-619.

NICARAGUA - THE LITERACY CRUSADE

Alexander, Titus, 'The Country that Turned Itself into a Classroom' Guardian, September 1982. A two-part Guardian Third World Review article on the campaign and the subsequent adult Basic Education Programme.

Assmann, Hugo, The Literacy Victory of Nicaragua. Documents and Testimonies of the National Literacy Crusade, MED and DEI, San Jose, 1981.

Cardenal, Fernando, S.J. and Valerie Miller, 'Nicaragua 1980: The Battle of the ABCs', Harvard Educational Review, 51, 1, 1981, pp.2-25. The leading article in a special issue on Education as Transformation: Identity, Change and Development.

Cardenal, Fernando and Valerie Miller, 'Nicaragua: Literacy and Revolution', Prospects, XII, 2, 1982, pp.201-212. Edited version of a study for the IIEP Workshop on Planning and Administration of National Literacy Programmes, Arusha, 1980.

Grigaby, K. 'The Utilization of Volunteers in Implementing Literacy and Post-Literacy Programme', in IIEP and Unesco, International Literacy Workshop Papers, Madras, 1982, pp.268-295.

Haley, Aileen, 'The Madonna as Revolutionary', The National Times (Australia), 13-19 May 1983, pp.26-27. Report on radical Catholicism on the occasion of the Pope's visit to Nicaragua.

Miller, Valerie, 'Nicaragua Literacy Crusade: Some Reflections', in H.S. Bhola, et al, The Promise of Literacy, Nomos, 1983, pp.194-199.

CHILE - THE EDUCATIONAL OPERATIVE UNITS

Gajardo, Marcela, et al, Las Unidades Operativas Educacionales: Antecedentes y Funcionamiento de Una Experiencia en el Campo de la Educacion de Adultos, PIIE, Santiago, 1978.

Gajardo, Marcela, 'Chile: An Experiment in Non-formal Education in Rural Areas', Prospects, XIII, 1, 1983, pp.83-94. An account of the Rural Informa-

tion Programme, an experiment combining educational activity with community information of
possible use for community organisation and
people's participation.

SOUTH KOREA - SAEMAUL UNDONG AND SAEMAUL EDUCATION

Brandt, Vincent S.R., 'Rural Development in South
    Korea', Asian Affairs: An American Review, 6, 3.
    Highlights the initial pressure by the govern-
    ment for involvement in the Saemaul Movement.
    The author says that the greatest contribution
    the Saemaul Movement has made is the improvement
    of institutional linkages and communication
    between village and city. He also cites continu-
    ing problems of excessive individualism and the
    poor not benefiting.
Brandt, Vincent S.R. and Ji Woong Cheong, Planning
    from the Bottom Up: Community-Based Integrated
    Rural Development in South Korea, IIED, 1979.
Cheong, Ji Woong and Kwan Eung Lee, 'Saemaul Educa-
    tion and Reduction of Rural Poverty', Journal of
    SNU Saemaul Studies, 1, i, 1981, pp.175-211.
Durio, Helen F., 'The Spirit of the Yushin in Korean
    Education', Clearinghouse, 53, 1, pp.25-28.
    Gives the historical background of Korea with
    its years of domination by other countries which
    is the basis for the programme launched in the
    1970s to emphasise Korean culture and nation-
    ality. It says that the emphasis of the Saemaul
    Undong is to provide better living conditions
    for rural people and build unity and prosperity
    among Koreans.
Kim, Jongchol, et al, The Saemaul Education in the
    Republic of Korea, The Korean Society for the
    Study of Education, 1974. This study explores
    the historical, philosophical and sociological
    background of Saemaul education in Korea. It
    analyses present practices and problems and
    makes suggestions for the improvement of
    policies on Saemaul education as well as its
    practices. The first part is theoretical while
    the second part is empirical, with a large-scale
    survey summary.
Korean Overseas Information Service, Saemaul Undong,
    Seoul, Korea, 1977. This pamphlet starts out
    with the historical background and philosophy
    behind the Saemaul Movement. It outlines the
    evolution of the movement from one stage to
    another and addresses the issues of planning and
    project selection and coordination between
    involved agencies. Finally, it lists lessons
    from Saemaul Undong which are important for
    rural development.

Further Reading

Lee, Man-Gap (ed.), Towards a New Community Life; Reports of International Research Seminar on the Seamaul Movement, ISUD, Seoul National University, 1981.
Saemaul Undong: English Summaries of Research Articles in Saemaul Undong, Vol. 7, Institute of Saemaul Studies, Republic of Korea, 1982. A collection of summaries of very specific studies conducted on Saemaul Undong in 1981; subjects range from the relation of Saemaul Undong to rural-urban migration, to yields of mechanically transplanted rice on newly reclaimed land.

SRI LANKA - SARVODAYA SHRAMADANA
Ariyaratne, A.T., Sarvodaya Shramadana: Growth of a People's Movement, Sri Lanka, 1970. The founder of the movement discusses the background and philosophy of Sarvodaya Shramadana and its inspiration from Buddhist thought, then specific programmes in detail such as the 100 Villages Development Scheme.
Ariyaratne, A.T., 'Mobilization of Private Philanthropy in Asia for Aid in Rural Development', Sarvodaya, 1972.
Ariyaratne, A.T., 'Role of Shramadana in Rural Development', Sarvodaya, n.d.
Ariyaratne, A.T., 'For a New Life-Style Based on Cooperation and Harmony', (paper presented to NOVIB Asian Seminar), 1981.
Colletta, N.J., R.T. Ewing and T.A. Todd, 'Cultural Revitalization, Participatory Non-Formal Education and Village Development in Sri Lanka: The Sarvodaya Shramadana Movement', Comparative Education Review, 26, 2, June 1982. The authors of this article got their information from interviews with 109 village leaders, heads of households and Sarvodaya field workers. They outline the beginnings of the movement and describe a Shramadana camp. Their critical evaluation of the movement concludes that it has created the social-psychological readiness for development but now needs input of technical, financial and managerial resources.
Hewage, L.G., 'The Role of Religious Institutions in Asian Development', Marga Institute, Colombo (reprinted from Religion and Development in Asian Societies), 1974.
Hewage, L.G. and David J. Radcliffe, 'The Relevance of Culture in Adult Education for Development', Convergence, 10, 2, 1977. Emphasises how the Sarvodaya Shramadana Movement has integrated the cultural heritage of Buddhism into its

development programmes. It says that the Movement has taken the 'Middle Path Approach' to development by trying to maintain a balance between the socio-economic and the religio-cultural.

Koech, Michael Kipkorir, 'Contributions of Alternative (Non-Formal) Education in Developing Countries', US Educational Resources Information Center, ERIC Document ED 233 447, 1983. This study details the development of the Sarvodaya Shramadana Movement and goes on to discuss objectives, clientele, funding, personnel and curriculum. Its evaluation of the Sarvodaya Shramadana Movement says that many positive outcomes have resulted; however problems have arisen due to overdependence on the top personalities and the rigidity of headquarters' policy and planning.

Ratnapala, Nandasena, The Sarvodaya Movement: Self-Help Rural Development in Sri Lanka, ICED, 1978.

Spee, Arnold A.J., 'Sarvodaya: A Ceylonese Experiment in "Change in Society", study report, Amsterdam, 1973.

Wickremesinghe, C.L., 'Religion and the Ideology of Development', Marga Institute, Colombo (reprinted from Religion and Development in Asian Societies), 1974.

ADULT EDUCATION, POVERTY AND DEVELOPMENT - GENERAL READING

Adiseshiah, Malcolm S. (ed.), Adult Education Faces Inequalities, (Unesco - University of Madras), Sangam, 1981.

Adult Education and Development, DVV, Bonn.

Adult Education and Development, 'Comments on "co-operating or campaigning for literacy"', 22, 1984, pp.49-53.

Ahmed, Manzoor and Philip H. Coombs, Education for Rural Development: Case Studies for Planners, Praeger, 1975.

Barratt Brown, Michael, 'Adult Education and Social Change' (review), Convergence, XIII, 4, 1980, pp.89-92.

Bataille, Leon (ed.), A Turning Point for Literacy, Pergamon, 1976.

Bhasin, Kamla and R. Vimala (eds.), Readings on Poverty, Politics and Development, ffhc/ad, FAO, 1980.

Bhola, H.S., Campaigning for Literacy, Unesco, Paris, 1982.

Bhola, H.S. et al, The Promise of Literacy. Campaigns, Programs and Projects, Nomos, 1983.

Further Reading

Bhola, H.S. with Joginder K. Bhola, Planning and
     Organization of Literacy Campaigns, Programs and
     Projects, DSE, Bonn, 1984.
Bhola, H.S., 'A Policy Analysis of Adult Literacy
     Promotion in the Third World: An Accounting of
     Promises Made and Promises Fulfilled', (prepared
     for International Review of Education, 1984).
Brandt, Willy, (chairman) North-South: A Programme
     for Survival, Pan, 1980.
Centro de Estudios Educativos 'Some Remarks on the
     Problem of Literacy for the Rural Population',
     Adult Education and Development, 22, 1984,
     pp.55-59.
Clark, Noreen, Education for Development and the
     Rural Woman, World Education, 1979.
Commonwealth Secretariat, Participation, Learning
     and Change, 1980.
Convergence, ICAE, Toronto.
Coombs, Philip H. (ed.), Meeting the Basic Needs of
     the Rural Poor, the Integrated Community-Based
     Approach, Pergamon, 1980.
Coombs, Philip H., 'Critical World Issues of the Next
     Two Decades', International Review of Education,
     XXVIII, 1982, pp.145-157.
Development Dialogue, Dag Hammarskjold Foundation,
     Uppsala.
Dore, Ronald, The Diploma Disease. Education, Quali-
     fication and Development, Allen & Unwin, 1976.
Duke, Chris (ed.), Adult Education, International Aid
     and Poverty, ICAE, 1980.
Duke, Chris, 'Adult Education and Poverty: What are
     the Connections?', Convergence, XVI, 1, 1983,
     pp.76-83 (also in Adult Education and Develop-
     ment, 22, 1984, pp.79-88).
Fisher, E.A., 'The World Literacy Situation: 1970,
     1980 and 1990', Prospects, X, 1, 1980.
Fisher, E.A., 'Illiteracy in Context', Prospects,
     XII, 2, 1982.
Fordham, Paul, Co-operating for Literacy, DSE, Bonn,
     1983.
Foubert, Charles, 'Development Theory and the Third
     World' (review), Ideas and Action, 149, 6, 1982,
     pp.19-24.
Freire, P., Pedagogy of the Oppressed, Penguin, 1972.
Freire, P., Cultural Action for Freedom, Penguin,
     1972.
Friberg, Mats, et al, 'Societal Change and Develop-
     ment Thinking; An Inventory of Issues', UNU,
     1979.
Ghose, Ajit K. and Keith Griffin, 'Rural Poverty and
     Development Alternatives in S. and S.E. Asia:
     Some Policy Issues', N.L.I. Bulletin, 5-6, 1979.

Further Reading

Hall, Budd L. and Roby J. Kidd (eds.), Adult Learning: A Design for Action, Pergamon, 1978.

Hallak, Jacques and Francoise Caillods, Education, Training and the Traditional Sector, Unesco/IIEP, 1981.

Healey, Patrick, 'Who Gains and Who Loses: The Political Economy of Adult Education', Convergence, XVI, 4, 1983.

Hettne, Bjorn, Development Theory and the Third World, SAREC, 1982.

Hinzen, Heribert, et al, 'Cooperating or Campaigning for Literacy: Let's Remove Doubtful Promises and Cope with the Practicable', Adult Education for Development, 21, 1983, pp.1-5.

Hinzen, Heribert, 'Literacy and Development', Adult Education and Development, 22, 1984, pp.61-72.

Hogheim, Robert and Kjell Rubenson (eds.), Adult Education for Social Change, Stockholm Gleerup, 1980.

Ideas and Action, ffhc/afd, FAO, Rome.

I.D.S. Bulletin, Rural Development: Whose Knowledge Counts?, 10, 2, 1979.

IIEP and Unesco, International Literacy Workshop Papers, Madras, 1982.

International Review of Education, XXVIII, 1982.

Kassam, Yusuf O., Illiterate No More. The Voices of New Literates from Tanzania, Tanzania Pub. House, Dar es Salaam, 1979.

Keesing, Roger, 'From the Ground Up: Towards Development without Dependency', Human Futures, Summer, 1980, pp.121-126.

Keyfitz, Nathan, 'Development and the Elimination of Poverty', Economic Development and Cultural Change, 30, 3, 1982, pp.649-670.

Kidd, Ross and Krishna Kumar, 'Co-opting Freire. A Critical Analysis of Pseudo-Freirean Adult Education', Economic and Political Weekly, 16, 1-2, 1981, pp.27-36. (A shortened version appears in Ideas and Action, 148/5, 1982.)

Kindervatter, Suzanne, Nonformal Education as an Empowering Process, U.Mass., 1979.

King, Kenneth, 'Formal, Nonformal and Informal Learning: Some North-South Contrasts', International Review of Education, XXVIII, 1982, pp.177-187.

Korten, David, Community Organization and Rural Development: A Learning Process Approach, Ford Foundation reprint from Public Administration Review, 1980.

La Belle, Thomas J., Nonformal Education and Social Change in Latin America, UCLA, 1976.

Lee, Jo-Anne, 'An Ideological Framework in Adult Education Poverty and Social Change', Learning, III, 3, 1981, pp.22-25.

Further Reading

Lythgoe, June, 'Paulo Freire: From Radical Reformer to Revolutionary Advocate', Learning, III, 2, 1980, pp.18-23.
Mackie, R. (ed.), Literacy and Revolution: The Pedagogy of Paulo Freire, Pluto Press, London, 1980.
Mbilinyi, Marjorie, 'Basic Education: Tool of Liberation or Exploitation?', Prospects, VII, 4, 1977.
Muyeed, Abdul, 'Some Reflections on Education for Rural Development', International Review of Education, XXVIII, 1982, pp.177-187.
Network Literacy, ICAE, No.1, May 1984 (Dialogue on Cooperating or Campaigning for Literacy).
Paulston, Rolland G., Conflicting Theories of Social and Educational Change: A Typological Review, U. of Pittsburgh, 1976.
Prospects, Unesco, Paris.
Rahman, Md. Anisur, 'Rural Development in Asia: Search for Another Path', Ideas and Action, 149, 6, 1982, pp.9-14.
Rigg, Pat and Francis E. Kasemek, 'Adult Illiteracy in the USA: Problem and Solution', Convergence, XVI, 4, 1983, pp.24-31.
Roling, Niels and Henk de Zeeuw, Improving the Quality of Rural Poverty Alleviation, IAC, Wageningen, 1983.
Simkins, Tim, Non-formal Education and Development. Some Critical Issues, Manchester, 1977.
Simmons, John (ed.), The Education Dilemma; Policy Issues for Developing Countries in the 1980s, World Bank/Pergamon, 1980.
Srinavasan, Lyra, Perspectives on Nonformal Adult Learning: Functional Education for Individual, Community and National Development, World Education, New York, 1977.
The NFE Exchange, Can Participation Enhance Development?, IISE, MSU, 20, 1981.
Torres, Carlos Alberto, 'From the "Pedagogy of the Oppressed" to "A Luta Continua". An essay on the political pedagogy of Paulo Freire', Education with Production, 1, 2, 1982, pp.76-97.
Thompson, Jane L. (ed.), Adult Education for a Change, Hutchinson, 1980.
Thompson, Jane L., 'Adult Education and the Disadvantaged', Convergence, XVI, 2, 1983.
UNESCO/UNDP, The Experimental World Literacy Programme: A Critical Assessment, Unesco and UNDP, Paris, 1976.

Index

seasonal rhythm 65, 162
self-help 50, 61, 64, 169
shramadana 190
   see also Sarvodaya
   Shramadana Movement
social awareness 69
socialist consciousness
   102
social mobility 33
social transformation and
   structural change 89,
   95-6, 103, 111-14,
   129-30
   structural transform-
   ation 102, 152, 220-1,
   232
spectrum of objectives
   and approaches, 221,
   230
spiritual aspect 162,
   168, 176, 197, 200-1,
   234
Somoza 101, 105, 106,
   108, 123
Soviet Union 101
surveys 56

Tamil Nadu
   see Indian National
   Adult Education
   Programme
tanha (craving) 196, 198
Tanzania
   'food is life'
   campaign 2
   literacy campaign 51,
   101
target groups 76
   see also priority groups
teachers see instructors
technologies of grass-roots
   origin 25
   see also traditional culture
   and ways
ten Basic Human Needs
   197-9, 200, 207
total education and
   development 208

traditional culture and
   ways 62, 102, 115,
   125, 229-30, 232
   see also technologies
   of grass-roots origin
trainers
   see instructors
'trickle down' 7, 9, 155,
   165, 233
Tunneman, Carlos 110

Unesco 6-7, 58
unintended consequences
   5, 40, 42, 128-9, 147-
   8, 155, 224
United States, influence
   of 105, 107, 129
University of Nairobi
   Institute of Adult
   Education 57
usefulness of partici-
   pation 145
unrealistic expectations
   94

volunteers 59, 186,
   188-9, 192, 222-3, 226
   see also instructors

Workers' Educational
   Association 3
workers' organisations
   and citizens' groups
   109-10, 116
women 10, 22, 47, 64,
   65-7, 76, 131, 142,
   144, 151, 228-9
   and innovation 66
   groups 62, 142

THE   INTERNATIONAL   COUNCIL

The ICAE is a non-governmental, voluntary partnership
of people and organisations working together to promote the education and the learning of adults for
responsible,   human-centred   social   and   economic
development.
        The decision to organise the Council was taken
by representatives of a number of countries in all
regions of the world. It was established officially
in early 1973. It now comprises national and regional
member associations in some 80 countries, and liaison
with other groups and organisations.
        The ICAE is linked internationally through the
Secretariat headquarters in Toronto, Canada.
        The ICAE is the only organisation of its kind to
provide an international network and coordinating
focus for action on a basic principle of adult education: people have the capacity to learn how to accomplish many things that can change the conditions of
their lives and improve their communities and
societies.
        Thus, adult education <u>as the power of learning
and of collective action</u> is integral to all economic,
social, individual and political development.
        The work of the ICAE centres around the
following:

  . Strengthening of the capacity for service and
        action of national and regional organisations.
  . Leadership training of practitioners at all
        levels.
  . Research that is participatory, practical and
        applied.
  . Information exchange, seminars/workshops,
        journals and other publishing.
  . Contributing to adult education as a field of
        study.
  . Advancing the knowledge, skills, competencies
        of individuals and groups.

Thus, all ICAE programmes and activities are cooperative in nature and emphasise:

. self-reliance;
. indigenous solutions;
. local-level experience;
. participatory approaches.

ICAE IN ACTION

The work of the International Council is carried on through national associations in all parts of the world and through regional bodies in Africa, Asia, Arab world, Caribbean, Europe and Latin America.

It cooperates with United Nations agencies and with non-governmental organisations that share its aims; with regional inter-governmental bodies; with universities and training centres and with people's voluntary groups.

The General Assembly of member representatives now meets every three years (following seven years of annual meetings) to consider, evaluate and delineate the broad lines of policy and development of the ICAE.

The responsible governing body is the Executive Committee, elected by the General Assembly and accountable to it. It comprises the Bureau of Officers, nine Vice-Presidents selected from the regions, and nine 'ordinary' members also selected from the regions. The Executive Committee meets yearly.